Our American Cousins

The United States through Canadian Eyes

Edited and with an Introduction by
Thomas S. Axworthy

James Lorimer & Company, Publishers
Toronto 1987

Design: Don Fernley
Cover photo: The StockMarket Inc., Toronto

Canadian Cataloguing in Publication Data

Main entry under title:

Our American cousins

ISBN 0-88862-877-3 (bound). — ISBN 0-88862-878-1 (pbk.)

1. United States — Foreign opinion, Canadian,
2. Public opinion — Canada. 3. Canadians —
United States. I. Axworthy, Tom, 1947-

| E183.8.C3087 1987 | 973.927 | C87-093645-X |

James Lorimer & Company Ltd., Publishers
35 Britain Street
Toronto, Ontario M5A 1R7

Printed and bound in Canada.
6   5   4   3   2   1   87   88   89   90   91   92

Table of Contents

V. The Southwest   131

VI. The Northwest   151

VII. The Far West   163

VIII. Postscripts   207

Acknowledgements

"Americans," by Gordon Sinclair, copyright 1973 by Gordon Sinclair. Reprinted by permission of the Gordon Sinclair Foundation.

["Trouble at the Border"], by Farley Mowat, copyright 1985 by Farley Mowat. Reprinted by permission of McClelland and Stewart Ltd.

"New York, New York...," by Hugh MacLennan, copyright 1958 by Hugh MacLennan. Reprinted by permission of the author.

["Four New York Poems"], by George Jonas, copyright 1973 by George Jonas. Reprinted by permission of the author.

"The Catskills," by Mordecai Richler, copyright 1965 by Mordecai Richler. Reprinted by permission of the author.

["Letters From Washington"], by Sondra Gotlieb, copyright 1985 by Acropolis Books Ltd. Reprinted by permission of the author.

"Another Time, Another Place, Another Me," by Hugh Garner, copyright 1971 by Hugh Garner. Reprinted by permission of McGraw-Hill Ryerson Ltd.

"Adventures in God's Waiting-Room," by Kildare Dobbs, copyright 1968 by Kildare Dobbs. Reprinted by permission of the author.

["Big Shots in Chicago"], by Roy Greenaway, copyright 1931 by Roy Greenaway. Reprinted by permission of Mrs. C. Roy Greenaway.

["With the Yippies in the Streets of Chicago"], by David Lewis Stein, copyright 1969 by David Lewis Stein. Reprinted by permission of the author.

"Life in Lawrence," by Elspeth Cameron, copyright 1987 by Elspeth Cameron. Published by arrangement with the author.

Introduction

I have always believed that one of the essential characteristics of every Canadian is a fierce ambivalence, one might almost say a schizophrenia, about the United States. Collectively and usually individually as well, the essays and stories in this collection make plain the fact that no one, least of all Canadian writers, can claim disinterest or inattention to America, the way the Americans so often do with us. The attitude we adopt towards the United States is not only very complex but highly fluid; it must be, in view of the way our neighbours themselves are always undergoing some change of mood or circumstance. I offer two incidents from my own experience, one profound, the other trite. Both occurred in Boston.

In October, 1969, I was invited by activists at the Harvard Law School to take part in the Moratorium Movement against the war in Vietnam. For a graduate student at Queen's University, Kingston, hardly a hotbed of radicalism, my first visit to Harvard was an opportunity to join with thousands of young Americans in protesting a war we passionately detested.

Despite the anti-intellectualism and senseless violence of the Sixties' ferment, when mobs took over university administration offices and free speech was prevented in the name of anti-war zeal, I couldn't help being moved and permanently transformed by the sight of thousands of idealistic students massing in Harvard Square for the march to Boston Common. This was American democracy at its best. On that October day, no one was thinking of future jobs or financial success or getting ahead. There was only the pervasive belief that the United States was reneging on the best of its heritage. The killing had to stop.

In the 1960s, the youth of America were connecting with the rest of the world. What happened at Berkeley or Columbia in the spring was replicated in Paris or Tokyo in the autumn. But American parochialism is at least as powerful as American universalism. The scene shifts to 1985. I had left public life in Ottawa to take up a Harvard appointment as the visiting Mackenzie King professor of Canadian Studies. I was soon introduced to that famous local institution, the Cambridge dinner party. This one was an especially international affair and the hostess made animated conversation with each guest in turn. The conversational juices flowed from terrorism in Iran to the Royal Family in Britain to auto parts in South Korea. Finally, the spotlight shone on me.

"And where are you from?" she inquired eagerly.

"Canada," I replied in a cheerful voice.

But a painful silence enveloped the crowd. Spirits sank. Foreheads knotted as people tried desperately to find some interesting connection. The hostess finally broke the tension by blurting out, "Oh, yes, you're clean and quiet like North Dakota, aren't you?" It was with relief that the table turned to something more palatable, such as human rights violations in Guatemala.

What I should have explained but didn't (*pensées des escalier!*) is that though every society is influenced by the ebb and flow of American politics, only Canada owes its very existence to a conscious rejection of the American Dream — without the United States to rebel against there would be no Canada. As Frank Underhill observed, Canadians are the world's oldest continuing anti-Americans. But there would have been little use speaking to that point. Americans are willing enough to accept that the two most important influences in the development of Canada, were, first, the wars between the French and the English and, second, the American Revolution. But they refuse to believe that the latter was a civil war as well as a revolution, though many people at the time certainly saw clearly that it was. John Adams, the second President, estimated that a third of his fellow colonists were what we call Loyalists and what the Americans, with a special contempt, have always called Tories. George Washington thought the Loyalists "ought to have...long ago committed suicide." At one point there were nearly as many Americans serving with the British forces as there were fighting with the Continental army. After the war, 100,000 of them, two or three per cent of the total population of the thirteen colonies, fled their homes, scarred by fighting, stung by the confiscation of their property, fearful of the mobs — and dedicated to order. Half of them came to Canada. John Holmes, that wisest of Canadian diplomats, has called them "the first anti-liberation resistance movement — sort of eighteenth-century Contras." But Contras with a difference, setting out to build something new — British North America — rather than continuing to fight a revolution they had already lost.

Right from the beginning, then, the fate of Canada has been linked inextricably with the course of American politics. Margaret Atwood has made the point that the cliché about the world's longest undefended border should be replaced by a more accurate metaphor — the world's longest one-way mirror. Canadians continually press their noses to the glass, looking with equal parts amazement, admiration and outrage at the antics of the great republic, while the Americans remain serenely oblivious to everyone but themselves. What do Canadians see in the mirror these days and how does it compare with what they've seen in the past? Offering answers to that question is the task of the articles, stories and poems in this book. However, a historical precedent may not be out of place.

In his famous book *Democracy in America,* published in 1835, the French writer Alexis de Tocqueville analyzed three central components of the new country. All of them continue to be relevant to American politics today.

The first is pluralism, the openness and dynamism of the United States. What struck de Tocqueville then and still amazes us today is the sheer diversity. "It is clear," he wrote, "that the opinions, prejudices, interests and even passions of the people can find no lasting obstacles preventing them from being manifest in the daily conduct of society." The American constitution is based on the contrary nature of the human spirit, so that ambition is made to counteract ambition and regional interest to fight regional interest — all of it carried out more or less in the open. To us with our British heritage, in which the supremacy of Parliament is the opposite of the separation of powers and most decisions are made behind closed doors, often by a powerful permanent public service, it all seems quite strange. It's terribly messy, noisy and inefficient, and anything but free from abuse, as events continue to show. But it has merit for the Americans. Their recent tax reform schemes have come to pass in a way Canada's probably never will because by their nature the plans were made in the open. Yet this same degree of theatrical, often almost confessional, openness makes the United States the most difficult country to negotiate with, because it takes so long to reach agreement amongst the different branches of government. Separation of powers means that before the United States can arrive at a treaty with Canada, its State Department must first arrive with something almost as complicated as a treaty between itself and, let us say, the Treasury.

The second focus of de Tocqueville's attention was the political party. My own overwhelming impression is that the two great American parties are mainly flags of convenience for people with ambition. The original organizers of American democracy thought political parties should be conduits of public opinion as well as the mechanism by which public opinion was changed. Now the first has been replaced by opinion polls and the second by television and media manipulation. It's money not the party that counts in American politics, for with money even the least likely candidate becomes viable and without it even Abraham Lincoln would have difficulty getting nominated. Of course, money is important to all political systems, but in Canada or Britain strict laws limit the amount of campaign spending and one must serve an apprenticeship within a party by proving oneself in Parliament: if not impossible, it's certainly very difficult indeed for an outsider to take a party by storm.

De Tocqueville's third point centres on what for convenience we can call citizenship. When De Tocqueville referred to America's "great democratic revolution," he was correctly pointing out that the United States virtually invented mass democracy — something that caused violent rumblings in the Canadas, with the well-intentioned rebellions of 1837-38. Now mass democracy is more alive in Canada than it is in the United States, where in presidential elections only 50 per cent of the citizens bother to vote. The country that invented modern democracy is the modern democracy with the smallest percentage of its citizens practising it. The implications are serious, as the political process becomes more responsive to special interest groups and the larger public interest grows less distinct. This is something we view from our side of the border with concern, but we should be careful that our concern does not become self-satisfaction: a natural temptation given human nature but one I believe most of the contributors to this collection have avoided as they have reacted, in a variety of styles, approaches, even levels of awareness, to the American reality.

To look at some of these questions through the eyes of Canadian writers is as useful as seeing how American writers have looked at us. Generally speaking, American authors visiting Canada — Walt Whitman is a famous example — have most often found here a sort of innocence that was largely a product of their own hopes and preconceptions. But Canadians writing about their adventures in the United States, as the two dozen included here do, have more varied, more intense experiences to share. Inundated at home with exported American culture, they have grown up, many of them, thinking of the States with a strange combination of longing and dread. They have seen it as a place always close at hand but never quite within reach, as demanding as it is unresponsive to their own way of life, with its subtle but crucially important differences. Regardless of their political views, what they have usually found in going south is a core of foreignness bathed in extreme familiarity, something they've either embraced or been disillusioned by — often both at once, in fact. The result has been the quality I mentioned earlier, the creative tension that can be mistaken for indecisiveness or a personality disorder. It is a feature, I feel, that is common to all the writers included here, though it is found in many different strengths and couched in many tones.

In a number of instances, it has been necessary for editorial reasons to give pieces new titles for the purposes of this collection. These ad hoc titles are indicated by square brackets, *viz* [   ], in the table of contents and the acknowledgements. The pieces themselves are reproduced in their original form; American spellings have not been changed.

Thomas S. Axworthy

PART

I

OVERVIEWS

Americans
GORDON SINCLAIR

Gordon Sinclair (1900–1984) was a nationally known news-
paperman-turned-broadcaster, much loved for his outspokenness,
his colourful wardrobe and his supposed parsimony. On June 5,
1973, he became a socio-political phenomenon when he broadcast the
following bit of comment on CFRB, a Toronto radio station. The piece
was widely reprinted across the United States and formed the basis of
several records which sold hundreds of thousands of copies.

T he United States dollar took another pounding on German, French and British exchanges this morning, hitting the lowest point ever known in West Germany. It has declined there by 41% since 1971 and this Canadian thinks it is time to speak up for the Americans as the most generous and possibly the least-appreciated people in all the world.

As long as sixty years ago, when I first started to read newspapers, I read of floods on the Yellow River and the Yangtse. Well, who rushed in with men and money to help? The Americans did. That's who.

They have helped control floods on the Nile, the Amazon, the Ganges and the Niger. Today, the rich bottomland of the Mississippi is under water and no foreign land has sent a dollar to help. Germany, Japan and, to a lesser extent, Britain and Italy, were lifted out of the debris of war by the Americans who poured in billions of dollars and forgave other billions in debts. None of those countries is today paying even the interest on its remaining debts to the United States.

When the franc was in danger of collapsing in 1956, it was the Americans who propped it up and their reward was to be insulted and swindled on the streets of Paris. And I was there; I saw that.

When distant cities are hit by earthquake, it is the United States that hurries in to help... Managua, Nicaragua, is one of the most recent examples. So far this spring, 59 American communities have been flattened by tornadoes. Nobody has helped.

The Marshall Plan ... the Truman Policy ... all pumped billions upon billions of dollars into discouraged countries. And now newspapers in those countries are writing about the decadent warmongering Americans.

Now ... I'd like to see just one of those countries that is gloating over the erosion of the United States dollar build its own airplanes.

Come on, now you ... let's hear it! Does any country in the world have a plane to equal the Boeing Jumbo Jet, the Lockheed Tristar or the Douglas 10? If so, why don't they fly them? Why do all international lines except Russia fly American planes? Why does no other land on earth even *consider* putting a man or a woman on the moon?

You talk about Japanese technocracy and you get radios. You talk about German technocracy and you get automobiles. You talk about American technocracy and you find men on the moon, not once, but several times ... and safely home again. You talk about scandals and the Americans put theirs right in the store window for everybody to look at. Even the draft dodgers are not pursued and hounded. They're right here on our streets, in Toronto most of them ... unless they are breaking Canadian laws ... are getting American dollars from Ma and Pa at home to spend up here.

When the Americans get out of this bind ... as they will ... who could blame them if they said 'the Hell with the rest of the world.' Let someone else buy the bonds. Let somebody else build or repair foreign dams or design foreign buildings that won't shake apart in earthquakes.

When the railways of France and Germany and India were breaking down through age, it was the Americans who rebuilt them. When the Pennsylvania Railroad and the New York Central went broke, nobody loaned them an old caboose. Both of them are *still* broke. I can name to you 5,000 times when the Americans raced to the help of other people in trouble.

Can you name to me even *one* time when someone else raced to the Americans in trouble? I don't think there was outside help even during the San Francisco earthquake.

Our neighbours have faced it alone and I'm one Canadian who is damned tired of hearing them kicked around. They will come out of this thing with their flag high. And when they do, they are entitled to thumb their noses at the lands that are gloating over their present troubles.

I hope Canada is not one of these. But there are many smug, self-righteous Canadians. And finally, the American Red Cross was told at its 48th Annual Meeting in New Orleans this morning that it was broke.

This year's disasters ... with the year less than half over ... has taken it all and nobody ... but nobody ... has helped.

Trouble at the Border
FARLEY MOWAT

By any system of reckoning, Farley Mowat (born 1921) is one of Canada's most popular authors at home and abroad. His many books on ecology, wildlife, the North and history include People of the Deer, Never Cry Wolf, Westviking *and* Sibir: My Discovery of Siberia. *In 1985, he joined the ranks of those denied admittance to the United States, and he responded with* My Discovery of America, *of which the following is a sample.*

Tuesday, April 23

Depart Pearson International Airport, Toronto, 1:15 p.m. Air Canada Flight #795.
Arrive Los Angeles, 3:30 p.m.
You will be met by a Prime Time Limo and taken to your hotel, the Beverly Wilshire.

"Promotion tours," I complained to my wife, Claire, as I dragged my suitcase to the front door, "are a royal pain in the ass. Don't know why I let myself get suckered into them. Jet lag in a dozen cities that all look and smell alike — rat-racing from radio studio to TV studio to do the same damn interview for the umpteenth time — autographing 'parties' where the only body that turns up is a fifth cousin, twice removed!"

"Think of the bright side," Claire said soothingly. "The adulation; the free booze, the swish hotel suites; the chance to twirl your kilt in public ... Besides, how else can we writers get the kind of publicity we need to sell our books?"

"I'll think about that," I grumbled, sliding into the passenger seat beside neighbour David Brooks, who was driving me to the airport. "Meanwhile, take care, honey. See you in ten days' time ... if I survive."

It was a magnificent spring morning, bright, warm, and tranquil, as we drove out of Port Hope, the little town on the north shore of Lake Ontario where I spend part of my year. David thought so, too.

"Nice day for a trip," he offered.

"Nicer day to stay home and plant the bleeding garden!" I snapped.

Sensing my mood, he said no more as we made the seventy-five-mile freeway trek to Toronto's Malton Airport — now pompously renamed Lester B. Pearson International in honour of a defunct Prime Minister.

But David was right. It *was* a charming day. And, despite myself, I began to feel little twinges of excitement, even anticipation, at the prospect of visiting the West Coast of the United States: Los Angeles, San Francisco, Sacramento and the little university town of Chico, then finally Seattle. Some of it was bound to be worthwhile, even if I did have to spend most of my time peddling my book, which had, by no mere coincidence, been published that very day in the United States.

Over the years I had received hundreds of good letters from Californians and Washingtonians who had read my earlier books. And Peter Davison, friend and editor of three decades' standing at Atlantic, had called to cheer me on.

"You'll find it stimulating. The West Coast has the worst, and some of the best of America to offer. Furthermore, people there *buy books* . . . and even read them."

Ah, well, I thought, as we pulled into the airport. It may not be so bad. After all, I *was* being sent First Class — a condition that makes air travel almost tolerable. In deference to this munificence on the part of my publishers, I had dressed soberly in a pair of impeccably creased grey slacks, a tweedy jacket, and something I almost never wear — a tie.

David bade me farewell and departed. Feeling quite chipper now, I made my way through the vast terminal building to an enclave occupied by U.S. Customs and Immigration. I presented myself to the Customs counter.

Having first determined where I was bound, a sallow fellow with a long-suffering face asked if I had anything to declare.

"Nothing but good intentions," I replied cheerfully, if stupidly.

He winced. "Open the bag!"

I did so and he rumpled aimlessly through it; but when he came to my kilt in all its yards of gaudy tartan, he stopped, raised his pale eyes to mine, and said accusingly:

"This is a *skirt!*"

"No," I explained. "It is a kilt."

"You wear that thing?"

"I do indeed. And proudly."

"A *skirt*," he reiterated. "'Frisco ought to suit you good."

A trifle less jauntily, I moved on to a sort of toll booth presided over by a uniformed young man whose shoulder flashes proclaimed him to be a member of the INS — the Immigration and Naturalization Service of the United States of America. He was wispy, sandy-haired, bespectacled, and mild of manner. I warmed to him at once. Here, surely, was the archetypal, shy, but friendly American.

He asked me the usual routine questions, accepting all my answers with a nod . . . until he came to the purpose of my journey.

"Business," I told him. And then I breached what fellow-author Max Braithwaite calls the cardinal rule for dealing with customs and immigration officials the world over. *Never Volunteer Information!*

"I'm off to the West Coast to promote my newest book. I'm an author, you see."

His head came up and his eyes, behind their windows, seemed to sharpen. Vaingloriously, I thought he might have recognized me.

"Show me your tickets."

I passed them over.

"Your name is Mao-it?"

"*Mo*wat — as in poet," I corrected him.

"So. Your first name Fairley?"

"*Far*ley," I said kindly. "As in barley." Since only my initials appeared on the airline tickets, I deduced from this exchange that he must know me by repute even if he couldn't pronounce my name. At any rate, he stamped my boarding pass and waved me into the corridor leading to the departure lounge.

I found a seat, got out a pocketbook, and prepared to read until the boarding call. But after five minutes or so, I became aware that the sandy-haired INS man had materialized beside me. He must have approached as softly as a cat.

"Ah ha," thought I smugly. "I'll bet he wants an autograph." I was actually reaching for my pen when he asked me to return to the

immigration section. His tone was soft, but it was an order nonetheless. Nonplussed, I followed him to a tiny cubicle equipped only
with a desk and one chair, which he pre-empted. Then, as I stood in
increasing bewilderment before him, he peppered me with questions that carried a penetrating chill of menace.

"Have you ever been turned back at the U.S. border?"

"Never!"

"Have you entered, or attempted to enter the U.S.A. illegally?"

"Of course not!"

"Do you have a criminal record?"

"Certainly not!"

"Is there a security file on you in the U.S.A.?"

"Now how would I know that?"

The impertinence of these questions was beginning to annoy
me. "What the devil's going on? You already passed me through —
remember?"

"I need further identification."

"Well," thought I. "They must be confusing me with someone
else. Thank God I've brought my passport." Although neither
passport nor visa is usually required of Canadians visiting the
United States, I invariably carry that magic little book whenever I
go abroad. With something of a flourish I produced it.

The INS man flipped it open, stared at the rogues' gallery portrait
contained therein, then without a word stood up and ambled off,
the passport in his hand.

"Excuse me," I asked of his retreating back. "Should I wait here or
in the departure lounge?"

"Wait there," he replied, without even deigning to turn his head.

Indignant at his rudeness, but baffled and bewildered, too, my
thoughts raced. What was happening here? It had to be some
minor bureaucratic muddle! There could be no earthly reason the
Americans, in this, the sixty-fourth year of my life, should decide to
keep me out! Probably a case of mistaken identity. But if that
sandy-haired gumshoe didn't hurry back, I might miss my flight.

Ten – fifteen minutes dragged by. Flight time was inexorably
approaching and I have a life-long fear of missing planes and trains.
Anxiously I peered down the long hallway and at last saw my man
approaching.

He took his time. Once he stopped to exchange badinage with a female clerk. Once he turned back, as if he had forgotten some-thing, then again reversed himself. But as he finally reached the cubicle, I saw there was a faint smile on his face.

My relief was monumental. I was so pleased to think that the *contretemps*, whatever it might have been about, had been resolved that I returned the pale one's smile with a broad and grateful grin. I held out my hand for my passport, and was about to hasten to the departure lounge where boarding was just beginning, when the INS man dropped his bombshell.

"You are excluded from entering the United States."

He issued this stunning dictum with a righteousness that would have suited St. Peter turning a poor sinner away from the Pearly Gates.

"I *what?*"

"You are not permitted to enter the United States of America." He was being patient now but, I suspect, enjoying himself.

I, most assuredly, was neither.

"Why in blazes can't I?"

"I can't tell you that."

"You *know*, but you bloody well won't tell me?"

"You could say that."

"*I* could say that! Who *will* tell me? What in Christ's sweet name is going *on* here? And what the hell am I supposed to do about it?"

I think I may have raised my voice a trifle. A few passengers being "processed" in other booths craned their necks in our direc-tion. Gumshoe picked up a fragment of paper and pencilled two telephone numbers on it — just the numbers, nothing else.

"You could call these," he said, in a tone that suggested the uselessness of such an exercise.

Furiously I snatched the paper and scanned it, noting that the area codes were unfamiliar and therefore doubtless too distant to be of any immediate assistance — even had he volunteered the use of a telephone, which he did not. In order to call these anonymous numbers, I would have to go and find a pay phone in the main terminal; *but there was no time.* There was barely time, I realized distractedly, to rescue my bag and my precious kilt. It was already too late to rescue my *sang-froid.*

"Piss on you!" I flung at my sandy-haired nemesis, and ran for the baggage area. First things first.

A few moments later, a black Customs employee was listening sympathetically to my incoherent story. He shook his head sadly. "Your bag's already left for L.A. I'm sorry. But don't worry. They'll put it on the first plane back to Toronto."

He noted the particulars and went off to send a retrieval telex to Los Angeles, and it was only then that I began to comprehend fully the incontestable reality — *I was not going on my journey to Los Angeles!*

Panic and confusion filled my thoughts. "What about my airline and hotel reservations?" was the first, inane reaction. Then, "Mother of God! What about all the people awaiting my arrival? ...publishers' representatives, media people, TV producers, book sellers, book *buyers*...who would straighten *that* mess out?

"And what about Susan DiSesa in Atlantic's New York office, who had sweated blood to make the publicity arrangements for the tour?...And Peter Davison in Boston?...and Michael Bauman in Chico?...

"And what about me, for God's sake?" Having been stopped from entering the United States by contemptuous officialdom, and without being offered a shred of explanation, I was actually feeling *guilty*, as if I was some wetback who had been caught trying to crash the border! "Why should *I* be feeling guilty? and why...why had they *done* this to me anyway?"

Confused, outraged, and growing angrier by the second, I knew I needed help. I made a mad dash for the nearest exit.

Outside, in the bright April sunshine, I swerved unseeingly toward what I took to be a taxi, flung myself inside, and snarled the address of my Toronto publishers.

Only then did I realize I was in no ordinary cab. This vehicle was an obscenely-stretched limousine, equipped with one-way windows, a bar, TV, and a curved divan upholstered in mauve velvet. It was the sort of harem buggy one associates with Hollywood celebrities, and a phrase from my tour schedule flashed before my eyes... *You will be met by a Prime Time Limo and driven to the Beverly Wilshire*...

The faceless, factory-like premises of McClelland and Stewart can have nothing in common with the *Beverly Wilshire*, and my limo created something of a sensation when it drew up at the front door.

"I thought it must belong to either the Premier of Ontario, or the Mafia," the receptionist told me. She also told me that Jack McClelland, chairman of the company, to whose comforting arms I was fleeing, had not come in this day from his country home. However, his executive assistant, Marge Hodgeman, was in her office.

Marge was astonished to see me. When I explained as best I could what had happened, fire flew from her eyes. Marge is nothing if not loyal.

"How could they dare!" she cried. "The little wimps! Wait 'til Jack hears this. I'll ring him right away. But first you need a drink. Hang on, I'll get you one."

Jack was equally astonished — then magnificently blasphemous.

"So what do you plan to do now?" he asked when he had run down.

"I don't really know. I guess I have to call New York and Boston and break the news. Then, well, I guess I'll catch the afternoon train back to Port Hope. Surprise the devil out of Claire! I really don't think there's any way the Yanks are going to let me make the trip. To tell the truth, Jack, there is no goddamn way I *want* to make it, after what I've just been through. Screw the lot of them! Maybe Claire and I'll go to the cottage for a couple of days and look at birds."

Jack was appalled. "You'll do no such bloody thing! My God, Farley, don't you realize what's happened here? Canada's foremost writer *proposing to slink away like a whipped cur because Uncle Sam lays one on him? And,*" he snorted like an angry horse, "*go off and look at effing birds?*"

Words temporarily failed him. Then:

"Listen, man. Let Peter know. Then have Marge call you a cab and get yourself out here. We are going to have a council of war. We are going to make those idiots wish they'd never heard your name. The media will go ape over this one ... Mowat barred from the U-S-of-A while Prime Minister Mulroney is trumpeting to the wide world how lovey-dovey we and the Yankees are. Oh, they love us down in Washington all right! *You be here in an hour's time.*"

This was vintage McClelland. Commander of a motor torpedo boat during the war, Jack has never lost his lust for combat, especially against heavy odds. As I polished off my drink, it struck me that Mowat and McClelland against the Empire of the Reagan Eagle *was* pretty heavy odds. I downed another drink. But what the hell ... Goddamn it, Jack was *right!*

I talked briefly to Claire, who was properly stunned by my news;

and then Marge got Peter Davison on the line. He was frankly incredulous, refusing to believe my rejection could be anything more than a tempest in an airport, as it were.

"Calm yourself, Farley, I'll make a call to Washington. We'll get to the bottom of this idiocy. Susan will see if she can shuffle your appointments and get you on a later plane tonight."

"Peter, I think you're absolutely wrong. God alone knows why, but I got the impression the guardians of your fair land want no part of me."

As is his fashion, Peter raised his voice and overrode me.

"*Nonsense, Farley. You are being irrational. This is just a simple error. I'll call Jack's place when we've cleared it up.*"

It took nearly an hour to drive from Toronto to McClelland's home near the village of Kleinberg — time for me to sort through some of the impressions and events and try to find some answers. One thing seemed clear — it would be a delusion to think that my exclusion had been a matter of mistaken identity. When the gumshoe went off with my passport, it could only have been to check with his superior in the flesh, or with that supreme superior, the computer. The result had been unequivocal. Farley McGill Mowat — he, himself, and no other — was *persona non grata* in the United States of America.

For whatever reason.

But what, indeed, could that reason be? Perhaps there was a clue in the questions gumshoe had fired at me. A criminal record? No — nothing there that I could think of. Turned back at the U.S. border? Perhaps someone *else* had been turned back, using my name? ... but that was too far-fetched. How about illegal border crossings? None of that either ... ah, but wait a moment ...

In 1967, Claire and I had sailed our little schooner up the St. Lawrence seaway *en route* to Lake Ontario. Passing out of the seaway locks near Cornwall at dusk one day, we were smothered in dense fog and I instinctively did what I have always done in such situations — scuttled for the nearest port. This happened to be Massena, on the New York side of the river.

The schooner felt her way to an abandoned dock where I thankfully made fast for the night. What I did *not* do was hie me to the nearest U.S. Customs and Immigration post to report my entry. Worse still, I landed an illegal alien.

He (or it may have been she) had come aboard surreptitiously somewhere along the Gaspé coast and had been hiding in the chain-locker ever since. We knew about his presence mainly because of footsteps on deck during the night. But after we left Massena (at dawn next day, to avoid attracting official attention), we heard no more from him. He had jumped ship. He may have been a rat, or perhaps a weasel — or even a singularly heavy-footed meadow mouse. Grasping at straws, I wondered if this incident had been observed by some gimlet-eyed immigration snoop.

Or — and another shrouded memory was unfurled — there was the day in 1968 when, southbound in a chartered float-plane from Old Crow in Yukon Territory, my pilot lost his way in low cloud and we unwittingly strayed into Alaska. Clawing through mountain valleys almost at deck level, we eventually encountered a road. Knowing it had to be the Alaska Highway (there was no other in that region), we turned east and followed it at an altitude of about fifty feet until we were safely back in Canada. On this occasion we certainly *were* observed, for we passed so closely over the border post that I saw two uniformed officials duck for cover.

But, no again . . . even if the U.S. knew about these two incursions, they could hardly be sufficient grounds to bar me out.

Then what about the reference to a mysterious "security file"? I was still chewing on that one when my taxi pulled up at the McClelland home.

With the scent of coming battle flaring his nostrils, Jack welcomed me and led the way to his den. Little lights on his several telephones were flickering impatiently. A full bottle of vodka, together with glasses and ice, stood ready for action. Jack, as dashing and debonair as ever, waved me to a chair while he continued an interrupted phone conversation with the company solicitor.

"Sorry, Bob. Farley just arrived . . . You really think he could be on the blacklist? How the hell do we find out? Okay, let me know if you come up with anything."

Jack hung up.

"We may have a problem, Farley," he said thoughtfully. "Bob thinks you have probably been barred under something called the

McCarran-Walter Act. You may have heard of it. Back in the 1950s, Joe McCarthy scared the U.S. Congress into passing a law that would exclude anyone, any time, on the mere suspicion of being a Commie or even a fellow traveller. Bob tells me that, under the law, the U.S. authorities don't even have to give reasons to the people they shaft. They don't even have to *have* a valid reason. Nevertheless, the impression that gets left with the public is that you are, or maybe were, a Commie. And there ain't *no* way to clear yourself."

"You've got to be joking!" I replied incredulously. "The Yanks got rid of all that fascist malarkey years ago!"

"I'm not joking. And they didn't. *And* if we make a stink about you being barred, and *they* claim they did it under the Commie clause of the McCarran Act, a lot of people could figure where there's smoke there must be fire; and that if U.S. Immigration claims you're Red, you likely are. It's dirty stuff, but it does what it was designed to do — scares the pants off anyone they finger. Makes the poor bastards lie down and play dead for fear of losing their reputations and their jobs; of seeing their friends and even their families turn against them. It's blackmail, man . . . and here's the pinch . . . are you prepared to take the chance of being clobbered if we go public? You never can tell for sure which way the media will jump."

This was definitely something to give me pause. The risk of being stigmatized as a Communist or a "com symp" by the U.S. government, and of subsequently being pilloried by right-wing elements in the United States and in my own country, was not attractive — especially not at a time when neo-conservatism was in the ascendancy in both Canada and the U.S.A. The prospect of just quietly slipping off to the cottage to look at birds began to seem exceedingly attractive.

I temporized. It was then only about 4:00 p.m. and Peter Davison *might* be having some success. While we waited to hear from him, I could ring the two anonymous numbers given to me and, perhaps, make some small progress toward straightening out the situation myself.

"Right, then," said Jack. "Go ahead and make your calls. Meanwhile I know a guy at the Canadian Embassy in Washington and I'll see what he can tell us."

My first call was answered by the U.S. Customs and Immigration border post at the Rainbow Bridge, linking Niagara Falls,

Ontario, with its namesake in New York State. The chap who answered seemed to be one of the duty officers whose task it is to check Canadian visitors entering the U.S.A. by car. He had never heard of me, nor did he seem to have any knowledge of my problem. He did offer to call me back after consulting his superiors. I never heard from him again.

The second number proved to be that of a U.S. Immigration office at Buffalo. Once again, the chap who answered apparently knew nothing about my case. "Hold on," he told me. "I'll get the superintendent on the line."

I waited five minutes, but nothing happened. Supposing that we had been disconnected, I hung up, then called again...with the same result, except that this time I waited nearly ten minutes for the elusive superintendent. Jack tried the third time; was told to wait; did so until his patience was exhausted; then slammed down the phone.

"They're giving you the goddamn run-around! Clearly nobody wants to talk to you. And my Embassy guy in Washington says he knows nothing about any problem with Farley Mowat, but says he's going to check it out with the INS brass. I'm going to try External Affairs in Ottawa, but don't hold your breath."

A light blinked for an incoming call and he motioned me to take it. A chastened Peter Davison was on the line.

"I'm afraid this really *is* a hell of a mess, Farley. We've talked to the Justice Department and they are not going to let you in. No reasons given. So we've had to tell Susan to begin cancelling your West Coast arrangements. What have you and Jack decided? Will you go to the press with this? Or do you want to let it drop?"

Jack had picked up the other handset. Now he cut in. "Peter? We are going to fight! We are going to blow the lid so goddamn high, it'll make a moon landing. Are you with us?"

"Oh, we're with you. Harry Evans, our new chief, is appalled, as I am, and he knows his way around in Washington and in the press, as former editor of the London *Times*. We'll start with the *New York Times*, the *Washington Post*, the *Boston Globe*, the *Los Angeles Times*, and go on from there. Good hunting on your side of the border."

Jack put the phone down and gave me his lopsided grin.

"Before you say anything, let *me* say this. You *have* to bite the bullet on this thing because, you see, it isn't just you; it's everyone who gets shit on this way by the Almighty Eagle. Consider it your *duty*, man...Now go and ask Elizabeth to cook some grub; then pour us both a drink. We've got a war to fight."

I sighed, but did as I was told. The die was cast.

We began our campaign with a string of calls alerting Canadian press services, then, through the good offices of Elsa Franklin, another stalwart friend, all major Canadian radio and television networks. Interest was immediate and electric. By 8:00 p.m., the story was on the national news on CBC, Global TV, and CTV. By 8:30, all the phones in the McClelland home were ringing off their hooks. Squeezed in among the media calls came a plaintive, somewhat desperate one from Claire.

"Farley, what on earth are you *doing*? The phone hasn't stopped for two solid hours. I can't get time to eat or even make a cup of tea. Some reporter just called from Vancouver and when he couldn't get you, tried to interview *me* on your so-called Communist history! *When'll* you be *home*?"

I did not know, and had to tell her so.

Jack and I, together with his wife, Elizabeth, were now fielding a steady torrent of inquiries, all zeroing in on the same question: what, exactly, *had* Mowat done? As Paul Taylor of the *Globe and Mail* inelegantly put it: "Why *did* the Yanks give you the bum's rush?" He had aready called the INS and had received no satisfaction from that source. As his published story said:

"U.S. Immigration officials are not telling Mr. Mowat or anyone else why they won't let him into their country...'I can't give any information — nothing at all,' said Hyman Jackson, a U.S. Department of Immigration official in Buffalo, New York."

"They'll just leave the implication hanging that you're a Commie baddie — one of the Kremlin's boys."

He seemed to be right, because there followed a number of forthright demands to know whether or not I was a Communist.

It was simple enough to tell the truth: that I was not and never had been either a Communist or a Communist sympathizer. It was not so easy to provide a credible alternative explanation. In some desperation I hazarded the guess that it might relate to an earlier book of mine, *Sibir* (*The Siberians* in the U.S.A.), an account of life in the Soviet far north based on two trips I made there in 1966 and 1969.

"That book treated the Soviets as human beings essentially like us," I explained to a reporter from the Associated Press. Although he did not seem entirely convinced that *Sibir* was the cause of my difficulties, he did agree that, given the current Evil Empire attitude of the Reagan administration, there might be something to it. Consequently, and for want of anything else to offer, it became my stock reply throughout the remainder of that hectic night.

Jack would not buy it. "That's old stuff, Farley, and there's no weight to it anyway. *I* think you're in trouble over *Sea of Slaughter.* You've no idea how powerful the hunting lobby and the anti-environmental kooks are in Washington. And they will hate the book for the way you cut them up in it."

"Nonsense, Jack! Are you seriously telling me a lobby group like that could get a U.S. government department to shut the door on me?"

"Farley, be your age! And ask yourself, why *did* they turn you back? There *had* to be more to it than *Sibir*! That's fifteen years ago!"

We were interrupted by a call from a CBC story producer who had been independently pursuing the question of cause, although without success. However, he *had* tracked down the man nominally responsible for turning me away — one Benedict Ferro, District Director of the INS, in Buffalo.

"He takes full responsibility for stopping you, Mr. Mowat. At any rate, he's officially carrying the can. He says you were barred because of serious accusations against you which are contained in a file they have. He won't divulge the nature of them because he says that would intrude on your privacy rights; but an INS spokesman in Washington confirms they come under the McCarran-Walter Act. I have Mr. Ferro's home number if you'd like it."

Would we like it?

Peremptorily waving me aside, Jack dialed. He got through immediately.

"Mr. Ferro? Jack McClelland here. Farley Mowat's publisher. He'd like a word with you . . . You say the matter's so sensitive you'd rather *not* speak to him personally? Okay, I'm his representative. We'd like to know the charges against him. We'd like to know why he was given no explanation for being barred and what, in fact, that explanation is . . . You mean you *won't*? . . . I'm sorry, but you'd better realize this will be an international incident by morning and I hope you can find some believable explanations by then ... Yes, I'll see that he gets that message."

Jack hung up and turned to me with a wry grin. "He won't talk to you, and he won't say why you were stopped; but it's obvious the media have already reached his bosses, and they'd clearly like to damp the story down. What he *does* say is that, if you come to the airport tomorrow morning, his people will, and I quote, 'review your file with you.'"

"Does that mean they'll let me in?"

"He didn't say. My guess is, it would depend on whether you'd be willing to let the whole thing drop, and even then, you might get the royal run-around."

"So what do you think we ought to do?"

"Tell them to go to hell? That you won't settle for anything less than full clearance and a public apology. I think they're beginning to realize they've got a tiger by the tail."

There was no doubt but that a tiger had broken loose that night. By 1:00 a.m., when we finally dropped into our beds, we had (according to Jack's telephone log) answered sixty-three media calls.

The question in my mind as I sought for sleep was could I ride this beast we had unleashed? Or would I end up in its gut?

Following a short but messy controversy in the media on both sides of the border, Mowat was allowed admittance to the United States — which he declined, pending, he said, an apology from the White House.

PART
II
THE NORTHEAST

A New England June
BLISS CARMAN

Bliss Carman (1861–1929) was in his day almost indistinguishable from the popular image of the poet: romantic, bohemian, given to visions and fits of inspiration. For decades he was also the Canadian poet, though he spent most of his mature life in New York, Massachusetts and Connecticut, and American audiences tended to forget, or to overlook, his Canadian birth. "A New England June" is typical of the pastoral verse he produced in great volume. It shows how genuinely he loved the landscape of the northeastern United States.

A NEW ENGLAND JUNE

These things I remember
Of New England June,
Like a vivid day-dream
In the azure noon,
While one haunting figure
Strays through every scene,
Like the soul of beauty
Through her lost demesne.

Gardens full of roses
And peonies a-blow
In the dewy morning,
Row on stately row,
Spreading their gay patterns,
Crimson, pied and cream,
Like some gorgeous fresco
Or an Eastern dream.

Nets of waving sunlight
Falling through the trees;
Fields of gold-white daisies
Rippling in the breeze;
Lazy lifting groundswells,
Breaking green as jade
On the lilac beaches,
Where the shore-birds wade.

Orchards full of blossom,
Where the bob-white calls
And the honeysuckle
Climbs the old gray walls;
Groves of silver birches,
Beds of roadside fern,
In the stone-fenced pasture
At the river's turn.

Out of every picture
Still she comes to me
With the morning freshness
Of the summer sea, —
A glory in her bearing,
A sea-light in her eyes,
As if she could not forget
The spell of Paradise.

Thrushes in the deep woods,
With their golden themes,
Fluting like the choirs
At the birth of dreams.
Fireflies in the meadows
At the gate of Night,
With their fairy lanterns
Twinkling soft and bright.

Ah, not in the roses,
Nor the azure noon,
Nor the thrushes' music,
Lies the soul of June.
It is something finer,
More unfading far,
Than the primrose evening
And the silver star;

Something of the rapture
My beloved had,
When she made the morning
Radiant and glad, —
Something of her gracious
Ecstasy of mien,
That still haunts the twilight,
Loving though unseen.

When the ghostly moonlight
Walks my garden ground,
Like a leisurely patrol
On his nightly round,
These things I remember
Of the long ago,
While the slumbrous roses
Neither care nor know.

A Letter on Western New York
WILLIAM LYON MACKENZIE

In its bare outline at least, the story of William Lyon Mackenzie (1795–1861) is familiar to all. The fiery editor of **The Colonial Advocate** *and various other newspapers hoped to persuade Upper Canada to embrace the sort of egalitarian democracy that was the most obvious feature of President Andrew Jackson's America. But his efforts were unsuccessful, and so in 1837, three years after he was chosen to be the first mayor of York (Toronto), Mackenzie led an armed uprising against the colonial administration before fleeing across the border. What's less well known is that, by the time of his return to Canada in 1849, his opinion of the United States had changed fundamentally. The following is an excerpt from* **Sketches of Canada and the United States** *(London, 1833), one of the books he wrote during his strongly pro-American period.*

Clyde, May 14th, 1829.

DEAR SIR, — I HAD no leisure to write until after I took the packet this afternoon; and as a crowded canalboat is not the most desirable situation for a letter writer, you will have to make the necessary allowances; and believe me when I assure you that I am anxious to give a faithful sketch of the country I am passing through, without fatiguing you with tedious and minute details.

I left York on the evening of the 8th, and next morning rode through the Credit woods, much pleased with the improvements which have been made on Dundas Street, on both sides of that beautiful river. On the evening of Monday I reached Fort Erie; but there was no getting across the Niagara; the ice from the great western lakes was floating down towards the Falls in large masses, forming one continued tract of moving ice, extending as far up and down the river as the eye could reach. On returning to the Falls I ascertained that there was good crossing at Queenston, and experienced no difficulty whatever. The weather was very cold, and the inhabitants considered the ice as having a powerful effect in lowering the temperature of the atmosphere.

The stage starts from Lewiston for Rochester at 2 A.M., and arrives at 3, 4, 5, or 6 P.M. the same day, passing through Lockport, where the passengers breakfast about six in the morning. The ridge road is naturally good, perhaps the best in America; but to go to Lockport we had to leave it for some time, and on doing so we passed over ten or twelve miles of as bad road as any in Canada; but it is newly made, and probably they will have it improved before another year. It surprised me much to find the road between Rochester and Fulham's Basin, on the Canal, all full of holes and broken up, so as to render it quite unpleasant for travellers. There are many very good roads in "the States," but it seems they are not all good more than with us. Lockport thrives amazingly; there are now two towns, the upper above the locks and the lower below them. Many of the buildings show signs of great wealth, and the appearance of the place, taken as a whole, evinces a sense of security, comfort and industry. They had been electing their officers under the new charter in Lockport the night before we arrived, and the Jackson ticket succeeded. The Presbyterians are the leading and predominant sect in this state; I meet their churches in every direction. Presbyterianism is exceedingly well suited to a republican system, being itself distinguished by a democratic form of church government, and which well accounts for the detestation in which it was always held by the Stuart family when on the throne of England. Episcopacy is on the increase; and, being freed from state nurture, is by no means unpopular (as in Canada now or in New England threescore years ago.) One of the Episcopal churches in Rochester is superbly finished inside; and I could distinguish several more chapels belonging to this sect as I passed along, by the square tower with which each of them is surmounted.

We entered Rochester at half-past five, having passed through a thickly settled country, in some places in a high state of cultivation; and Mr. _____ and myself remained for the night at the Eagle Tavern, one of the mammoth caravanseras in that extraordinary town. The accommodation is good and the charges moderate; but I am told that the Rochester House is more retired, and therefore preferred where families are travelling. The postmaster of Rochester, Mr. Reynolds, has built an arcade or exchange for the merchants; it is one of the greatest curiosities in the place, — very handsome and convenient, — a pleasing evidence of American enterprise, and of the confidence capitalists entertain in the security of property and the permanency of their free institutions. Two lines of daily stages ply on the ridge road; — the old line, by Mr. Barton, Mr. Adams, and others, which conveys the mail, and the new or Pioneer line, which is distinguished from its elder opponent by resting from its labours on the Christian Sabbath. Manufactures of various kinds thrive in Rochester; there is one daily and about a half dozen of weekly newspapers, besides job and book printers. The flouring mills of Rochester are famed for the flour they turn out, and the papermills supply that article in greater variety, at least twenty-five per cent cheaper than with us. Every necessary and luxury of life is to be had in abundance; law is cheaply administered, and there is the utmost confidence in the purity of the administration of justice. The seminaries for education are upon a grand and efficient scale; and it is a fixed principle with all parties, that to make good citizens the people must be well informed, — and so they are. There is of course much party feeling in a free government like this, but it is very evanescent, constantly assuming new forms. I have never yet met an American who would prefer another system of government to his own; local circumstances may cause him to emigrate, but an American is at heart an American still, and the more I see of this country the better I can account for the objections made by persons in office in Canada to the admission of its citizens to the benefit of naturalization among us.

Along the line of canal below Rochester I am now travelling for the first time. About eight years ago I went by the land route *via* Canandaigua and Auburn, which is by far the finest. The canal route, however, has its peculiar beauties and attractions; every few miles bring you to a village or a hamlet, — and the elegant church spire or commodious belfry tells you at every crook and curve of the liquid highway that you are in a Christian country, among an opulent and religious people. I am much pleased to find that the country through which the canal passes is agreeably diversified in its scenery by hill and dale, — here a valley and there a gentle swell, and so on in succession in all directions. For a few rods you find yourself in the midst of a wood, then again in a rich well-settled country, having all the outward signs of plenty and content. The modern Palmyra is a town about two-thirds of the size of York; but the houses in general are finer and more substantial. Lyons, Newark, Montezuma, Port Gibson and several other villages we passed to-day are curious as having sprung into existence like Rochester, as if by the wand of an enchanter. Our boat has already passed twelve or fifteen other large vessels crowded with passengers, and filled with goods and baggage for the west. Among others we met The General Jackson, The La Fayette, The John Hancock, The Dulcinea del Tobosa, and The Napoleon. The boat I am now writing in (11, P.M.) is called the Buffalo, the expense for conveyance on board of which, including board and lodging, being four cents a mile, or six dollars and one-third from Rochester to Utica. You may take the canal all the way through, or only for a mile or two, paying in proportion to the distance. The accommodations and fare are much better than I could have anticipated. The Erie Canal, unlike British canals, is not puddled, and of consequence the risk of accidents to its banks is much greater. Mr. Merritt expects to have the Welland Canal open and in use some time in June, and the whole line to the Grand River navigable by the month of August. Although a great part of the work will be finished in a very superficial manner, and soon require repair, and although it will be impossible to reconcile the cost with the progress and execution of the work, I shall, nevertheless, feel great satisfaction at witnessing its completion. A canal in a colony is a wonder under any circumstances, and as for economy, it is out of the question. They have begun to excavate the banks of the Niagara at the mouth of the Welland River, by which its entrance will be greatly improved; towing paths are also being made, which will prevent the banks of the Niagara from being washed away by the stream, from which at present they are suffering great injury.

As a proof of the merit of Scott's novels, you meet them everywhere, — in boarding houses, taverns, steamboats, and packet-boats; and the superiority of Irish and Scottish national airs may be inferred when you hear the American packet buglers strike up Paddy Carey or the Yellow-haired Laddie on entering one of their villages, changing to Moore's Legacy, or Tannahill's Jessie, from time to time, for variety's sake. A gentleman on board the packet informs me that there are 150 houses lighted up with natural gas from the rock in the village of Fredonia on Lake Erie. He has his store, his counting room and dwelling-house so lighted, and the flame is as pure and clear as that from the coal-gas of New York or London.

There are many pleasant reflections associated with the Erie Canal, — that splendid monument of the departed Clinton's comprehensive genius. He may with truth be said to have made the wilderness to blossom as the rose, and created pastures for the lamb in the everlasting forests. The yell of the savage and the howl of the wolf are succeeded by the song of praise, and the glad tidings of salvation to fallen man.

New York, New York...
HUGH MACLENNAN

Hugh MacLennan was born in 1907 in Nova Scotia but is indelibly associated with Montreal. He is famous as the author of Barometer Rising, Two Solitudes *and* The Watch That Ends the Night, *but in addition to novels has published several collections of essays. The following, written in 1958, is a well-known sample.*

The first time I understood that New York taxi-drivers are a unique tribe within the human family was in 1929 on the occasion of my first visit there. I was with my father, who hated New York and never missed an opportunity of saying so, who dreaded New York not for its own sake but for all of our sakes, because New York by its very colossality seemed a constant temptation inviting Providence to get to work on it. On the way to Penn Station, my father grumbling with some justification about the way the traffic was not being handled — they used cops then instead of lights and prohibition had softened the cops up — the driver stopped his car and turned around.

"Listen mister, you wanna know what is the trouble with New York? It is very simple. New York is the trouble with New York."

At the time this struck me as a courteous way of suggesting that what was the trouble with my father was my father, but I don't really think this is what the man meant. He simply meant that New York is New York, and as such that it is so transcendent, so irrefragably self-confident, that for most of us it has an unrivalled capacity among the cities for arousing extreme sensations of love, hate, admiration, and nausea. I don't know what your experience has been with this city, but mine is nearly always the same. I arrive full of excited anticipation; I depart frustrated and with my pockets empty. I can't imagine a world without New York; I find it increasingly difficult to imagine the world surviving indefinitely with New York a part of it. New York, for years, has been my Great White Whale. Year after year between my first visit and 1952 I kept going down to New York and once I lived there for eight consecutive months, during which it seemed entirely different from the city I knew when I visited it. Then for five years I stayed secure in Montreal and left the Whale to itself and the rest of humanity.

But a time came — it always does — when I had to return to New York, and on this occasion it was because I had finished a novel on which I had been working for five years. I was tired and with reason. During the previous five months I had been working night and day in the most intense creative drive I had ever known. So I slept for a week, then bought a ticket for the Great White Whale because it seemed essential that I consult my agent. "With this little book," whispered a little thought in the back of my little mind, "I will stick my little bodkin into the Whale. This little book will make the Whale admit that I exist."

So I slept soundly on the train, and with the usual feeling of expectant excitement I stepped out of Grand Central into a cab driven by Joe Przwyk, to whom I carelessly mentioned that I had not been in New York for five years.

"Where you bin?" said Przwyk. "In jail?"

There it was again: that cheerful, humiliating, friendly assumption that if you are absent from New York you are not alive, and that only the most ignominious failure or the direst calamity can keep you away until, after having been preserved on ice, you return. No wonder Moby Dick heaped Ahab; no wonder the Whale was his wall. Ahab was a whaler by trade; I am a writer by trade, and New York, among other things, happens to be the centre of the book market.

Przwyk drove with a competent insouciance delightful after the paranoic behaviour of Montreal taxi-drivers, and the familiar kaleidoscope unreeled, historical climacterics of a quarter-century flashing past as he drove from Grand Central to my hotel. There was the corner on which I had stood, that November night in 1932, when Franklin Roosevelt was elected president and the New York crowd, anticipating 3.2 beer and everything else that happened during Roosevelt's regime, sang "Happy Days Are Here Again." There was the barbershop where I read about Dollfuss's bombardment of the Viennese workers in 1934. Coming out of that theatre I had seen displayed in banner headlines the news that Adolf Hitler had become the master of Germany. In this block my shoes were shined while I looked at a *Daily News* photo of Hitler doing a jig in the

Forest of Compiègne. New York had certainly appreciated the news value of the war, but it was from another member of its taxi-driving tribe that I learned what I believe was its real attitude toward that half-forgotten conflict.

"This town," the man said, "is pretty big for the war."

The news in New York on this particular occasion was widely analysed elsewhere on the continent and will be analysed in special circles long after New York has forgotten it. In Brooklyn, which might be described as the belly of the Great White Whale, a prominent school authority had just committed suicide; a famous judge had just been accused of calling the Superintendent of Schools a bastard; a grand jury had announced that the schools were rife with "hoodlums, rapists, thieves, extortionists, arsonists, and vandals"; the mayor had ordered policemen into some of these schools to protect the teachers against their pupils.

"Naw," said Przwyk, "that stuff has *always* been here. I could tell you a story."

He deposited me in front of the hotel where, in the spring of 1933, I had lived on credit for eight days while the nation's banks were closed. The hinterland had trembled, several Wall Street bankers had contemplated a choice between suicide and the penitentiary, but the Great White Whale had basked blissfully indifferent and carried on as usual while the world panicked. The most disreputable strangers were given almost unlimited credit in the hotels. New York, after all, had to continue being New York just as it now had to continue being New York in spite of the blackboard jungle.

"Yeah," said Dominick Tintoretto as he drove me that night to a remembered jazz-spot in the Village, "definitely and strictly it is a very wonnerful thing people like you coming from all over here. You see how things is done here, you go home and you make your improvements. It is all very wonnerful. Seeing how things is done here, you *gotta* make improvements or how can you odderwise live? Up in Mo-ree-al how are things?"

I asked him how he knew I was from Montreal, since I had not told him.

"You talk like an English fella," said Tintoretto, "only you don't talk like an English fella, so I figure it is from Mo-ree-al that you come."

I asked how he knew how an English fella talked.

"I bin all over. First World War. Wincheser, Durby, Oggsferd, Wales. I guess England's okay if you like the Village. The Mayor is gonna do something about the Village. Now take the Mayor."

He arrived at my destination before he had time to take the Mayor, and I entered the familiar place to find it with a new decor, a quadrupled cover charge, but the same sprightly, spring-fresh jazz played by young Negroes who looked just like the ones I had first heard a quarter-century ago before they became middle-aged and famous and much duller than they had been when they played here. Next to me was a couple holding hands sitting opposite another couple doing the same, and they all seemed so intimate I thought they were old friends until the second couple departed for the bar and I overheard that the first couple had met them only half an hour before. The girl, speaking a beautiful English in a Dutch accent, was explaining something to her inarticulate American escort.

"But New York is the *only* place where people don't have to live with *each other*. They only have to live with *themselves*."

Her escort, who admitted that his home town was Washington Courthouse, Ohio, opined that New York had everything, and the Dutch girl said she wasn't sure about that, but she was certainly sure — a glance from lowered lids into the eyes of the Washington Courthouse man — that New York was a place where the most delicious things could happen to a girl night after night.

"You know what's the trouble with Arnold Toynbee?" said Isadore Goldberg three hours later as he drove me back to my hotel.

I have been driven through New York by a student of Immanuel Kant, by several Marxian scholars, by one anthropologist, by a variety of ex-pugs and bootleggers, but now, in Goldberg, I had discovered someone who outmoded the lot of them.

"What's history," said Goldberg, "but psychology, and what's psychology but the ree-searches of Sigmund Freud? Toynbee writes history like Freud was not in it. That's what's the trouble with Toynbee."

New York, which is everything, is also the Metropolitan Museum, and I spent four hours there on my second day, my chief purpose being to revisit the Rembrandts and the Grecos. They were there, they were cleaned, and they were wonderful, but once again I found that the White Whale had continued its habit of

surpassing and outmoding even itself. I left the Museum overwhelmed not by Rembrandt and Greco, but by the colossal nude
bronze statue of the Emperor Trebonianus Gallus, who was the
greatest man in the world between 251 A.D. and 253 A.D., when he
was murdered by his own soldiers. Black, terrible, huge, and
naked — the nakedest statue I ever saw — this awful apparition
dominates the atrium of the Metropolitan, his face and horrible
labourer's body telling more about the decline and fall of the
Roman Empire than Gibbon and Toynbnee put together. Was it
always there in the Metropolitan and I had not seen it? But New
York had incorporated Gallus now, and Goldberg, who as a Freu-
dian understands that history is a prolonged process of gods eating
gods, religions eating religions, civilizations eating civilizations,
might possibly agree with my terrified apprehension that the Great
Whale has now swallowed the Roman Empire along with the
British.

The Whale, I discovered a few hours later, had swallowed and
incorporated another big fish: Franklin Roosevelt, together with
his whole family, who have survived him and still live, I understand, interesting and exciting lives of their own, had been legend-
ized into a show off Broadway with Ralph Bellamy in the lead. Mr.
Bellamy had never seemed to me to resemble Franklin Roosevelt in
any way whatever, but there he was, and I had the odd sensation
that so far as the Whale was concerned, the thirty-first president
had never been quite real until he was dead enough to be converted
into *The Roosevelt Story*. The Whale was browsing as usual on a large
variety of sexual shows (when will it outmode sex?) and also on the
dramatized versions of two novels which seemed to me to have
been contemporary only yesterday, but were treated by the critics
in the manner adopted by fashionable shops to the dress styles of a
year ago. *A Farewell to Arms*, a novel which seemed to me to have
been written only yesterday, was playing in a movie at the Roxy,
and one of the Whale's special correspondents found it interesting
because it demonstrated how out of touch was the writing of the
early 1930s with the reality of Now. "Catherine Barclay," the
writer complained, "*used* to be every man's ideal girl." That other
anti-war novel of the thirties, *Paths of Glory*, was also on display in a
movie version and I saw it and found it tremendous. But the
Whale's press was uninterested in it, and the taxi-driver James

Westerley (his foreign-sounding name attributable to the fact that he was a Negro) had the final word on its importance.

"They don' fight wars that way any more," said Westerley. "No, sir, not any more do they fight wars that way."

The next morning I decided I could put it off no longer and went to see my agent with the manuscript, which I delivered just before lunch. As we sipped our coffee after lunch I asked him a few questions about the book trade and his answers did not sound cheerful. He told me what I knew only too well: that the general market for cloth-covered fiction was away below the level of what it had been a dozen years ago. Paper-backs had changed the entire shape of the market. Television had cut heavily into the time available for reading. Some eighty-five percent of American families now owned television sets and the average burning-time of a set in America was more than five hours in twenty-four. According to some fairly reliable opinion-samplers, only one American in five read even one book a year and only seventeen percent of Americans *bought* as many as one book in a lifetime.

I left my good friend feeling that the effort of the last years had probably been wasted, and walked around for a while trying to forget that in my little mind my little bodkin was broken.

My favourite part of Manhattan — I am obvious in my tastes — is the stretch of Fifth Avenue between the Plaza and Forty-eighth Street, and this stretch I now began to pace. My favourite shop in New York is Scribner's, which has the finest window of any book-shop I have ever seen. Mr. Van Duym, who dresses it, is a famous man in the trade; he loves and understands books, and if he really likes a book he has the art of setting it out in the window in such a way that you realize it is a thing much more precious than the diamond tiara you just looked at in Cartier's. I first saw Scribner's window in 1932 and I have looked into it on every visit to New York since that time. I used to think that if ever a book of mine were given even a modest corner of that window, all the work and strain of half a lifetime would have its reward. So now I spent ten minutes studying the window, went inside and browsed, bought a book, and emerged for another walk. Ah well, if not with this novel, perhaps with the next. The Whale had never been interested in anything Canadian, and this novel of mine was set in Montreal.

That night I took my departure with the Whale scintillating as he always does on a clear night, and as I rode to Grand Central and saw the towering television masts on the top of the Empire State and the Chrysler, I asked myself why this place seemed to annihilate the value of everything I had ever learned to do in my entire life. But encouragement came in this dark moment from an unexpected quarter.

"This Tee-Vee," said Steve Svoboda, "ain't gonna last much longer. People all over is getting very weary indeed of Tee-Vee."

At a traffic light Svoboda pondered further: "They'll come up with sumpin new. When they gotta, they do."

I paid him off, counted the money remaining in my wallet, discovered as always that the Whale had swallowed more than I had expected that even he would be able to swallow, got into the train, and slept well. The white snow of Montreal looked comfortable after the White Whale and I muttered that it would be never before I tempted him again. But I knew I was fooling myself, for I always go back to New York. So does everybody. And this brings me to a postscript to the story of my dealings with the Great White Whale.

My forebodings about the book I had written turned out to be well founded, for six weeks after my return I was informed that the publisher to whom the novel had been sent did not wish to publish it. This was a shock, for it meant that for the first time since I became a professional novelist I was without an American publisher. After a very minor revision, the book was despatched to one of the Whale's most ancient and honourable publishers, and there it reposed while the editor considered it. By this time spring had broken out, and when my work in the university ended for the season, I boarded a freighter and sailed to England on the first holiday I had enjoyed in a dozen years. The ship took twelve days getting there, and I reached London on a Saturday night. When I picked up my mail at the bank in Cockspur Street the following Monday morning, the first letter I opened contained the news that the second publisher had also rejected the script, his reason being that the prose was turgid and the characters uninteresting. Prospects now were beginning to look alarming. It is worse than grim, it is like writing on the wall, when an established novelist gets two rejections of a script in succession. It is worse still when this happens to what he believes is his best book, for he has always known that at any moment he may cease to please, and that a time comes in the life of every writer when such talent as he possesses fails. Generally he himself is the last person to understand this, just as a faithful wife is often the last person to know what her husband has really been up to on some of his absences from home. Well, I thought, let's forget it and get on with the vacation. So I spent six weeks in England and Scotland and then flew home.

The first letter I opened on my arrival in Montreal was also from my agent, and it told me that the manuscript, as he had all along predicted, was now in safe hands. Scribner's was going to publish it some time in the course of the next year. The months went by and in a rush of new work I pushed the novel into the back of my mind. Proofs arrived and I corrected them, but I diligently kept away from the Great White Whale and professed incredulity when some interesting rumours about the novel floated north. The book appeared on the luckiest day of the year: Friday, the thirteenth of February, and still I kept away from New York. I was afraid of spoiling the pitch, for no writer, least of all a foreign one, could possibly have received more generous reviews than I was getting from the Whale's special correspondents at that particular moment. My publishers finally invited me down, and down I went.

My mind was confused in that month and I forgot my dates. When I began walking that Monday morning after breakfast the ghastly thought occurred to me that once again something unaccountable might have happened, for at ten-thirty the streets were almost deserted and all of the shops were closed. Had the Whale suffered some unexpected disaster during the night? Had the next depression begun? Had Wall Street collapsed? Was an atomic attack impending? As anything is possible in that city, none of these ideas seemed entirely unreasonable.

Then I began noticing that in window after window there was a picture of George Washington, and at last I understood that this was the man's birthday. It is true that the Whale had done no fighting for Washington during the Revolution; indeed, such effort as he expended in that war was mostly on the side of the King. But when the King lost, the Whale of course contrived to make his arrangements with the new government and now he was celebrating this. The holiday would mean a crowded Metropolitan in the afternoon, but it would also mean fairly empty streets. The air was brisk and I continued walking down Fifth until I reached Scribner's window. Honestly I had expected to find nothing there, but what I did find nearly knocked me out.

The entire window had been given over to that little novel of mine, and in my prejudiced eyes Mr. Van Duym had performed the finest work of art in his career. Stacks and stacks of the book were arranged in patterns; in addition there were five large photographs of Montreal, one of Ottawa, and another of a Canadian lumber camp. Blown-up photostats of reviews from the *Times* and the *Herald-Tribune* were in the window, and two strangers were bending forward to read them, while every fifth person who walked by stopped to stare.

For myself, I stayed there no longer than fifteen seconds, and when I bolted around the corner I was afraid that I had stayed at least ten seconds too long for my safety. The beastie was at my heels and my father's ghost was on the heels of the beastie. He was reminding me of the winter Sunday years ago when I had come home from a walk and discovered, absolutely out of the blue, that a telegram had arrived informing me that I had won a Rhodes Scholarship months after I had believed that I had lost my last chance of getting one. My father had risen to this occasion in the spirit of his ancestors. "Go out and shovel the snow," he said, and it was the only occasion when he ever ordered me to work on the Sabbath Day. So on that Washington's Birthday, as there was no snow to shovel in New York, I walked and I walked and I walked.

Four New York Poems
GEORGE JONAS

George Jonas was born in Budapest in 1935 and came to Toronto in 1956, part of the intellectual gain made by Canada from the abortive Hungarian uprising. Alone or in collaboration he has written several award-winning books about crime, terrorism and the law, including **Vengeance** *and* **By Persons Unknown.** *He is also a librettist and the author of three collections of poetry, one of which,* **Cities** *(1973), includes responses to America such as these.*

GREENWICH VILLAGE

The girl who shares this upstairs room
with a cat, a guitar and a chesterfield
left her native town, Sarnia,
because it was the end of the world.

First she moved on to Montreal
then crossed the ocean to Prague,
quickly returned to Los Angeles
and now she's bitterly crying.

She's bitterly crying I suppose
because she'd seen much sea and land
without once having glimpsed that world
of which Sarnia is the end.

LAW OFFICE ON BROAD STREET

My 23rd floor lawyer
looks in the cold morning light
at a quarter of a million
dollars worth of worthless
pre-war bonds and stocks
being optimistic.

Planners drill
                      tunnels
raise   towers,   monuments   design
                      parks
erect   structures of permanence   but
this is no city,
no century for planners.

Except as these
clouds are perfect for soaring
this night
perfect for darkness
these streets are
perfect for kisses and for knives
nothing else.

The elevator takes me down
past 23 floors of practical men
buying and selling stocks in a dream.
I note that no one cries.

Cautious downtown
                      emptied

by long silent rails for the night
of briefcases, aspirins and
the subway faces of defeat
                              where
do the elect live whose malice could injure
whose goodwill could heal
this wounded, patient world?

CARNEGIE HALL

Because sadness is costly
and inadequate
        and after a while
siege guns scale down to overtures

and finally our houses become ruins or monuments

also because of the hope that there will be a mind
to remember or to forget these cities
where bodies are even now being discharged
from hospitals and morgues
                or admitted
into offices and jails and high society
                   This is
for the explorers of ephemera

This is for students of coded words
exhumers of graves and connoisseurs of explosions
collectors of potsherds
             or readers
of the writing on the wall

This is trumpets for the ears of those whose hearing
has not become too subtle for loud music
it is kettledrums
        the rending
of foundations
        it is grenades
shattering granite

WHITE ANGLO-SAXON PROTESTANT
IN CENTRAL PARK

I find the moonlight much too sharp
to hide my preference for pain.
Checkered shadows follow the lane
police advise me not to take across
  this lonely park
but I am set in my ways
the night is bright and my mood is dark.

Well, city, kill me if you can
having killed stronger men and better men.
I have a wallet, there's my watch to pawn,
  black man white man
drug addicts, losers, whiners, victims come
  and take me on.

Indeed a man emerges from the bushes
but, on seeing me, turns and disappears.
Perhaps it is the aura of my breath
that makes the pale trees threatening and still,
for desperate as I have been for peace
  I am ready to kill.

I built this country. Shall I be the first
to yield what is best in it to the worst?
Why should I give in patiently? Jefferson's light
  is programmed in computers.
The dreamers and the hidebound, Left or Right,
the envious, the weak, the slow of wit
have it reduced, transistorized and geared
to the requirements of human shit.

Are all lessons of history in vain?
All gifts of man to man painful and bitter?
Wealth by its nature choked in its own litter?
Ripe fruit a necessary poison to its root?
May I not seek a maximum of good,
and still retain a minimum of truth?

Men are equal in birth and death. Between
men are stupid and wise, they're kind and mean,
diligent/indolent, aggressive/shy,
tolerant/biased, timid/bold, dull/keen
the evidence of which we all have seen
      and seen fit to deny.

In every act there is a final choice
in spite of all complexities
between the silence and the voice.
Happiness not a right, but a pursuit:
we talk to God privately, and he makes
      reply to suit.

But even if I were alone
in not wanting my privacy defended
by a wire-tap on my telephone
      I'm not alone
in needing no more well-meaning policemen
to keep me from a lonely walk across
a city park of pale trees, slow and sane,
in which checkered shadows follow the lane
and shafts of moonlight far too sharp
to hide my preference for pain.

Pain, for I am not free. Cops and robbers
play games around me, both protected by
my tolerance and money. I have tried
far too long too many substitutes.
      I am not free
for I have valued comfort more than truth.
It is my city, I am not a stranger,
I myself could be danger if there's danger,
I myself could be murder if there's murder.
Not more policemen to escort me further,
Liberty, walk with me. I look to you again
      for my Law and Order.

The Catskills
MORDECAI RICHLER

The important novels of Mordecai Richler (born 1931) include The Apprenticeship of Duddy Kravitz *and* Joshua Then and Now. *He is one of the Canadian writers with a large following in other countries, especially Britain, where he lived and wrote from the late 1950s to the early 1970s, and the United States, where he brings to magazine journalism the same strain of black humour associated with his fiction. The following article on the Catskills, the New York State resort area that has inspired generations of stand-up comics, was written in 1965.*

A ny account of the Catskill Mountains must begin with Grossinger's. The G. On either side of the highway out of New York and into Sullivan County, a two hour drive north, one is assailed by billboards. DO A JERRY LEWIS—COME TO BROWN'S. CHANGE TO THE FLAGLER. I FOUND A HUSBAND AT THE WALDEMERE. THE RALEIGH IS ICIER, NICIER, AND SPICIER. All the Borscht Belt billboards are criss-crossed with lists of attractions, each hotel claiming the ultimate in golf courses, the latest indoor and outdoor pools, and the most tantalizing parade of stars. The countryside between the signs is ordinary, without charm. Bush land and small hills. And then finally one comes to the Grossinger billboard. All it says, *sotto voce*, is GROSSINGER'S HAS EVERYTHING.

"On a day in August, 1914, that was to take its place among the red-letter days of all history," begins a booklet published to commemorate Grossinger's 50th anniversary, "a war broke out in Europe. Its fires seared the world.... On a summer day of that same year, a small boarding house was opened in the Town of Liberty." The farm house was opened by Selig and Malke Grossinger to take in nine people at nine dollars a week. Fresh air for factory workers, respite for tenement dwellers. Now Grossinger's, spread over a thousand acres, can accommodate fifteen hundred guests. It represents an investment of fifteen million dollars. But to crib once more from the anniversary booklet, "The greatness of any institution cannot be measured by material size alone. The Taj Mahal cost a king's ransom but money in its intrinsic form is not a part of that structure's unequalled beauty."

Grossinger's, on first sight, looks like the consummate kibbutz. Even in the absence of Arabs there is a security guard at the gate. It has its own water supply, a main building — in this case Sullivan County Tudor with picture windows — and a spill of outlying lodges named after immortals of the first Catskill Aliya, like Eddie Cantor and Milton Berle.

I checked in on a Friday afternoon in summer and crossing the terrace to my quarters stumbled on a Grossinger's Forum Of The Air in progress. Previous distinguished speakers — a reflection, as one magazine put it, of Jennie Grossinger, in whom the traditional reverence for learning remains undimmed — have included Max Lerner and Norman Cousins. This time out the lecturer was resident hypnotist Nat Fleischer, who was taking a stab at CAN LOVE SURVIVE MARRIAGE? "I have a degree in psychology," Fleischer told me, "and am now working on my doctorate."

"Where?"

"I'd rather not say."

There were about a hundred and fifty potential hecklers on the terrace. All waiting to pounce. Cigar-chumpers in Bermuda shorts and ladies ready with an alternative of the New York *Post* on their laps. "Men are past their peak at twenty-five," Fleischer shouted into the microphone, "but ladies reach theirs much later and stay on a plateau, *while the men are tobogganing downhill.*" One man hooted, another guffawed, but many ladies clapped approval. "You think," Fleischer said, "the love of the baby for his momma is natural — *no!*" A man, holding a silver foil sun reflector to his face, dozed off. The lady beside him fanned herself with *From Russia, With Love.* "In order to remain sane," Fleischer continued, "what do we need? ALL OF US. Even at sixty and seventy. LOVE. A little bit of love. If you've been married for twenty-five years you shouldn't take your wife for granted. Be considerate."

A lady under a tangle of curlers bounced up and said, "I've been married twenty-*nine years* and my husband doesn't take me for granted."

This alarmed a sunken-bellied man in the back row. He didn't join in the warm applause. Instead he stood up to peer at the lady. "I'd like to meet her husband." Sitting down again, he added, "The *shmock.*"

There was to be a get-together for singles in the evening, but the prospects did not look dazzling. A truculent man sitting beside me in the bar said, "I dunno. I swim this morning. I swim this afternoon — indoors, outdoors — my God, what a collection! When are all the beauties checking in?"

I decided to take a stroll before dinner. The five lobbies at Grossinger's are nicely panelled in pine, but the effect is somewhat undermined by the presence of plastic plants everywhere. There is plastic sweet corn for sale in the shop beside the Olympic-size outdoor pool and plastic grapes are available in the Mon Ami Gift and Sundry Shop in the main building. Among those whose pictures hang on The Wall of Fame are Cardinal Spellman and Yogi Berra, Irving Berlin, Governors Harriman and Rockefeller, Ralph Bunche, Zero Mostel, and Herman Wouk. The indoor pool, stunningly simple in design, still smelled so strongly of disinfectants that I was reminded of the more modest "Y" pool of my boyhood. I fled. Grossinger's has its own post office and is able to stamp all mail "Grossinger, N.Y." There is also Grossinger Lake, "for your tranquil togetherness"; an 18-hole golf course; stables; an outdoor artifical ice rink; a ski trail and toboggan run; a His'n Hers health club, and of course a landing strip adjoining the hotel, the Jennie Grossinger Field.

The ladies had transformed themselves for dinner. Gone were the curlers, out came the minks. "Jewish security blankets," a guest, watching the parade with me, called the wraps, but fondly, with that sense of self-ridicule that redeems Grossinger's and, incidentally, makes it the most slippery of places to write about.

I suppose it would be easiest, and not unjustified, to present the Catskills as a cartoon. A Disneyland with knishes. After all, everywhere you turn the detail is bizarre. At the Concord, for instance, a long hall of picture windows overlooks a parking lot. There are rooms that come with two adjoining bathrooms. ("It's a gimmick. People like it. They talk about it.") All the leading hotels now have indoor ice skating rinks because, as the lady who runs The Laurels told me, our guests find it too cold to skate outside. True, they have not yet poured concrete into the natural lakes to build artificial filtered pools above, but, short of that, every new convenience conspires to protect guests from the countryside. Most large hotels, for instance, link outlying lodges to the main building through a system of glassed-in and sometimes even subterranean passages, all in the costly cause of protecting people from the not notoriously fierce Catskills outdoors.

What I'm getting at is that by a none too cunning process of selected detail one can make Grossinger's, the Catskills, and the people who go there, appear totally grotesque. One doesn't, because there's more to it than that. Nothing, on the other hand, can prevent Sullivan County from seeming outlandish, for outlandish it certainly is, and it would be condescending, the most suspect sort of liberalism, to overlook this and instead celebrate, say, Jennie Grossinger's maudlin "warmth" or "traditional reverence" for bogus learning.

Something else. The archetypal Grossinger's guest belongs to the most frequently fired at class of American Jews. Even as *Commentary* sends out another patrol of short story writers the *Partisan Review* irregulars are waiting in the bushes, bayonets drawn. Saul Bellow is watching, Alfred Kazin is ruminating, Norman Mailer is ready with his flick-knife, and who knows what manner of trip wires the next generation of Jewish writers is laying out at this very moment. Was there ever a group so pursued by such an unsentimental platoon of chroniclers? So plagued by moralists? So blamed for making money? Before them came the *luftmensh*, the impecunious dreamers — tailors, cutters, corner grocers — so adored by Bernard Malamud. After them came Phillip Roth's confident college boys on the trot, Americans who just happen to have had a Jewish upbringing. But this generation between, this unlovely spiky bunch that climbed with the rest of middle-class America out of the depression into a pot of prosperity, is the least liked by literary Jews. In a Clifford Odets play they were the rotters. The rent-collectors. Next Jerome Weidman carved them up and then along came Budd Schulberg and Irwin Shaw. In fact in all this time only Herman Wouk, armed with but a slingshot of clichés, has come to their defence. More of an embarrassment, I'd say, than a shield.

Well now here they are at Grossinger's, sitting ducks for satire. Manna for sociologists. Here they are, breathless, but at play, so to speak, suffering sour stomach and cancer scares, one Israeli bond drive after another, unmarriageable daughters and sons gone off to help the Negroes overcome in Mississippi. Grossinger's is their dream of plenty realized, but if you find it funny, larger than life, then so do the regulars. In fact there is no deflating remark I could make about minks or match-making that has not already been made by visiting comedians or guests. Furthermore, for an innocent goy to even think some of the things said at Grossinger's would be to invite the wrath of the B'nai Brith Anti-Defamation League.

At Grossinger's, guests are offered the traditional foods, but in super-abundance, which may not have been the case for many of them in the early years. Here, too, are the big TV comics, only this is their real audience and they appreciate it. They reveal the authentic joke behind the bland story they had to tell on TV because Yiddish punch-lines do not make for happy Neilson ratings.

The "ole swimmin' hole," as one Catskill ad says, was never like this. Or to quote from an ad for Kutsher's Country Club, "You wouldn't have liked The Garden of Eden anyway — it didn't have a golf course. Kutsher's, on the other hand...." There are all the knishes a man can eat and, at Brown's Hotel, they are made more palatable by being called "Roulade of Fresh Chicken Livers." In the same spirit, the familiar chicken soup with *lockshen* has been reborn "essence of chicken broth with fine noodles" on yet another menu.

The food at Grossinger's, the best I ate in the Catskills, is delicious if you like traditional kosher cooking. But entering the vast dining-room, which seats some 1600 guests, creates an agonizing moment for singles. "The older men want young girls," David Geivel, the head waiter told me, "and the girls want presentable men. They want to line up a date for New York where they sit alone all week. They've only got two days, you know, so they've got to make it fast. After each meal they're always wanting to switch tables. The standard complaint from the men runs... 'even when the girls are talking to me, they're looking over my shoulder to the dentist at the next table. Why should I ask her for a date, such an eye-roamer?'"

I picked up a copy of the daily *Tattler* at my table and saw how, given one bewitching trip through the hotel Gestetner, the painfully shy old maid and the flat-chested girl and the good-natured lump were transformed into "sparkling, captivating" Barbara, Ida, "the fun-loving frolicker"; and Miriam, "a charmladen lass who makes a visit to table 20F a must." I also noted that among other "typewriter boys" who had stayed at "the G." there was Paddy Chayefsky and Paul Gallico. Dore Schary was a former editor of the *Tattler* and Shelley Winters, Betty Garrett, and Robert Alda had all once worked on the special staff. Students from all over the United States still compete for jobs at the hotel. They can clear as much as a hundred and fifty dollars a week and, as they say at the G., be nice to your bus boy, next year when he graduates he may treat your ulcer. My companions at the table included two forlorn bachelors, a teenager with a flirtatious aunt, and a bejewelled and wizened widow in her sixties. "I hate to waste all this food," the widow said, "it's such a crime. My dog should be here he'd have a wonderful time."

"Where is he?"

"Dead," she said, false eyelashes fluttering, just as the loud-speaker crackled and the get-together for singles was announced. "Single people *only*, please,"

The teenager turned on her aunt. "Are you going to dance with Ray again?"

"Why not? He's excellent."

"Sure, sure. Only he's a *faigele*." A homosexual.

"Did you see the girl in the Mexican squaw blanket? She told her mother, 'I'm going to the singles. If I don't come back to the room tonight you'll know I'm engaged.' What an optimist!"

The singles get-together was thinly attended. A disaster. Bachelors looked in, muttered, pulled faces, and departed in pairs. The ladies in their finery were abandoned in the vast ballroom to the flatteries of staff members, twisting in turn with the hairdresser and the dance teacher, each of whom had an eye for tomorrow's trade. My truculent friend of the afternoon had resumed his station at the bar. "Hey," he said, turning on a "G-man" (a staff member), "where'd you get all those dogs? You got a contract with New York City maybe they send you all the losers?"

The G-man, his manner reverent, told me that this bar was the very place where Eddie Cantor had discovered Eddie Fisher, who was then just another unknown singing with the band. "If you had told me in those days that Fisher would get within even ten feet of Elizabeth Taylor —" He stopped short, overcome. "The rest," he said, "is history."

Ladies began to file into the Terrace Room, the husbands trailing after them with the mink stoles now slung nonchalantly over their arms. Another All-Star Friday Nite Revue had finished in the Playhouse.

"What was it like?" somebody asked.

"Aw. It goes with the *gefilte* fish."

Now the spotlight was turned on the Prentice Minner Four. Minner, a talented and militant Negro, began with a rousing civil liberties song. He sang, "From San Francisco to New York Island, this is your land and mine."

"Do you know Shadrach?" somebody called out.

"Old Man River?"

"What about Tzena Tzena?"

Minner compromised. He sang Tzena Tzena, a hora, but with new lyrics. CORE lyrics.

A G-man went over to talk to my truculent friend at the bar. "You can't sit down at a table," he said, "and say to a lady you've just met that she's, um, well-stacked. It's not refined." He was told he would have to change his table again.

"Allright. O.K. I like women. So that makes me a louse."

I retired early, with my G. fact sheets. More than 700,000 gallons of water, I read, are required to fill the outdoor pool. G. dancing masters, Tony and Lucille, introduced the mambo to this country. Henry Cabot Lodge has, as they say, graced the G. roster. So has Robert Kennedy. Others I might have rubbed shoulders with are Baron Edmund de Rothschild and Rocky Marciano. It was Damon Runyon who first called Grossinger's "Lindy's with trees." Nine world boxing champions have trained for title bouts at the hotel. Barney Ross, who was surely the first orthodox Jew to become lightweight champion, "scrupulously abjured the general frolic-some air that pervaded his camp" in 1934. Not so goy-boy, Ingemar Johansson, the last champ to train at Grossinger's.

In the morning I decided to forgo the recommended early riser's appetizer, a baked Idaho potato; I also passed up herring baked and fried, waffles and watermelon, blueberries, strawberries, bagels and lox, and French toast. I settled for orange juice and coffee and slipped outside for a fast cigarette. (Smoking is forbidden on the sabbath, from sunset Friday to sundown Saturday, in the dining-room and the main lobbies.) Lou Goldstein, Director of Daytime Social Activities, was running his famous game of Simon Says on the terrace. There were at least a hundred eager players and twice as many hecklers. "Simon says put up your hands. Simon says bend forward from the waist. The *waist*, lady. You got one? oi. *That's* bending? What's your name?"

"Mn Mn," through buttoned lips.

"Allright. Simon says what's your name?"

"Sylvia."

"Now that's a good Jewish name. The names they have these days. Désirée. Drexel. Where are you from?"

"Philadelphia."

"*Out.*"

A man cupped his hands to his mouth and called out, "Tell us the one about the two *goyim*."

"We don't use that word here. There are people of every faith at Grossinger's. In fact, we get all kinds here. (Allright, lady. Sit down. We saw the outfit.) Last year a lady stands here and I say to her what do you think of sex. Sex, she says, it's a fine department store." Goldstein announced a horseshoe toss for the men, but there were no takers. "Listen here," he said, "at Grossinger's you don't work. You toss the horseshoe but a member of our staff picks it up. Also you throw downhill. Allright, athletes, follow me."

I stayed behind for a demonstration on how to apply make-up. A volunteer was called for, a plump matron stepped forward, and was helped on to a make-shift platform by the beautician. "Now," he began, "I know that some of you are worried about the expression lines round your mouth. Well, this putty if applied correctly will fill all the crevices. . . . There, notice the difference on the right side of the lady's face?"

"No."

"*I'm sure* the ladies in the first four rows can notice."

Grossinger's has everything — and a myth. The myth of Jennie, LIVING SYMBOL "HOTEL WITH A HEART" runs a typical *Grossinger News* headline. There are photographs everywhere of Jennie with celeb-rities. "A local landmark," says a Grossinger's brochure, "is the famous smile of the beloved Jennie." A romantic but mediocre oil painting of Jennie hangs in the main lobby. There has been a song called *Jennie* and she has appeared on *This Is Your Life*, an occasion so thrilling that as a special treat on rainy days guests are sometimes allowed to watch a rerun of the tape. But Jennie, now in her seventies, can no longer personally bless all the honeymoon couples who come to the hotel. Neither can she "drift serenely" through the vast dining-room as often as she used to, and so a younger lady, Mrs. Sylvia Jacobs, now fills many of Jennie's offices. Mrs. Jacobs, in charge of Guest Relations, is seldom caught without a smile. "Jennie," she told me, "loves all human beings, regardless of race, colour, or creed. Nobody else has her vision and charm. She personifies the grace and dignity of a great lady."

Jennie herself picked Mrs. Jacobs to succeed her as hostess at the G.

"God, I think, gives people certain gifts — God-given things like a voice," Mrs. Jacobs said. "Well, I was born into this business. In fifty years I am the one who comes closest to personifying the vision of Jennie Grossinger. The proof of the pudding is my identification here." Just in case further proof was required, Mrs. Jacobs showed me letters from guests, tributes to her matchmaking and joy-spreading powers. You are, one letter testified, T-E-R-R-I-F-I-C. You have an atomic personality. "There's tradition," she said, "and natural beauty and panoramic views in abundance here. We don't need Milton Berle. At Grossinger's, a seventy-five dollar a week stenographer can rub shoulders with a millionaire. This is an important facet of our activities, you know."

"Do you deal with many complaints?" I asked.

Mrs. Jacobs melted me with a smile. "A complaint isn't a problem — it's a challenge. I thank people for their complaints."

Mrs. Jacobs took me on a tour of Jennie's house, Joy Cottage, which is next door to Millionaire's Cottage and across the road from Pop's Cottage. A signed photograph of Chaim Weizmann, first president of Israel, rested on the piano, and a photograph of Jack Benny, also autographed, stood on the table alongside. One wall was covered from ceiling to floor with plaques. Inter-faith awards and woman-of-the-year citations, including The Noble Woman of the Year Award from the Baltimore Noble Ladies' Aid Society. There was also a Certificate of Honour from *Wisdom* magazine. "Jennie," Mrs. Jacobs said, "is such a modest woman. She is always studying, an hour a day, and if she meets a woman with a degree she is simply overcome...." Jennie has only one degree of her own. An Honorary Doctor of Humanities awarded to her by Wilberforce University, Ohio, in 1959. "I've never seen Jennie so moved," Mrs. Jacobs said, "as when she was awarded that degree."

Mrs. Jacobs offered me a box of cookies to sustain me for my fifteen minute drive to "over there" — *dorten*, as they say in Yiddish — the Concord.

If Jennie Grossinger is the Dr. Schweitzer of the Catskills then Arthur Winarick must be counted its Dr. Strangelove. Winarick, once a barber, made his fortune with Jeris Hair Tonic, acquired the Concord for $10,000 in 1935, and is still, as they say, its guiding genius. He is in his seventies. On first meeting I was foolish enough to ask him if he had ever been to any of Europe's luxury resorts. "Garages with drapes," he said. "Warehouses."

A guest intruded; he wore a baseball cap with sunglasses fastened to the peak. "What's the matter, Winarick, you only put up one new building this year?"

"*Three.*"

One of them is that "exciting new sno-time rendezvous," King Arthur's Court, "where every boy is a Galahad or a Lancelot and every damsel a Guinevere or a fair Elaine." Winarick, an obsessive builder, once asked comedian Zero Mostel, "What else can I do? What more can I add?"

"An indoor jungle, Arthur. Hunting for tigers under glass. On *shabus* the hunters could wear *yarmulkas*." Skullcaps.

It is unlikely, however, that anyone at the Concord would ever wear a skullcap, for to drive from the G. to *dorten* is to leap a Jewish generation; it is to quit a *haimeshe* (homey) place, however schmaltzy, for chrome and concrete. The sweet but professional people-lovers of one hotel yield to the computer-like efficiency of another. The Concord, for instance, also has a problem with singles, but I would guess that there is less table-changing. Singles and marrieds, youngs and olds, are identified by different coloured pins plugged into a war plan of the dining-room.

The Concord is the largest and most opulent of the Catskill resorts. "Today," Walter Winchell recently wrote, "it does 30 million Bux a year." It's a fantastic place. A luxury liner permanently in dry dock. Nine storeys high with an enormous lobby, a sweep of red-carpeted stairway, and endless corridors leading here, there, and everywhere, the Concord can cope with 2,500 guests who can, I'm assured, consume 9,000 *latkas* and ten tons of meat a day. Ornate chandeliers drip from the ceiling of the main lobby. The largest of the hotel's three nightclubs, the Imperial Room, seats 2,500 people. But it is dangerous to attempt a physical description of the hotel. For even as I checked in, the main dining-room was making way for a still larger one, and it is just possible that since I left, the five inter-connecting convention halls have been opened up and converted into an indoor spring training camp for the Mets. Nothing's impossible. "Years ago," a staff member told me, "a guest told Winarick you call this a room, at home I have a toilet nicer than such a room. And Winarick saw that he was right and began to build. 'We're going to give them city living in the country,' he said. Look at it this way. Everybody has the sun. Where do we go from there?"

Where they went was to build three golf courses, the last with 18 holes; hire five orchestras and initiate a big-name nightclub policy (Milton Berle, Sammy Davis Jr., Judy Garland, Jimmy Durante, etc.); install a resident graphologist in one lobby ("Larry Hilton needs no introduction for his humorous Chalktalks. . . .") and a security officer, with revolver and bullet belt, to sit tall on his air-cushion before the barred vault in another; hire the most in life guards, Director of Water Activities, Buster Crabbe ("This magnificent outdoor pool," Crabbe recently wrote, "makes all other pools look like the swimming hole I used to take Jane and the chimps to. . . ."); buy a machine, *the first in the Catskills*, to spew artificial and multi-coloured snow on the ski runs ("We had to cut out the coloured stuff, some people were allergic to it"); and construct a shopping arcade, known as Little Fifth Avenue, in the lower lobby.

Mac Kinsbrunner, the genial resident manager, took me on a tour beginning with the shopping arcade. A sign read:

SHOW YOUR TALENT
Everyone's Doing It
PAINT A PICTURE YOURSELF
The Spin Art Shop
50 cents
5 x 7 oil painting
Only Non Allergic Paints Used

Next door, Tony and Marcia promised you could walk in and dance out doing the twist or the bossanova or pachanga or cha-cha.

"We've got five million bucks worth of stuff under construction here right now. People don't come to the mountains for a rest any more," Kinsbrunner said, "they want *tummel*."

Tummel in Yiddish means noise and the old-time non-stop Catskill comics were known as *tummlers* or noise-makers.

"In the old days, you know, we used to go in for calisthenics, but no more. People are older. Golf, O.K., but — well I'll tell you something — in these hotels we cater to what I call food-cholics. Anyway I used to run it — the calisthenics — one day I'm illustrating the pump, the bicycle pump exercise for fat people — you know, in-out, in-out — zoom — her guts come spilling out. A fat lady. Right out. There went one year's profits, no more calisthenics."

We went to take a look at the health club. THRU THESE PORTALS, a sign read, Pass The Cleanest People In The World. "I had that put up," Kinsbrunner said. "I used to be a school teacher."

Another sign read:

FENCE FOR FUN
Mons. Octave Ponchez
Develop Poise — Grace — Physical Fitness

In the club for singles, Kinsbrunner said, "Sure they're trouble. If a single doesn't hook up here she goes back to New York and says the food was bad. She doesn't say she's a dog. Me, I always tell them you should have been here last weekend. Boy."

The Concord, indeed most of the Catskill resorts, now do a considerable out-of-season convention business. While I was staying at the hotel a group of insurance agents and their wives, coming from just about every state in the union, was whooping it up. *Their* theme-sign read:

ALL THAT GLITTERS
IS NOT GOLD
EXCEPT ANNUITIES

Groups representing different sales areas got into gay costumes to march into the dining-room for dinner. The men wore cardboard moustaches and Panama hats at rakish angles, and their wives wiggled shyly in hula skirts. Once inside the dining-room they all rose to sing a punchy sales song to the tune of "Mac the Knife," from *The Threepenny Opera* by Bertolt Brecht and Kurt Weill. It began, "We're behind you/Old Jack Regan/To make Mutual number one...." Then they bowed their heads in prayer for the company and held up lit sparklers for the singing of the national anthem.

The Concord is surrounded by a wire fence. It employs some thirty security men. But Mac Kinsbrunner, for one, is in favour of allowing outsiders to stroll through the hotel on Sundays. "Lots of them," he told me "can't afford the Concord yet. People come up in the world they want to show it, you know. They want other people to know they can afford it here. So let them come and look. It gives them something to work toward, something to look up to."

The Concord must loom tallest from any one of a thousand *kochaleins* (literally "cook-alones") and bungalow colonies that still operate in Sullivan County. Like Itzik's Rooms or the Bon-Repos or Altman's Cottages. Altman's is run by Ephraim Weisse, a most engaging man, a refugee, who has survived four concentration camps. "The air is the only thing that's good in the Catskills," Ephraim said. "Business? It's murder. I need this bungalow colony like I need a hole in the head." He shrugged, grinning. "I survived Hitler, I'll outlast the Catskills."

Other large hotels, not as celebrated as Grossinger's or the Concord, tend to specialize. The Raleigh, for instance, has five bands and goes in for young couples. LIVE "LA DOLCE VITA" (the sweet life), the ads run, AT THE RALEIGH. "We got the young swingers here," the proprietor told me.

Brown's, another opulent place, is more of a family hotel. Jerry Lewis was once on their social staff and he still figures in most of their advertisements. Brown's is very publicity-conscious. Instead of playing Simon Says or the Concord variation, Simon Sez, they play Brown's Says. In fact as I entered the hotel lobby a member of the social staff was entertaining a group of ladies. "The name of the game," he called out, "is not bingo, It's BROWN'S. You win you yell out BROWN'S."

Mrs. Brown told me that many distinguished people had stayed at her hotel. "Among them, Jayne Mansfield and Mr. Haggerty." Bernie Miller, *tummler*-in-residence, took me to see the hotel's pride,

The Jerry Lewis Theatre-Club. "Lots of big stars were embryos here," he said.

Of all the hotels I visited in the Catskills only The Laurels does not serve kosher food and is actually built on a lake. Sackett Lake. But, oddly enough, neither the dining-room nor the most expensive bedrooms overlook the lake, and, as at the other leading resorts, there are pools inside and out, a skating rink, a health club, and a nightclub or two. "People won't make their own fun any more," said Arlene Damen, the young lady who runs the hotel with her husband. "Years ago, the young people here used to go in for midnight swims, now they're afraid it might ruin their hairdos. Today nobody lives like it's the mountains."

Finally, two lingering memories of the Sullivan County Catskills.

As I left the Laurels I actually saw a young couple lying under a sun lamp by the heated indoor pool on a day that was nice enough for swimming in the lake outside the picture window.

At Brown's, where THERE'S MORE OF EVERYTHING, a considerable number of guests ignored the endless run of facilities to sit on the balcony that overlooked the highway and watch the cars go by, the people come and go. Obviously, there's still nothing like the front-door stoop as long as passers-by know that you don't have to sit there, that you can afford everything inside.

Letters from Washington
SONDRA GOTLIEB

Sondra Gotlieb (born 1936) won the Leacock Medal for Humour for her 1978 novel True Confections. *She is married to Allan Gotlieb, Canada's ambassador to the United States. She is renowned as a Washington hostess, but has managed to escape the confining role of diplomatic wife and become a public figure — a sometimes controversial one — in her own right. One means of doing so has been a* Washington Post *column in which letters to a friend back home point up the differences between the two countries. The following are two examples.*

Doing the Shuttle-Huddle...

Dear Beverly,

I'm glad you're coming to Washington at last although I'm not sure what you mean by "doing some market research on muffin shops." If you're looking for a profitable site, Mr. Ambassador thinks Georgetown has the greatest number of the classic muffin-eater type.

But I'm worried about you flying in on the shuttle from New York. Taking the shuttle for the first time at your age is like learning to ski without an instructor. The shuttle has a set of rules particular to itself which covers everything from social behavior to arrival expectations.

Beverly, you really ought to have an old shuttle salt put you through the paces because it will be a shocking experience. I know you think Washington is a glamorous town but even Popsie Tribble, on her way to a gala benefit in New York, looks like a deportee when she's on the shuttle.

So if you actually make it from New York, don't expect me to introduce you to any Important Job hanging around the airport. You won't be in bandbox condition. Oddly enough, Popsie Tribble actually believes the shuttle encourages spontaneous travel because you don't need reservations and it is supposed to leave every hour. She says, "When I get pooped out shopping at Bergdorfs I grab a cab to La Guardia and soon I'm flying back to Georgetown in time for Baron Spitte's costume ball."

Well, Beverly, Mr. Ambassador and "wife of" have never been that lucky. Here's our shuttle drill from Washington's National (a must, Beverly, because of your interest in architecture; Early Greyhound, I'd say).

We try to arrive with a positive attitude because they said on the phone that the weather was hunky-dory and planes were leaving on time. But Mr. Ambassador, who has a bionic nose, sniffs fog over the East River in New York. And the terminal is ominously empty as we make our way to Shuttle Gate 18.

Beverly, at Gate 18, we meet with Shuttle Reality.

An assemblage of bodies looking like the cast from Mother Courage, with 50-pound bundles strapped to their backs, are doing the Shuttle Huddle. They do the Shuttle Huddle because there is no seat selection. Those who stand clamped nearest to the door where they think the plane is supposed to park will get the best places. Since no plane has left for New York since 6 a.m. (fog over East River) about 500 refugees are ready to risk suffocation in order to avoid the dreaded middle seat.

On normal plane trips, Beverly, the rules of social behavior are cut and dried. Don't make eye contact, keep your skirts drawn in, and place your carry-on luggage on the seat beside you so a stranger won't sit down.

These rules are more embarrassing to follow on the shuttle, even though we all make the attempt.

You see, Beverly, except for the odd tourist like you, everyone on the shuttle knows each other.

There's Lionel Portant, World Famous Columnist and TV Commentator, who broke bread at our residence two days before, with his head buried in *The New York Times* avoiding eye contact with Mr. Ambassador. Melvin Thistle Jr. from State is pretending to sleep standing up, because Joe Promisall, the famous lobbyist, talking anxiously on the pay phone, might hang up and talk to him. Joe Promisall used to have Thistle's job in a past administration, and, who knows, might get it again in the next.

Beverly, Powerful Jobs become Profitable Jobs when Powerful

Jobs leave government. Profitable Jobs are more sociable unless they suffer from "decompression," a Washington code word for an emotional state caused by loss of power.

In the bleakness of Shuttle Gate 18, decompressing former Mr. Secretaries who used to fly on government planes to New York now have to press their bodies against people whose phone calls they never returned.

Some Profitable Jobs, like Joe Promisall, don't practice normal airplane rules. Joe behaves as if Gate 18 is one more Washington cocktail party. Wordlessly, he pats a former Four Star General on the back, slides over to Mr. Ambassador for a handshake and explains how he used to run the shop to Melvin Thistle, Jr., who is forced to open his eyes. Lionel Portant, with his instant TV recognizability, is now standing facing the wall praying nobody can see him.

Beverly, we have now been standing at Gate 18 for two hours and Mr. Ambassador is angry because I packed four pair of shoes and the electric hair curlers in one of the carry-on bundles. But it's a good thing I did, because Mr. Ambassador uses it as kind of a counter-missile to advance our boarding position and we are able to requisition an aisle and window seat.

Beverly, always glance at the bulkhead seats, because the shuttle, despite the no-reservation rule, will keep the bulkhead for famous people. Some of the Famous suffer from reverse snobbery and believe it's politically safer to sit discreetly several seats behind. No reverse snob, the dusty diplomat, Baron Spitte, is already ensconced in the bulkhead as we walk by.

The problem now is what to do with the bundles. Storage space is not a Shuttle Priority. Mr. Ambassador parks the counter-missile on top of Baron Spitte's cashmere coat in the overhead space for the Famous. I crawl on the floor and wedge my bundle in front of the dreaded middle seat (no space in front of mine) which has been taken over by unhappy Melvin Thistle.

It's another half-hour sitting on the runway and the atmosphere is deadly. Everybody except us foreigners is afraid to talk because an enemy is bound to be within hearing range. I don't dare ask Thistle why he's going to New York because if he answers he might reveal his foreign policy intentions to Joe Promisall, who's breathing heavily behind us.

Finally, we hear our pilot.

"Morning folks. I'm Charlie Williams. Just relax and have a nice chat with your neighbor. We're number 14 on the runway."

Twenty minutes later, Thistle speaks to me.

"If you trade seats with me, you will be closer to your luggage."

Before I answer, Charlie makes a second announcement. "Good news, folks. We have clearance from the tower. And I'm thrilled to say we have a truly famous person on our airplane."

Lionel Portant, all the ex-Mr. Secretaries, and even Thistle, try to remove a smug look from their faces.

"Let's welcome to our shuttle this morning the famous dog trainer and author of 'No Bad Dogs,' Barbara Woodhouse." Then he pauses and says, "We're ready for takeoff. Stewardesses, here is your command. Sit."

Beverly, I hope your trip to Washington is tax-deductible.

Your best friend,

Sondra

The Upper Media and Georgetown Chic

Dear Beverly,

I'm not surprised that you wonder why I keep mentioning George-town in my letters when I don't even live there. Georgetown is a district of Washington where you can walk your dog, peer into a candle-and-pillow shop and try and figure out where one house ends and the other begins. The average Georgetown dweller must have some money because even the brick row houses sell for a sum that Sonny Goldstone, the Gilded Bachelor, wouldn't deride.

But there is something about Georgetown that provokes a curl of derision on the lips, a tone of suspicion in the voice of many a Washingtonian who doesn't live there. At first I thought it was because the houses looked so inconspicuous and cost so much. It's not only that, Beverly. Georgetown has become kind of a myth for those who dwell within as well as out.

I've heard phrases like "Georgetown Elite," "Georgetown Snobbism," "Georgetown Has-Beens," and even "Georgetown Conspiracy." I've also heard of "Georgetown Chic" (although I must admit the last phrase is mostly used by those who dwell within). I'm not sure why this innocent-looking neighborhood arouses such strong feelings, Beverly, but I'm doing my best to find out.

I was lunching with "wife of" Thistle Jr. from State and her 8-year-old twins at Armand's Pizzeria (not far from her home in Cleveland Park) when she used the phrase "that Georgetown set."

"I take it," I said, "you're not a Georgetownophile?"

"Too much faded chintz and uninformed gossip," she said shortly, helping herself to the last wedge of deep-dish pizza.

I wondered if she was referring to the fact that Dexter Tribble is lobbying for her husband's job and had invited a few of the Upper Media (Lionel Portant and the likes) for dinner to leak Thistle Jr.'s problems.

About the chintz, Beverly. "Wife of" Thistle Jr. may have put her finger on something. When Popsie Tribble redecorated her Georgetown house she put down her $80-a-yard fabric in the sun for three weeks, "for maturation." It's the same method Thistle Jr.'s teenage daughter uses to fade her jeans.

Anyway, the next day I lunched with Popsie at the Jockey Club (not too many children eat there) and I repeated what "wife of" Thistle said.

"Sheer jealousy," Popsie sniffed. "Don't you know her background?"

"No," I said. "What is it?"

"She was actually born in Cleveland Park," Popsie replied.

Cleveland Park, Beverly, is a nice family neighborhood where a lot of young congressmen and senators live. You know the kind of place. No fences around the houses and perhaps a few too many purple azalea bushes.

Popsie continued.

"'Wife of' Thistle couldn't cope with a civilized dinner party even if she had the entire Protocol section of State helping her. Eat at the Thistles' in Cleveland Park and come to the Tribbles' for dinner in Georgetown. Then you'll see the difference. In Georgetown, we know how these things are done. I wouldn't live anywhere else. It's so cozy. And I can walk to all the parties, except when I have to fly to New York."

It's a queer thing, Beverly. Popsie talks about walking in Georgetown. I walk there all the time, but I never see Popsie strolling in front of her house. Or anyone else I know. Maybe Georgetown dwellers don't want to be confused with the tourists.

About a week after my conversation with Popsie, I sat beside Senator Pod at the Washington Hilton at the annual meeting of the Dermatologists Association of North America. The Senator had to be there because he was trying to corner the market on dermatologists' campaign funds in his state. We were there because of the word "North" in North America.

I asked the Senator what he thought about Georgetown.

"I don't think about it. It's Eastern Establishment. Who thinks about Eastern Establishment these days? No power there since the Kennedy period. The Democrats like Georgetown, except for Lyndon Johnson, of course. I agree with Johnson. It's a low-lying place and becomes dank in the summer. I call it Washington's Mosquito Belt."

"Do you ever go to Georgetown parties?" I asked.

The Senator changed his tone a little. "Sometimes I cross the moat," he said a little defensively.

"Why?" I asked.

"Because of the parlor-room access."

"Parlor-room acess to whom?" I asked.

"To the Upper Media," the Senator replied. "It's more agreeable to set things right with the Upper Media over the fingerbowls. They still use those things in some houses in Georgetown. A few 'Used-to-be-Close-to's' and former Mr. Secretaries live there along with members of the Powerful Press. In Virginia they gossip about horses at dinner. In Georgetown, they gossip about politicians."

Beverly, I don't know if setting things right over the fingerbowls means that Senator Pod is leaking information. Or giving his version of the story, off the record, of course, to Lionel Portant. I just hope there are no listening devices in all those faded chintz settees.

Your best friend,

Sondra

PART
III
THE SOUTH

Another Time, Another Place, Another Me

HUGH GARNER

Hugh Garner (1913–1979) was Canada's premier working-class novelist, best known as the author of **Cabbagetown** *and of many short story collections. When asked, he was also a forthright admirer of interesting American landscape and plain American ideals. Between service in the Spanish Civil War and the Second World War, he travelled extensively in the United States as a hobo. This short story, set in the Appalachian Mountains, is drawn from that experience.*

I don't know why I should think back again after all these years to the night spent with the dying old man, but I do. It was really only an incident out of many in my first youthful confrontations with disease and death. Perhaps, I sometimes think, it is because I have now reached the age that the old man had reached when he died; sometimes it seems to be something that happened to somebody else.

The cold October rain came down in ragged sheets across the railroad yards filled with empty coal gondolas, and now and then you could catch a glimpse of the black bulk of the hills in the distance, but how far away they were you couldn't tell. The red and green switch lamps twinkled through the darkness like a lighted Christmas tree seen from outside a rain-drenched window. The sign on the soot-covered stone station read, PARKERSBURG W.V.

I was soaked to the skin and cold with a feverish shivering cold that my wet shirt and thin windbreaker pressed against my skin. The water ran from the broken peak of my cap making rivulets, I guess, through the coal dust on my cheeks. The trip through the mountains on top of a B & O freight, through the old stone-lined tunnels, hadn't improved my looks, but blackface was a common disguise in 1933.

I'd been released from the county can in Keyser, West Virginia, the day before, after doing seven days on a vag charge. I'd hurried through the jailhouse yard and the turnkey's house into the street, hating every hillbilly bastard prisoner in the place since it was built. They'd known from my accent that I wasn't from around there, and had put me through a kangaroo court on the charge of "breaking into jail as a vagrant bum." If you've never done hard time in a hillbilly can during the Depression its no use me telling you what it was like. You wouldn't believe it. By the time I was sprung I hated the whole goddam coal-dusted state of West Virginia, and the Baltimore & Ohio Railroad too.

Now the noise of the splashing rain shut out the smaller noises of the nearby town and the railroad shops, and as I stumbled along the tracks and across the switch ties I felt more alone than I'd ever felt before in my life. The only other human being in sight was a man in a lighted switch tower near the coal-tipple, who was staring in the direction of the yard diamond, at the same time taking gulps of something that looked warm and good from a thermos cup.

I steered clear of the lights from the station, passed by the coal-tipple and the water tower, and kept on until I spied a low windowless shack that showed a crack of light beneath its door. I crossed the mainline tracks, opened the door an inch or two, and glanced inside. It was the sand-house, as I'd expected it to be, its piles of warm dry sand banked high against the bubbling radiators that lined the walls. I stepped into the welcoming warmth, shutting the door quickly behind me.

For a minute or two I just stood there enjoying the heat, leaning with my wet face pressed against the door frame, letting the heat seep through my clothes as it raised small wisps of steam from my shoulders. The steam carried with it the familiar smell of months of boxcars, flophouses, and the new stink I'd learned in the Keyser county can.

A low moan from somewhere behind me raised the uncut hair from my neck and I swung around to see who or what it was. Sprawled on a pile of sand in a dim corner of the shack was a ragged old hobo, his legs thrust out at an awkward angle from his body and his arms thrashing at his sides. My sudden fright was replaced by a happiness to find I was not alone, as I'd been alone all day. I stumbled through the sand to his side, feeling its stickiness cake on my sodden shoes and crunch like sugar under my broken soles.

"Anything wrong, Cap?" I asked, staring down at the old man's sweating twisted face. A battered felt hat had rolled away from him and his thin dirty grey hair was sand-filled and stuck to his forehead.

His rheumy old eyes opened, and looking at me without hope he said, "Wa'er."

"Water?"

He closed his eyes again but managed to nod.

I looked around me for a cup or a tin can, but there was nothing. "What'll I get it in, Cap?" I asked him.

The rheumy old eyes opened again and he pointed to a pocket of his oversize wrinkled coat. "Bottle," he said.

I groped in a pocket and found a small bottle. Holding it up to the light I could read the heavy print on the label, RUBBING ALCOHOL.

Going outside again into the cold and rain was the last thing I wanted to do, but I slipped out and ran down the yards to a standpipe near the water tank. After rinsing out the bottle a couple of times I filled it with water. By the time I returned to the sand-house the old man had passed out, his legs twitching and kicking in the sand and his face grimacing like a kid in a nightmare. I sat down in the warm sand beside him, waiting for him to wake up.

I guess my weariness and the life-giving warmth of the shack made me doze off myself, but I was awakened by the wheezing voice of my companion pleading for water again. I held his head in my arms, put the bottle to his lips and let him take a long slow drink.

When he'd finished he stared at me and then said, "Tell Edna May — Springfield —" and passed out again. Springfield! There must be a score of towns with that name in the U.S., scattered over as many states. I sat staring at the poor old guy, listening to his labored breathing against the knocking of the hot radiator pipes. After a while his legs stopped twitching and his breathing quieted down. I picked a fresh pile of sand against the wall and fell asleep myself.

The loud scraping of a shovel woke me and I sat up and stared scared at an overalled workman turning over some sand near the door. When he noticed I was awake and staring at him he said, "It's okay, Bud, nobody'll bother you here. The yard bull's home with the flu." His accent was neither Yankee nor cornpone Southern but a mountain mixture of the two, just like those of the prisoners in the county can.

"What time is it please, mister?"

"Nearly two o'clock."

The shack trembled as a heavy manifest freight pounded through a few feet outside the door.

When the train had passed the workman asked, "What's wrong with your friend over there?"

"I don't know. He was there when I came in."

"I seen him earlier. He looks po'ly."

I glanced at the old man. His face was dead white now against the yellow sand, and his mouth had fallen open revealing his rotten teeth. His breath was being forced out of his chest in long shuddering gasps and he'd slipped from the pile of sand and was lying huddled on the sandy floor.

I talked to the workman, trying to keep him there, not wanting to be left alone with the sick old man. My pack of *Bugler* tobacco from the county can was damp but I managed to roll an uneven cigarette. In a minute or two the workman finished his shovelling and left the shack, while I sat with my back against a radiator unable to take my eyes off the old man.

After a while he croaked, "Wa'er!" again.

I was glad to leave the sand-house this time even though it meant getting wet all over again. I ran down to the standpipe, filled the bottle and ran back to the shack again.

I managed to lift the old man's head but I had to pour the water slowly down his throat. A lot of it spilled over his chin and chest but he didn't even open his eyes.

His breathing had now become harsh and uneven and I knew he was going to die. I prayed that somebody would come and take him out of there, not for his sake but for mine. Until then I'd never seen anyone die and my own death was something I was still too young to contemplate. I was scared to be left alone with a dying old man in a railroad sand-house, a long way from home and shut off from the rest of the world by the pelting rain. Crawling to him warily I placed him on his back and loosened his dirty collar. He looked more comfortable but his breath still escaped in long tortured sobs. I crawled back to my own place against the wall.

I guess it was more than an hour before the workman returned with his shovel to the sand-house. This time I told him I was certain the old hobo was dying. He walked over to the side of the old man and stared down at him briefly. Then he left, saying, "I guess I'll go call the doctor."

Left alone with the dying old man again I put my fingers in my ears to shut out the terrible sound of his breathing. From the corner of my eye I saw him raise himself off the floor, his body arched so only his heels and the back of his head touched the sand. Then he collapsed and lay still, looking like a pile of old clothes thrown into a corner. I took my fingers from my ears and found the room was quiet again, and I knew the old man was dead.

It was a long time before the doctor arrived, followed by two ambulance men carrying a stretcher. The doctor shook the rain from his yellow slicker, unbuttoned it to reveal he was wearing a pajama top pushed into his pants, and took his stethoscope from his bag. He opened the old man's shirt and listened for a heartbeat, then pushed up the old man's eyelids and closed the eyes again. Some yard workers crowded into the sand-house.

"What was it, Doc?" one of the railroad men asked.

The doctor shrugged and held up the rubbing alcohol bottle, which he placed in his slicker pocket. The ambulance men lifted the body from the floor to their stretcher, and the workmen stepped aside as the old hobo was carried out into the rain.

After the ambulance men had gone the workman who had been turning over the sand said to me, "You hungry, kid?"

I nodded. I was always hungry.

"Come with us down to the roundhouse an' I'll give you a sandwich."

The workman and I followed the others down the yards.

In the roundhouse locker room I sat with my friend and three or four yardmen and ate a lettuce-and-baloney sandwich washed down with a mug of coffee one of the others gave me.

When I was finished and was rolling a cigarette I said, "I feel sorry for that old guy. He sure scared me though. It was the first time in my life I actually saw anybody die."

"How old are you, boy?" asked the man who'd given me the coffee.

"Nineteen."

He looked around at the others and shook his head.

"It's an awful way to die," I said.

"It's a hell of a way for people to have to live too," another man said.

The man who'd given me the coffee said, "I heered they're closin' down No. 6 colliery over to near Deerwalk. That'll mean a couple a hunnerd more families on county aid."

"An' less coal to haul, so who can tell who'll be next?"

When I thanked the men and got up to leave the roundhouse one of them said, "If you're heading west there's a way freight pulls out for Chillicothe at eight in the mornin, an' you can catch her easy at the diamond. A 'bo told me las week that they're givin out free meals at dinnertime at the nuthouse in Athens, Ohio. That's not too far along the main line."

I thanked him, and said I'd make the way freight for sure.

When I reached the sand-house again I threw myself down in the sand and fell asleep. When I woke up in the morning I saw that the rain had stopped, and that the sun was just coming over the top of a wooded hill to the east. As I was leaving the shack I looked back at the place where the old man had died a few hours before. The sand had shifted and settled into different shapes since I'd fallen asleep. My eye caught a silvery glitter just about where the old hobo had been lying, and thinking it might be a quarter that had fallen from his pocket I hurried over and picked it up. It was much bigger than a half-dollar even, a World War I medal attached to a torn shabby ribbon. Around its edge had been cut the name *J.C. Waltham* and a service number.

It may have belonged to the old hobo, or maybe not. It was no good to me so I hung it by its ribbon on a nail above the inside of the sand-house door. If it *had* been the old man's that had died it was probably the only thing he'd left behind to show that he too had once lived as a member of the human race.

When the westbound way freight had been made up and was leaving the yards I jumped her. We reached Athens just in time for me to hurry to the state mental hospital and join the line-up of men waiting outside the kitchen door. After a long wait a kitchen worker handed us each a tin plate of macaroni-and-cheese, and we squatted on our haunches in the yard and ate it. It sure tasted good.

There's an awful lot of cities and towns called Springfield in the United States, but I can't drive through one even yet, almost forty years later, without remembering the dying old man in the sand-house in Parkersburg, West Virginia, and some girl or woman in his life named Edna May.

Adventures in God's Waiting Room
KILDARE DOBBS

Kildare Dobbs is one of Canada's most knowledgeable travel writers but also a literary generalist, the author of fiction, verse, historical works, an autobiography and two collections of essays. An Irishman, born in India (in 1923), in Canada since the early 1950s, he writes with an unaffected cosmopolitanism, as in this sketch of Miami Beach.

A s far as I can make out, everyone in the U.S. is in show business — but everyone. The triumph of style over content seems nearly complete. Ordinary Americans have surrendered to abstraction, have made themselves over as image. And all their world's a stage. I noticed this in Miami Beach recently, where Eastern Airlines had kindly flown me with a crowd of other free-loaders to inaugurate a new Whisperjet flight from Toronto by way of Buffalo, N.Y. The first portent: part of the highway from the airport was called Arthur Godfrey. But I was happy to see palm trees again and summery light, eager to breathe subtropical air just as soon as I could get at it — the bus, like everywhere else, was air-conditioned. Some of the other portents were vaguely disquieting: a building with a huge sign that said *National Exterminators*; a restaurant named the Robin Hood Inn which would have been fine except for the neon sign that went, "Eat, drink and be merrie." From the wreckage of my religious education a still, small voice insisted on completing the text.... Florida, I remembered, was God's waiting room, a balmy refuge for the twilight years. At every bus-stop the city had thoughtfully provided benches for the Waiting Ones. And paid for them by selling advertising-space on the back-rests, some of them plugging a $150 funeral service which, though hardly tactful, was certainly a nice thing to know about in the evening of life. Thrifty. For tomorrow we die.

But to return to the cardboard-and-tinsel, I discovered that the visitor too is expected to be a star. "Pardon me," a woman said in the marble fastnesses of the Hotel Fontainebleau (pronounced, incidentally, *fountain-blue*), "but aren't you the comedian from last night?"

I denied it. Her wide seat, I noted by way of preliminary put-down, was jammed into peach stretchie-pants. "The night before, then!" she said with conviction. "No, no," I insisted. "I've only just arrived." This the woman refused to accept. "What's your last name?" I disclosed it, adding in a hard voice, "What's *your* first name?" She received this with a happy smile, "Why...Ellie!" The stretchie-pants winked away with a complacent roll, their owner convinced she'd been proved right.

Just as soon as I could, I found the beach. This, at all events, is real. The sea is warm, reassuringly salty and restless, the sand is sand. And after I had swum and baked myself and swum again, I ordered lunch in full view of my own sector of the ocean. You should always take the chance to eat seafood, the local specialty, so I attempted Individual Can of Honeybee Tuna which comes fresh on the can, the American way. I thought of the rest of Miami Beach, one hundred hotels every mile along the shore for five miles (or is it six?). All those cans of Honeybee. And a sprinkling of bikinis, charming! A treat for the prostatectomy crowd.

And that night Eastern Airlines gave us all a big dinner at the Hotel Carillon where there was a show on stage, French follies and lovely girls almost as exiguously clad as the bikinied sirens on the beach. But the songs were a little too familiar, the effect a bit wholesomely close to geriatrics. "I don't know about you," I said to my photographer friend as we came out, "but I need something sordid to take away the taste."

He agreed, and we climbed into a cab with another enterprising Canadian and asked the driver to take us somewhere disreputable. Which was how we found ourselves in the Place Pigalle, a splendid place, dark and raffish. We had agreed not to waste money on drinks for B-girls and after a sporting try they left us alone. The Korean singer was doing his stuff on stage.

When we next looked round there was this astonishing young woman sitting beside us. "This," said the photographer, "has to be the most beautiful girl in Florida!" She was too. Sitting there in a black dress with sort of see-through panels over her astounding bosom. "We don't mind buying *you* a maple syrup," we told her. "Or whatever it is they bring you." She gave this dirty laugh. "I like maple syrup," she confided in a Cuban accent. And went on to tell us about some of her other enthusiasms in language that would not have disgraced a sailor. Me she addressed as Quasimodo, alleging that her own name was Dulcinea. She really was beautiful, it wasn't just the poor light. Her skin was like silk, and we couldn't think what a lovely girl like her was doing in a joint like this, etc.

It turned out she was Chelo, Chelo Castillo, the Latin Bombshell who was the star stripper of the show and the main attraction of the Place Pigalle. So she too was in show business!

But Chelo is real. Real as the white sand, the unpredictable sea, the spend-thrift Florida sun, Chelo is a force of nature on her own. Chelo, darling of the nightclubs, famous among taxi-drivers, hymned by conventioneers, rung up in a thousand expense accounts! "That girl's a *nut*," a citizen told me the next day, his face melting at the mere rehearsal of her name. "When Chelo goes some place — her night off she likes to visit places with a bit of class — the whole joint kind of lights up. You know? You hear that dirty laugh, the waiters start smiling, the band plays more lively, even the kitchen-help's happy. Ain't no way to describe her — Chelo's something all to herself!"

Chelo talked on softly and outrageously, knocking back that maple syrup as if it really was good brandy, which was what the management had the gall to charge for. But who cared? she was worth every cent of it in entertainment, in sheer animal vitality. Born in Havana, she has packed a dizzying world of experience into her twenty-six years. Married and divorced, she has enough to support her baby son with the three to five hundred dollars she earns every week. She began her career as a chorus-girl. For six years she travelled the world, appearing in Thailand, Singapore, Denver, Kowloon, Wichita, Korea, Louisiana, Tokyo, Cleveland. In Cambodia and Saigon she lived with a magazine-writer, and somewhere in her wanderings she must have acquired something of an education, since Garcia Lorca is her favourite poet — and even to have heard of The Hunchback of Notre-Dame and Don Quixote's lady is unusual in a strip-tease performer. Chelo has a passion for fresh air. She loves men, but finds all too many of them disappointing. She plays the piano by ear, cries when she listens to classical music, and Chopin and Tchaikovsky are her favourite composers.

Naturally we stayed for her act. A sharp, collective intake of breath greeted her first disrobing. "I just don't believe it!" I heard a man near me muttering as he dabbed the sweat from his temples.

Chelo doesn't particularly do anything other strippers don't do, but what she does she brings off with an audacity, a wicked grace that's uniquely engaging. Even the naturally shy men in her audience are startled and aroused. To which she responds with amusement and a curious battlecry of her own invention that sounds like "Ark!" Nothing less than physical perfection would be tolerable in such an act, and, though Chelo's endowments may seem slightly over-stated, they amount to a kind of hyperbole that is the burlesque equivalent of Elizabethan blank verse, Marlowe's mighty line declaimed in a gorgeous rhetoric of young and healthy flesh. Burlesque is, in its origins and common performance, an entertain-ment of Puritans, the imprisoned and choked-down passions burst-ing from their jails of instinct in ugly and misshapen forms and gestures. It is Chelo's genius to bring to this sometimes squalid art a Latin ease and freedom, and above all to preserve even in her more immodest passages an entirely Spanish dignity.

Should we see in Chelo yet another symbol of American abstrac-tion, a ceremony of pure sex, sex without object or content? Nor-mally the stripper, a humbler manifestation of the love-goddess, recalls Jay Macpherson's Mermaid:

> The fish-tailed lady offering her breast
> Has nothing else to give . . . .

But no. This is not Chelo, never. Too much is manifest in her of the impurity of lived life, of the comedy of fallen humanity. This mistress when she walks treads on the ground. Behind the insub-stantial façade of dream and image which is Miami Beach, at least one human person survives in her uniqueness. Buy your ticket now from the airline of your choice.

PART
IV
THE MIDWEST

Big Shots in Chicago
Roy Greenaway

When Roy Greenaway (1891–1972) wrote this Canadian's eye-view of the Chicago underworld in 1931, he was a recognized authority on rumrunning and related matters. In his almost 50 years as a reporter with the Toronto Star, *a career recounted in his memoir* The News Game *(1966), he helped to cover the discovery of insulin by Drs. Banting and Best and other key events of the era.*

I

AUGUST 14, 1930. A little after midnight. A double garage, the common type of low wooden affair, with two heavy frame doors opening on a dingy lane lined with other garages and weather-beaten high board fences.

At length a heavy roadster drove in beside the large touring car standing all evening on the right side. A woman stepped out first, followed by a man. She was good-looking, dark, 46, and wore a white dress. In a second or two more, she would have reached the electric switch beside the door opening towards the house. But she never touched it. Minion of the dark, she died in the dark.

From across the hood of the big touring car on the right two shot guns blazed. Apparently as unmoved as hunters shooting rabbits, the killers, if they did not wear gloves, unconcernedly wiped off all traces of finger-prints, even leaned one gun against the wall in the corner. At the opening of the lane, a parked car was waiting for them. It drove them away into the tutelary void that invariably swallows up all good Chicago gunmen.

The whole point, of course, is that this was not Chicago. This was Hamilton, Ontario, Canada; the land advertised these days to the gangster-harassed United States cities as the "sure capture" spot for gunmen and killers.

In this way died Mrs. Rocco Perri, common law wife of Rocco of that name, self boasted "King of the Bootleggers." The casket into which a New York undertaker tucked Frankie Yale's body was only $2,000 more expensive. She had a "nice" funeral, and thousands of citizens, literally driven away from her doorway, later witnessed the pompous parade to the graveside.

For a country inclined to swagger a little bit lately, to say the least, about how it handles its criminals, this is not the most pleasant case for detailed examination. Certainly, on a foundation of illegal alcohol, for more than 15 years, this woman blossomed; on an additional crust of dope, it was claimed in court, she died as much "on the spot" as Aiello, Zuta, or Oberta, underworld vermin of Chicago. For more than 15 years in this land where the United States public is told that "organized crime cannot live under the present legal structure," Bessie Perri tantalized more than the local police force. Over a period of some months, a bank manager in 1927 gave evidence that bank accounts known to be hers totalled $506,000. "One of the biggest drug operators in the game," was the way she was described in a Toronto court room by Constable Mathewson of the Royal Canadian Mounted Police, unsuccessfully trying to link her with four Italians and a large supply of narcotics captured at a Dundas Street West house just before Mrs. Perri arrived with an empty suit-case. This was more than a year after the shooting of Arnold Rothstein at the Park Central Hotel, New York, and yet Canadian police were still searching for the Rothstein dope they were sure she had.

The blast of buckshot that eliminated Bessie Starkman, known as Perri, now belongs to a long list of typical gangster assassinations around the city of Hamilton. 17 is the total. 17 fairly recent exceptionally brutal homicides around this one small Canadian city with a population of approximately only 156,000. All typical gang killings. Ruthless; barbarous; flint-hearted. All unsolved — for the present. The Dominion Department of Justice, as well as police headquarters at the Ontario Parliament Buildings and Hamilton, have added up the total, so unpleasant that it is being kept secret.

As a matter of fact, there is no reason why the list should be confined only to Hamilton. The escape of William Boivin with almost $300,000 worth of negotiable securities and cash from a mail car in the new Union Station in June, 1928, the John Kennedy murder a month before, a series of bank robberies in Toronto and Montreal from 1926 to 1928, the Rumbold case, not quite a month before the Perri killing, are just as scarifying to the doubtful foundation for our advertised pride.

Philip Rumbold, to all outward intents and purposes simply a respectable, 57-year-old Tonawanda real estate man, sitting in his car on the lonely Mineola Road, near Port Credit, on the night of July 22, 1930, strangled with a window sash cord tourniquetted twice around his neck and his head crushed by a hammer, might have been just an ordinary revolting murder if there was not sufficient evidence to trace it to the door of the alcohol gangs of Hamilton although not enough to score it from the records of unsolved Canadian crime.

The series of disquieting unsolved bank robberies between October, 1926, and April, 1928, involving Toronto and Montreal as well as Cleveland, Indianapolis and other cities across the border, stand out, because they were committed by gangsters on a foray from the United States, apparently not paralyzed with fear by any supposed inevitability of capture and conviction in Canada. From his notebook, one night in his room at the Fort Shelby Hotel, Detroit, Captain Fred Armstrong, head of the Michigan State Police Secret Service, joined together for me the links of the completed story. The robberies listed in it were:

> Standard Bank, Elm and McCaul, Toronto, Oct. 4, 1926, $6238.
>
> Bank of Toronto, King and Bathurst, Toronto, April 21, 1927, $18,000.
>
> Bank of Nova Scotia, Ossington and Dundas, Toronto, Oct. 19, 1927, $9,000.
>
> Bank of Montreal, St. Catherine and Papineau, Montreal, Sept. 21, 1927, $2,300.
>
> Banque Canadienne Nationale, St. Denis and Boucher, Montreal, Jan. 19, 1928, $9,200.
>
> Standard Bank, Elm and McCaul, second time, April 26, 1928, $37,000.

All of them were done by the Haight gang of Detroit, named after their leader, Fred Haight. Product of Herrin, Illinois, he was a type of trigger man who did not help to dispel its rather legendary reputation of "bloody Herrin." Four times in Toronto alone the Haight gang successfully swooped on banks, taking away $81,738 before the ungoverned emotions of their leader, culminating in his violent death, the discovery of bank deposit receipts in his pockets, and the registration number of his pistol gave clues enough to Captain Armstrong to round off a case fit for the records of

Scotland Yard or the Royal Canadian Mounted, beside whom, in my humble opinion, the Michigan Secret Service need take no second place. Yet it still remains for the Canadian public to begin to appreciate the fact that a United States police force has been playing a major part in keeping Canada free from crime.

I mention the killing of John Kennedy of Windsor, Ontario, not just because, assigned by my paper, the *Toronto Daily Star*, I saw the battered body of the bookkeeper of the Carling Breweries brought back to Canada from the marshy bush where he was found near Munroe, but because I am forced to believe from secret information in my possession that this was a straight case of Canadians employing professional United States gunmen to "bump off" a Canadian citizen. The hellish impassionateness and effrontery of this thing, as one stood there that May afternoon in 1928, seemed to burn the blood in revolt. A couple of weeks before he was to have been the principal Crown witness in the $421,000 action by the government against his firm for back gallonage taxes, Kennedy, accepting an invitation to cross the river to Detroit for dinner, expressed to friends he met on the ferry a premonition of how he might come back. To a self-righteous, unenlightened Canadian public this Kennedy murder was the deliberate work of a gang of cold-blooded killers operating out of Detroit. To better-informed, naturally resentful Michigan State Police Secret Service, this was the deed of Canadian criminals as ratlike as anything bred in the United States, whom, if there is still any Nemesis left in the world, they intend to bring to justice some day before long.

Taking only type cases, one follows the crime records into 1931, rounding back, suspiciously like a circle to Hamilton again. There are still the same old fumes of alcohol, the same sugary decks of white man's dope, the same nauseating sweetness of the poppy drip, the same Rocco Perri, an even more conspicuous Tony, or Frankie, Ross, right name Sylvester, and, in addition, some new opposing force, promising drama while it tries hard not to let the mousetraps smell of cheese.

Crime records, when considered, often seem inescapably summarizing. Take, for instance, the month of September last year on the Kingston Road in juxtaposition with the month of January this year (1931) in Montreal. In September, Ontario provincial police shot down Paul Comet of Thorold just west of Whitby as he was speeding west with 150 gallons of straight alcohol. At Prescott and Brockville in the same month, two captured trucks altogether carried 658 gallons of alcohol in cans. Then, on January 19, 1931, comes the finished picture. Montreal police, breaking into a place at 4410 St. Lawrence Boulevard, find five men in charge of six vats of alcohol whose total capacity equals 24,000 gallons. In another raid 11 days later, a 32,000 gallon plant is discovered, capable of producing 400 gallons daily. Ample evidence collected next week in Hamilton shows Sicilian and Jewish alcohol rings considerably disconcerted, with Poles, Ukranians, and Russians throughout the Niagara Peninsula and its adjacent small cities questing frustrated for the powerful kick and quick drunk coming from this beverage, cheaper than government liquors, most akin to their beloved vodka.

This, very briefly, is the background of the Canadian picture. So far as the actual processes of law are concerned, in any society's dealings with the criminal, they must run in somewhat the following order:

1 — Prevention.
2 — Detection.
3 — Trial.
4 — Sentence.
5 — Punishment.

Obviously, one and two belong to the police; three and four are the care of the courts and lawyers; while five is plainly a problem for specialized prison authorities.

It is also almost axiomatic that the chief deterrents of crime are just two in number: first, the certainty of detection, and second, the certainty of conviction. All of these specific cases of Canadian crime, very briefly advanced, apparently have most to do with the problem of detection. If these cases, I contend, mean anything, they show that whenever Canadian police have been faced with typical United States gang crimes, the Royal Canadian Mounted not excluded, for they worked on the Kennedy murder, they have been no more successful in their solution than the disparaged forces across the line.

The fault, very likely, is above any individual police force. Criminal detection, it may reasonably be argued, has not altogether marched with the times. Perhaps, even in Canada, it is necessary to recognize that the prevention and detection of crime are more national than local problems; that the time is fast approaching in Canada, as well as in the United States, for national supervision of the national problem of crime. Even yet, it is very doubtful whether even one out of every ten local detective chiefs in the small cities of Canada ever heard of Dr. Wilfrid Derome and his local scientific crime laboratory at Montreal.

"Granted ideal laws, an unbribable police force, a wonderful judiciary, everything to facilitate the certainty of speedy conviction," I remember Colonel Isham Randolph once saying in Chicago, smiling as he said it, "it is then, perhaps, worth while considering that you have to catch your gangster before you cook him."

II

If it is difficult to see much difference between our crime news and that of Chicago, except for quantity and spectacular magnitude, it is just as hard to find much intrinsic dissimilarity between its representative human products: Alphonse Capone and Rocco Perri.

The variation seems principally to be between the product of concentrations of 156,000 and 3,300,000 people. Both Capone and Perri are manifestations of the same microbe. But Capone is to Perri as scarlet fever is to scarlatina. Not having had the disease as badly as Chicago, Hamilton recovered quicker, with a temporary immunity.

Both of these Big Shots I have seen lately, and have been struck by the remarkable resemblance between them. Both are far removed from the true moving picture gangster. Neither began life with a bullet-shaped head, nor acquired in later years a broken nose and a cauliflower ear. Neither resembles in the least the stage impersonation of a low-browed person with evilly glinting eye, a plaid cap drawn down over beetling brows, and a swagger in itself sufficient to warn the world of a man bent on devilment. A gangster of this type was New York's Monk Eastman. As for Capone, he approximates more to the Monk's rival, Paul Kelly, who looked not unlike a theological student or a bank clerk out for a holiday.

Aptly enough, the French romantics divided mankind into two classes, the flamboyant and the drab. Among the flamboyants of crime today in these two countries undoubtedly rank Alphonse and Rocco. Flamboyant alone describes the flashiness of Al with his vaselined handsomeness, Napoleonic exaggeration, infernal cunning, impish humor, rococo villa and diamonds, red leather slippers and silk dressing gowns; his dexterity with the pea-shooter and the grand manner, his theatrical and effective entrances and exits.

Rocco, philosophising, might have been preparing Al's breviary back in those palmy days of 1924 when there was psuedo-prohibition in Ontario and a temporary protective alliance between the King of the Bootleggers and the local police in Hamilton until the attorney-general ordered an investigation.

"I'm a bootlegger," openly boasted Rocco. "I'm not ashamed of it. And a bootlegger I shall remain. . . ." On this text Al enlarges in an alarming manner: "All I ever did was to sell beer and whisky to our best people. . . . They call me a bootlegger, and some people call bootleggers criminals. I am simply supplying the demand of millions of law-abiding and law-making citizens. I sell liquor to judges, bankers, senators, governors, mayors; and I have preachers I sell wine to. It is no more criminal to supply this liquor than to barter for, possess and consume it. I am willing to be classed in the same category with judges, bankers, senators, governors, mayors and other well-known people, call them what you like."

In this matter of talking at least, so far as I can discover, Rocco even out-Caponed Al. In this land whose proud boast is that one law is supreme and organized crime cannot exist, Rocco outlined a higher law — the law of the Sicilian gunmen. "We do not go to the police to complain," said Rocco. "That is useless. We take the law into our own hands. I would kill a man on a question of honor, but not if he merely informed on me. We believe that we have the right to inflict our own penalties."

And in Canada, as in the United States, an astounded, law-abiding population listened impotently to this boastful effrontery, because a boast is no proof of guilt; because even if Capone in a court of law in the United States confessed to every crime that could be committed, His Honor would have to say, as John Stege, former superintendent of Chicago detectives, once graphically phrased it: "That's all right, Mr. Capone, under the constitution of the United States you are forbidden to give evidence against yourself. You are discharged."

As a matter of fact, Al wasn't discharged on February 25, 1931, when I talked to him in a Chicago court room for half an hour while he was waiting to answer a charge of contempt. Already Rocco the Little had suffered for his original ideas in Hamilton. Now, even Al the Great, of Chicago, felt occasional qualms of doubt about the result. The problem of meeting him at last had resolved itself by chance into reaching the court room at what proved to be the psychological moment, 35 minutes before the trial was to begin. As luck would have it, Chicago's "Public Enemy No. 1" was also early. His guards, tricking the crowds, slipping in with the Big Shot half an hour before the doors were opened.

It was as if Mussolini and his staff had arrived for a review. In fact, as one of Al's courtiers remarked: "If Mussolini came into Chicago on the same day as you, Al, you'd have the bigger crowd."

You fastened your glance at once on Capone because of the irrepressible exuberance of his personality and the sumptuousness of his dress. While he looked exactly like his later photographs, they never even suggest his size, his coloring, and his stylishness. For, above all, Capone is big: bigger than anything I had been led to expect from press clippings whose writers either never saw Capone or have unconsciously gathered evidence in support of the fantastic story that the real Capone was killed in 1925 and his place filled by a half-brother. The Capone that I saw was over six feet tall, with shoulders wider than anybody else's in the whole court room. Out of a thousand people he would have attracted attention by his animation, his laugh, his raven-black brilliantined hair and eyebrows standing out against the ruddiness of his Miami-tanned face like patent leather against red paper. His large lips registered in the memory, and the two scars on the left side of his face, one a pink welt a quarter of an inch wide extending from the sidebar almost to the corner of the lip, the other along the line of the jaw-bone. They were noticeable only close up against the purplish-black coloring of the shaven skin, which would otherwise have supported a heavy black beard.

He was affable enough in spite of the way I introduced myself. He shook hands, with one of those handshakes you remember, because it was moist and soft like a sponge. Dan Healy, the Chicago policeman who recently had shot "Schemer" Drucci, was with Capone. He was in plain clothes. "Mr. Capone," he explained, like a private secretary, "doesn't like all this crime stuff. It's been the way he has been written up in the Chicago papers that has made him so antagonistic to the press."

Al agreed, and smiled. For a moment his dignity was enormous. Only recently he had employed a skilful press agent to build up a background for his social ambitions. Then he chewed gum. Then he smiled again. Every time he smiled three sharp crows feet wrinkled up in the corners of his eyes. They are striking eyes; a bluish-grey, whose pupils dilate until they seem benevolent, then contract, under antagonistic emotion, until they point, motionless, adamant, menacing.

Questions regarding a possible acquaintanceship between the Perris and Capone at first amused him, then offended his dignity. The final masterpiece of his replies was, "I don't even know what street Canada is on." He showed all the satisfaction of a wit who has spoken something memorable and was gloating over it. But one last question, asked as a joke, had the effect on Capone of a banderillero's dart. "What do you think of 'Bugs' Moran?" His back was turned, and he noticeably stiffened. When he turned around his face had literally darkened, his eyes contracted. Silently he walked away again, then, suddenly, jerked round the second time. "Ask him," he almost hissed back at me.

For three days it was a great show, this vaudeville of Al in the Chicago court room. Capone dressed for the show: a rich blue suit for the first day; pearl grey for the second; a deep brown fabric with a slight blue stripe for the farewell performance. Each day, his diamond-studded platinum watch chain was strung across his vest. On the small finger of his left hand flashed a large diamond. On the other hand glowed a rare agate. For comedy relief he sometimes reverted to horseplay. At other times, he sparkled with smart repartee, sometimes smart-aleck repartee. He was the grown-up street kid trying to answer back: sometimes, in the process, achieving a real thrust of wit.

"Capone," one Chicago reporter shot at him, "You can't be a vagrant. A dark suit yesterday, a grey one today. Two suits!"

"I'm buying this one on time," Capone grinned.

It was Kathleen Breen, of the *American*, who became so flurried when she approached this fabulous creature — the czar of darkness — that she could only stutter: "I was supposed to ask you a question, but I can't think what it is." Capone stood smiling, attentive. "Oh, I know," suddenly remembered the girl reporter: the old gag — "What do you think of the American girl?" There was no clumsy fumbling for his answer. "I think you're beautiful," said Capone, pointing the compliment, bowing gallantly almost to the floor. "I think the American girls are wonderful," he later generalized, "and, surely, the most beautiful in the world," he amplified.

For three days, then, Al Capone dressed up for the knock-out that was coming, for his pictured moment of triumph, a throng congratulating him at the verdict in his favor. It was a knock-out all right, but the knock-out was against Capone. Alphonse Capone, as Judge Wilkerson called him, got six months in the Cook County jail. Those of us who watched him get it will long remember the way Capone stopped chewing his gum. For the three days of this contempt charge hearing he seemed never to stop chewing gum. For one moment now, he stopped and made no movement. His face paled. Then the flush came back and the smile, and he commenced chewing gum again. It was significant that he said: "There are other courts that can overrule this court." Somehow, it didn't seem so sure this time. Charges of failure to pay income tax, with a possible two or three year sentence, would follow. In spite of the handicap of a welter of protective legal technicalities, it seemed at last that the federal authorities had caught their gangster and were at least about to singe him.

III

In our attitude towards the crime records of the United States we Canadians are fast developing a pharisaical superiority complex that is irritatingly comic. Just recently a Toronto editor glowing with pious self-approval, satirized the spectacle of 200 New York police firing 1,000 shots into the apartment of 19-year-old "Two-Gun" Crowley. Better judgment would have recollected that, only five months before this, 400 Toronto police with all the furore of warfare finished in suburban fields what was described as an "epic of police vengeance" and "one of the greatest pieces of police work in the world," by shooting down and capturing 23-year-old John Brokenshire several hours after he had thrown away his gun. Strange! all this difference should be 'twixt Tweedle-dum and Tweedle-dee!

One reason United States crime statistics seem so high in comparison with England's, is that the United States includes not only minor breaches of the traffic and liquor laws as criminal offences, but also trivial assaults, which in the eyes of the general public are not, and perhaps, never will be so regarded. Criminal offences in Great Britain are comprised of the two main classes of felonies and misdemeanors. After an analysis of the latest British crime figures and of a copy of the *News of the World*, that matchless publication devoted to what passes through the British Criminal courts, C.F. Jamieson, barrister-at-law of Calgary, has recently published a reasonable opinion that it would not be difficult to prove that if both classes of offences were considered in reference to population that the percentage of crime is greater in Great Britain than in the United States.

An English newspaper lately has heaped case on case to show how our boasted swiftness in the execution of justice has repeatedly resulted in such cases as that of Oscar Slater who, in 1928, emerged from a British prison after serving 18 years of a life sentence for a murder that he never committed. And for all those weary, wasted years the British Government not long ago gave him $30,000.

On the other hand, all things considered, there is a general recognition that the United States perhaps protects the criminal at the expense of the public. Personal liberty, so ingrained in the minds of the idealistic patriots who framed the constitution under the stress of reaction from the autocracy then prevalent in Great Britain, has been overemphasized. Personal obligation, upon which they set equal store, has been underemphasized by their descendants. Admittedly, in many states, some of the present code was never fashioned for the 13 million alien-born residents that use 76 languages and dialects to cuss American institutions and help break the prohibition law.

Pessimistically in Chicago, John Stege, former head of detectives, sketched for me, as he saw it, the veritable network of silly technicalities that forms a protective barrier around the accused. These have permitted unscrupulous lawyers to secure indefinite postponements, drag out trials, and intimidate and bribe witnesses and juries. Not until recently, as a result, has the better class of men and women come back to jury service, urged by a determination to put an end to civic corruption, and the political alliance with crime. In Canada, for instance, bail is never allowed in most serious crimes and never for murder, attempted murder, or any other offence punishable by death. The prisoner must be brought before a court within eight days of his arrest, usually on the same day or the following. But in the United States a supreme court orders that a man must not be tried for 30 days from the time he is charged. First of all, he must be taken before a grand jury, then before a judge. In the meantime, he walks the street on a bond. In this respect, for the past few years in Chicago, at least, a condition has existed that made it almost impossible to keep a murderer in jail who was capable of producing a $35,000 bond. Never were these interminate delays better illustrated than in the Sacco-Vanzetti case that lasted seven years before these two men were sent to death. Nobody at least, could complain of lack of time to prove innocence. Nobody could charge that delays could evade the inevitable punishment.

Yet don't become excited over your opinion that because the United States system gives more protection to the accused than in Canada it is worthless. Your neighbor may like it. For the first time, you may hear surprising arguments why he thinks it better that judges be elected for short periods rather than appointed for life; why he even supports the appointment of the police and detective chiefs solely by the mayor in comparison to the large cities of Europe where the commissioners of police are chosen by and responsible only to the state. In Europe, it is argued a national organization is built for permanency; in the United States, a local organization is constructed to meet the exigencies of a political administration. In New York, for example, where the mayor has the sole right of appointing the police chief, there have been in the last 27 years 14 police commissioners; while, in London, in the 85 years between 1829 and 1914, Scotland Yard has had only six. Yet, as a result of harsh and unreasonable police methods in London it recently became necessary to place the reorganization of the whole force in the hands of Lord Byng of Vimy.

The anomaly of the crime situation, for instance, in Chicago, perhaps not understood by one Canadian in thousands, is that while for the past three years crimes have seemed to crescendo steadily from lower to higher heights of apprehensive frightfulness, still just as steadily, though less picturesquely and less explained, have the forces of the challenged Shot of Shots — the state — been lopping away from the head downwards the Len Small-Bob Crowe-Bill Thompson political machine that, it has been continuously alleged, made such conditions possible.

The Granady killing, the murder of Philip H. Meagher, building superintendent whose firm was represented in the Chicago Chamber of Commerce, in February, 1930, had resulted in the final determination of the bar and big business to get a decision once for all to the question of who was to be the Big Shot in the United States — the criminal or the government. The St. Valentine's Day Massacre did not raise up vigilantes; no sporadic, spectacular civic mass vengeance. For the gangster, it brought something worse than that: it produced the newspaper-named Secret Six, cool-headed, determined business men, members of the Chicago Association of Commerce, wealthy men prepared at last to match gangsters dollar for dollar, with their president, Colonel Isham Randolph, 47, noted engineer, World War commander of engineers at St. Mihiel, smiling, imperturable, to lead them.

"That Secret Committee of Six is all a myth," William Russell, former Commissioner of Police of Chicago had roared at me. "That Secret Six is all damned newspaper bologna." The smile of Colonel Randolph was unforgettable when I passed on the information. That early April evening in 1930, I had gone across the South Side of Chicago to the Colonel's home in the wealthy residential section of Riverside. In the big chintz living-room the Colonel did not say anything when I told him. He simply looked at me and smiled. When the first smile had died down, he smiled the second time, the smile that Bugs Moran and Al Capone just then were seeing in their nightmares. That fact I had already learnt in half a dozen "spots" of the Capone Beer Syndicate in the Loop, or downtown section of the city. It was the smile of another Big Shot; bigger, as events were to prove, than Chief William Russell, Big Bill Thompson, and Al Capone put together. For even then this man said with finality that "they were through." On April 7, 1931, Cermak swept out Thompson by the largest majority ever polled for a mayor in the city. Six weeks previous to that, as I have already described, I believe I saw Capone, as the Colonel predicted, commencing to toboggan down the chute.

Yet Randolph was one of those who strenuously defended the United States system of considering every man not guilty until it was proved. He defended safeguards even for the possible criminal on the principle that it is better for a hundred people to escape punishment than for one innocent person to be condemned. He maintained that, even as the code was in Illinois, there were plenty of legal weapons to wipe off the map Capone and the alliance between corrupt politics, police, and the gangs. Most of the gang killing in the United States, he admitted, is based upon competitive war between Big Shots for the millions of profit in liquor, gambling, vice and labor rackets. Still not for one moment had he the idea of imposing prohibition on a city that votes five to one for liquor. Mayor Dever, sincere enough in his intentions to clean up Chicago, tried to do that and only paved the way for the last return of Big Bill Thompson and the "wide-open city" slogan.

Nor do Randolph or other United States leaders, surprising as it may seem to Canadians, show much enthusiasm for the system of provincial government control as it is now in force in Canada. About the one good thing that can be said for it, in their opinion, is that it is better than theirs. With liquor costing in the liquor stores 200% more than in the United States saloons before prohibition, the Canadian system is referred to by bootleggers in the United States as the perfect consummation of a whisky manufacturer's dream. The result, they see, is that Canada has many bootleggers. The important question, plainly to them, in considering the adoption by the United States of a state control analogous to Canadian provincial control, is who would control the state? The only safe way, as they see it, is to eliminate all private gain from the liquor trade, if the 18th amendment is ever repealed: to inaugurate federal government control, not only of distribution, but also of manufacture.

All the Secret Six set out to do, however incongruous it seems to a Canadian outsider, is to break the league between corrupt politics, legal administration, and the gangsters. All they are trying to do is to make the booze trade orderly for the present. The severing of the alliance between organized crime and corrupt politics and police in the United States, they seem well on their way in Chicago and New York to prove, depends on eight parts public exposure and only two parts legal prosecution.

Randolph was correct. There was enough law and law enforcement left. For one thing, there was prosecution possible by the federal government against gangsters who had not paid their income taxes. "We could expect no help from the city police," he explained, "so we formed a pact with the federal government authorities, with the federal government prosecutor and the United States district attorney, Geo. E. Q. Johnson. The Secret Six forged a military intelligence system. It took the security and secrecy from the gangster and his political confederates. In its turn it became the agent of fear: the unapproachable, the cross-checked, the unbribable, whose agents knew not one another. It supplied the federal officers with adequate intelligence, the sinews of prosecution, and protection for all witnesses, and, once again, juries began to convict.

The white light of exposure began to throw its disrupting path of disgrace even to the high places. In quick succession came the capture of the Rothstein, Vitale, Genna, Zuta, Cooney, Jack "Legs" Diamond and "Mike De Pike" Heitler strong boxes with their startling disclosures of narcotic, liquor, gambling and vice operations, as well as the names of law enforcement officers and politicians on the payroll who are standing prosecution in the courts.

For the first time, in Chicago, the Secret Six really exposed and surveyed its enemy, the Capone Beer Syndicate. It found 20,000 speakeasies in Cook County with its 3,900,000 people. Since each of these used an average of 5 barrels of beer a week, this meant a total of 100,000 barrels, or 25 million pints, or 6 pints a week for every inhabitant of Chicago. To brew a barrel cost Capone $1.80. Cooperage and other costs brought the first charge to $3. The speakeasies paid $55 a barrel, obviously leaving a clear profit of $52. Deducting salaries of armed guards, brewers, truck men, collectors, fixers, custodians of brothels, gambling houses and handbooks, whose number was found to be roughly 2,000, Colonel Randolph figures that Capone could still have a handsome profit, after setting aside, if necessary, $20 a barrel for a slush fund; in other words, the staggering sum of $2 million a week for corrupting politicians, police, and other law enforcement officials. The operatives disclosed the other interesting fact that Capone kept 35 trusted gunmen for his own personal protection and 200 more as a sort of Praetorian Guard close to the throne.

As George E. Q. Johnson has reason to say: "One of the most hopeful signs in the crime problem is that invisible government is becoming visible. Organized crime cannot live except by an alliance with corrupt politics and corrupted police. When we fully grasp this fact and become sufficiently angry about it, organized crime will shrivel up and die."

There are people to whom the Great War was merely the running amuck of a criminal lunatic. To them the Germans were different in kind from all other peoples, utterly separated from the rest of us by their crimes. There seems to be a growing tendency in Canada, so far as the crime problem in the United States is concerned, to adopt such an attitude, based on the lack of information that there are less policemen in proportion to population in Chicago than in Toronto; that already eight of the most famous Capone leaders including Capone's brother, Ralph, are deported or in prison; that Capone himself has already been sentenced; that a governor who dispensed pardons lavishly, the state's attorney, and the mayor of Chicago with one of the strongest entrenched political machines in history have been ousted; and that there may even be police forces on the border who keep criminals out of Canada and apprehend them after they have left.

Canada has a vital interest in the United States crime situation. In a sense, it would not be out of place to say that Canadian cities owe nothing but gratitude to Chicago for providing on a great scale, not only an intensive example of what to avoid, but how to avoid it. For 45 years, Chicago has been the experimental laboratory for the whole continent. On the part of organized society, it has been the test tube for experiments in how to wipe out crime, just as, on the other hand, it has been the experimentary ground on the part of organized criminality for its rackets, the focal point from which to spread them out to surrounding cities.

On the result in Chicago and other cities across the border will depend to a large extent the future complexion of town and city life in the United States and Canada. If the gangsters win the war, and all ends in futility, it is obvious that the repercussions on orderly society on the continent must be tremendous. The question must soon be settled — which is the Bigger Shot; the gangster or the state?

With the Yippies in the Streets of Chicago

DAVID LEWIS STEIN

To Canadians as to many other nationalities, Chicago is forever identified with two historical events: the rise of Al Capone in the 1920s, as recorded in Roy Greenaway's article beginning on page 79, and the riots during the Democratic Party's national convention in August 1968. David Lewis Stein (born 1937) was an eyewitness to the latter, as recorded in his 1969 book Living the Revolution: The Yippies in Chicago, *from which the following is an excerpt. Stein is a novelist and short story writer as well as a journalist, and his fiction often deals with American values in conflict.*

D riving in from the airport, whipping through the tangle of throughways, the taxi driver said he was all in favour of what Mayor Daley was doing to protect the city because you've got to have order and you've got to keep people in line. But he was against the war in Vietnam. He had himself been in Korea and he told me, "It seems like every generation we got to go over there and fight and get killed. And for what?"

I asked what he was going to do about Vietnam then, but he evaded the question. He went off into a long talk about his philosophy: Avoid trouble. Even when he was a kid and growing up in, well, a tough neighborhood, he never got into trouble. He loved to go dancing, but if he heard there might be gangs at the dances, you know, kids who go looking to start fights, he stayed away. And after he got married, he moved into a quieter neighbourhood because he didn't want trouble with anyone. And when he was selling insurance, he was once invited to a weekend at Mackinac Island for salesmen who had written one million dollars' worth of policies in one year. He brought his wife along, but none of the other salesmen did, and as soon as he walked into the hotel lobby to register, he could see how hot and bothered they were for women. So he and his wife spent the weekend going on long trips around the island and came back to the hotel only for supper and to go to sleep. He just didn't want the kind of trouble he could get if some guy went and made a pass at his wife.

I said I was a little surprised at middle-aged insurance salesmen carrying on like a bunch of horny high-school kids, and he, in turn, was surprised at my naiveté. I would be amazed, he said, at how many middle-aged, respectable men come to Chicago for a convention and go out at night looking for action. They were always coming up to his cab and asking him to take them to some whores. He had a stock reply: "Do I look like a pimp? Get the hell out of here!"

This, he explained, was only common sense. A taxi driver could never tell when some respectable-looking guy who comes up looking all excited and asking for whores will turn out to be a cop. You can't be too careful in Chicago. The cops are always after the taxi drivers. Mind you, if some customer asked to be taken to a good restaurant or a good, respectable nightclub, he'd take them — as long as they didn't look like the kind of people who might come hunting for him later in case they had a lousy time. And he would take people to any address they gave him, except in the ghettoes. After all, why go looking for trouble? The Negroes have their own taxis to take them where they want to go.

I thought at first that I ought to argue with him. It is my responsibility to point out that if everybody goes through life avoiding trouble, how will we ever build a better world? How will we ever get out of Vietnam? But then I figured, oh, the hell with it. He'll just think I'm some kind of nut. Besides, what am I doing for the world? I am coming to Chicago as a free-lance reporter for the *Toronto Star* and what good is that going to do anyone?

As we came up to the hotel, I asked about the area. He said it was a pretty good neighborhood and a long way from the black ghettoes. Scratch one nightmare. In fact the last few days in New York, I had lived with the terrible fear that the Yippie Festival of Life might trigger the riot to end all riots and I would get caught alone in the middle of it.

Keith was on the john when I arrived. He got up, let me into the hotel room and went back to the john.

From the window of our room, I could see into Lincoln Park. The view was obscured by a line of dark, leafy trees, but I could see that the park was quite large, running from Clark Street, the main thoroughfare that our hotel faced, down to Lake Michigan. It looked quite pleasant and pastoral.

Keith came out of the john and announced that he was on his way down to the courthouse. I dropped my suitcase and typewriter and joined him. Riding down on the bus, he filled me in on what had been happening.

First, there had been the fight with the Chicago group, but that had calmed down and the New York Yippies were using the *Seed* offices as a headquarters. Then there had been a fight inside the New York group itself. Rubin and Abbie had fought over what Yippie should be doing in Chicago and the others had been compelled more or less to pick sides. Rubin had accused Abbie of letting Yippie become too much of a personality cult. He argued that the leaders had done their job and now they should fade into the crowds. Every action should be collective now and they shouldn't allow the media men to pay special attention to any single personality, as the "Yippie spokesman" or the "Yippie leader." Abbie had argued that this was guerrilla theatre and they must use every means available to them to get the Yippie message across. It was an honest quarrel over philosophy and tactics, but it had brought some personal resentments to the surface and harsh words had been exchanged. The meeting broke up at midnight with a sort of friendly truce. Abbie and Jerry would divide responsibility for different projects and other people could join in where they felt most comfortable. But it still sounded as though Yippie was falling apart.

We stepped out of the relative coolness of the bus into the thick, gummy heat of downtown Chicago. The temperature was over 90. In a walk of half a dozen blocks we were dripping with sweat. Keith went on about how, in the middle of all their internal problems, the Yippies were having to cope with the pressure from outside. The cops were tailing Abbie and Paul Krassner 24 hours a day, but apparently they still didn't recognize Jerry Rubin on sight. They had picked up another New Yorker, David Boyd, and they were following him around because they thought he was Rubin. Boyd was trying to look as conspicuous as possible so that Rubin could operate freely, but it was obvious that the cops would realize their mistake pretty quickly.

On the twenty-fourth floor of the Federal Building, the Yippie contingent was just coming out of the courtroom when we arrived. Reporters immediately surrounded them and the boys gave an impromptu press conference.

"What is a Yippie? A Yippie is a hippie who has been hit over the head with a policeman's club."

"We were suing Mayor Daley and the city of Chicago because they wouldn't give us a permit to sleep in the park. But we dropped the case this morning. We're through talking. We're not talking to no one no more."

"If the administration can suspend the rules to allow a square mile of barbed wire around the Amphitheatre, it can allow people to sleep in the parks."

A cop came and herded everybody over to an alcove. Got to keep the corridors clear for the people coming through. The Yippies, Krassner, Abbie, "Dan Cupid," who had just changed his name to "Peter Rabbit" because the heat in New York was getting too much for "Dan Cupid," and three or four other people whom I didn't recognize, all quietly obeyed the cop. The Yippies looked bizarre up against the reporters in their crisp summer suits. But the reporters were fawning over them with notebooks and microphones and the Yippies were obviously delighted at all the attention. Abbie told the crowd around him:

"The judge said, 'I'll find you a place to sleep tonight if you need one, young man,' I told him. 'I already got a place to sleep, Lincoln Park.' Well, I didn't actually say that out loud. I said it under my breath."

But downstairs, in front of a little half circle of microphones, Abbie forgot about the under-the-breath part and told the assembled television cameras how he had really told off that judge:

"He was a former law partner of Mayor Daley and that was too much for us. We talked to Judge Lynch and we got lynched. We talked to Stahl about the permit for the park and we got stalled. That's the way it's been going here, like some kind of comic book."

The people I had known as just people at Yippie meetings in New York had become stars in Chicago. The cops were guarding O'Hare airport against guerrilla assault and guarding the reservoirs to prevent anyone poisoning the city's water supply with LSD and the National Guard had already been mobilized. And here, out in the streets still walking around, were the savage Yippies. They had become celebrities.

I drifted off and sat down to rest on one of the benches in the little black and white granite plaza of the Federal Building. The Yippies were depressing to watch in action. They looked ridiculous, a little band of long-haired braggarts standing in front of the Federal Building, 27 stories of Mies van der Rohe steel girders and bronze-tinted glass. The revolution had a long way to go before it dislodged or even dismayed the power housed inside that tall, cold building. A potbellied old man, a courthouse aficionado in shirt sleeves and firehouse suspenders, leaned over and asked me sarcastically, "What I want to know is, who's *paying* these people?"

I told him they knew how to live without money.

Abbie read the Yippie platform. The little plaza became quiet. No smirking questions and wisecrack answers now. This was serious stuff. At last, the Yippie platform:

(1) An immediate end to the war in Vietnam, and a restructuring of our foreign policy which totally eliminates aspects of military, economic and cultural imperialism. The withdrawal of all foreign-based troops and the abolition of the military draft.

(2) Immediate freedom for Huey Newton of the Black Panthers and all other black people. Adoption of the Community Control concept of ghetto areas. An end of the cultural domination of minority groups.

(3) The legalization of marijuana and all other psychedelic drugs. The freeing of all prisoners currently in prison on narcotics charges.

(4) A prison system based on the concept of rehabilitation rather than punishment.

(5) A judicial system which works toward the abolition of all laws related to crimes without victims — that is, retention only of laws relating to crimes in which there is an unwilling or injured party, i.e., murder, rape, assault.

(6) The total disarmament of all the people beginning with the police. This includes not only guns, but such brutal devices as tear gas, Mace, electric prods, blackjacks, billy clubs and the like.

(7) The abolition of Money. The abolition of pay housing, pay media, pay transportation, pay food, pay education, pay clothing, pay medical help, and pay toilets.

(8) A society which works toward and actively promotes the concept of "full employment," a society in which people are free from the drudgery of work. Adoption of the concept "Let the machines do it."

(9) A conservation program geared toward preserving our natural resources and committed to the elimination of pollution from our air and water.

(10) A program of ecological development that will provide incentives for the decentralization of our crowded cities and encourage rural living.

(11) A program which provides not only free birth control information and devices, but also abortions when desired.

(12) A restructured education system which provides the student power to determine his course of study and allows for student participation in overall policy planning. Also an educational system which breaks down its barriers between school and community. A system which uses the surrounding community as a classroom so that students may learn directly the problems of the people.

(13) The open and free use of the media. A program which actively supports and promotes cable television as a method of increasing the selection of channels available to the viewer.

(14) An end to all censorship. We are sick of a society which has no hesitation about showing people committing violence but refuses to show a couple fucking.

(15) We believe that people should fuck all the time, anytime, whomever they wish. This is not a program demand but a simple recognition of the reality around us.

(16) A political system which is more streamlined and responsive to the needs of all the people, regardless of age, sex or race. Perhaps a national referendum system conducted via television or a telephone voting system. Perhaps a decentralization of power and authority with many varied tribal groups — groups in which people exist in a state of basic trust and are free to choose their tribe.

(17) A program which encourages and promotes the arts. However, we feel that if the Free Society we envision were to be fought for and achieved, all of us would actualize the creativity within us. In a very real sense, we would have a

society in which every man would be an artist.

(18) Eighteen is a blank. You can fill in anything you want there.

While Abbie read this, a small group — Paul Krassner, Peter Rabbit, Keith and a couple of girls — stood motionless around him. It looked almost like a parody of a family portrait. The TV men listened respectfully to Abbie, but when he got to the parts about "fucking," I saw one of the cameramen look away in disgust. From his point of view, Abbie had just ruined a fine piece of film. I don't think any part of the Yippie program was ever broadcast.

We were in the darkroom at the back of the *Seed* offices later that afternoon when we heard that the cops had shot and killed a hippie. Two men from CBS television were trying to talk to Abbie when someone came in with the papers. The police story was that they had stopped two kids in the early morning for an identity check. Chicago has a 10:30 curfew for kids under seventeen and these two looked as if they were violating it. But instead of producing identification, one of the kids pulled a gun and opened fire. The police said he missed even though he was only a couple of feet away from them. The kid ran and the police fired after him. Their third bullet pierced his heart. They took the other kid into custody and discovered that he had a butcher knife taped to his chest and that both boys had been carrying illegal drugs. That was all that was known at the moment except that the dead boy's name was Dean Johnson, he was seventeen years old, and he came from Sioux Falls, South Dakota. But the newspapers described him as wearing "hippie clothing," and in the emotional atmosphere of the *Seed* office, that was enough to make him a "brother."

The two men from CBS were trying to get a schedule of Yippie activities so that they could be in the right places with their mobile crews. "We don't go anywhere we're not invited," one of them said.

"You can go anywhere you want," Abbie said. "Just don't kill no more of our people."

They were sitting on the floor of the darkroom looking very uncomfortable and Abbie was sitting on an upturned pop case playing games with them. He had already conned one of them into exchanging a necktie for his beads. Abbie was just twisting the necktie nervously in his hands, but the CBS man had tried to live up to his side of the bargain. He looked silly in his spotless blue sport shirt with Abbie's motley and soiled string of beads around his neck.

"A Yippie is a Yiddish hippie," Abbie said.

"Abbie, I have a feeling we don't trust each other."

"Why don't you come around and take pictures of today's Czechoslovakian demonstration?"

"We might do that. But what about the pig?"

"How much would you guys pay for an exclusive interview with the pig?"

"I wouldn't pay anything. Frankly, it doesn't mean that much to me — to pay for it."

Abbie was shocked. He seemed to believe that reporters in the street had been given huge bankrolls to go out and buy stories with. He explained that he just wanted the money so that he could buy hot dogs and give them out to the people in Lincoln Park. The CBS men were sympathetic but they just were not going to give Abbie any money.

"We just want to tell the truth," one of them said.

"Whaddaya mean the truth?" Abbie said. "If I say, 'President Johnson is a fucking bastard,' you going to let me say that on television?"

The CBS men got up to leave and one of them explained to me on the way out that until Monday and the start of comprehensive TV coverage, they could only hope to get the Yippies on for a few minutes of the evening newscast. But later, when they had hours of dead convention time to fill, he was sure he would be able to get a lot of Yippie coverage on the air. It was something he really wanted to do. I never saw him again.

After the CBS men had cleared out, the people in the *Seed* office decided to hold a funeral service for Dean Johnson and to combine this with some kind of requiem for the young Czechs who had been killed by Russian troops. Keith immediately got up a delegation to visit SDS headquarters and try to bring the SDS people in on it.

Abbie was very upset by what had happened to Dean Johnson. He flung himself around the *Seed* office banging tables and smashing his fist into walls and pillars. The office was decorated with psychedelic and antidraft posters and the tables were littered with copy, bits of artwork and campy pieces of junk. The ambience was undergraduate. The *Seed* as an underground newspaper was more oriented toward drug culture, the psychedelic revolution, than it was toward New Left political action. But now a hippie kid had been shot and the police said he had been carrying drugs. In the fearful spring, New York hippies had told each other somberly that ten people might well die in action during convention week. And the police had already killed one kid and the convention hadn't even started yet. Abbie looked stunned. The CBS men had left; this was no media freak show. He stomped around the *Seed* office muttering, "Don't let them kill no more people. We've got to stop them killing our people."

The SDS office was in the Church of Three Crosses, a couple of blocks west of Lincoln Park. A carload of plainclothesmen sat out front trying to look inconspicuous. SDS had decided not to take part officially in any of the demonstrations, but Chicago was still the organization's national headquarters and the national officers could not just *ignore* all that activity going on in their own back yard. So they set up half a dozen SDS centers around the city, and eventually 300 to 400 people who identified themselves as members of SDS came to Chicago and the national office put out daily wall posters.

The church was the chief movement center of SDS during the convention, and in contrast to the lighthearted mess of the *Seed* office, it looked very militant and businesslike. There were trestle tables with typewriters and neat stacks of literature. In a corner, some kids were putting a stencil on a mimeograph machine. Over their heads was a poster of Ché Guevara with the slogan, "In a revolution, one wins or dies."

Keith found Tom Neumann of Up Against the Wall Motherfuckers. Neumann was from New York and the Motherfuckers were a Lower East Side chapter of SDS. Neumann wasn't really the right person to have gone to, but Keith knew him, he was there and there wasn't much time.

Neumann was impressed by the idea of holding a funeral service for Dean Johnson, but he was against combining it with a requiem for the murdered Czechs. The trouble was that there were "two diametrically opposed positions" on Czechoslovakia among SDS people. Keith told him this was bullshit, but Neumann was adamant. After a few minutes of fierce haggling, Keith backed down so that at least a service for Dean Johnson could be held. It would be sponsored by SDS and Yippie and the SDS people would get out the leaflet.

But driving back in the car, the Yippie delegation had second thoughts. The issue was clear enough. The international conspiracy of old men was killing young people in the streets of Prague and the streets of Chicago. Every other consideration was ideological hairsplitting. The Yippies decided to hold their own service and requiem and to issue their own leaflet. "Fuck SDS," someone said. "We've got our own constituency."

It was cool at last when we gathered in the washhouse by the park. Most of the crowd had long hair, ragged, exotic clothing, bits of castoff army uniforms, blue jeans and Indian headbands. One moon-faced Puerto Rican boy sat naked to the waist daubing himself with Day Glo war paint. Members of two motorcycle gangs, with their names, "Hell on Wheels" and "Headhunters," stenciled onto the backs of their black leather jackets, stood to one side, silent and watchful. Then there were some straight people, middle-age park strollers who had stopped to see what all the fuss was about and college kids in chinos and miniskirts who looked like early dropouts from McCarthy. One very sweet-looking lady who was very pregnant stood holding hands with her husband on the edge of the crowd. They were like representative good white liberals. Did they understand what was happening? Beside me, a long-haired boy introduced a girl to his friends with, "This is Helen. She used to be nonviolent, but she's gone through some spiritual growth and now she's with us."

Tom Neumann addressed the crowd through a bullhorn. The joint Yippie-SDS service seemed to have become a complete SDS show. While Neumann talked, uniformed cops and plainclothesmen circled the crowd and we could see the paddy wagons pulling into a line off to one side. The wagons were small and painted bright blue and white. They looked quite friendly, almost as though children could go up to the doors in back and buy Eskimo pies.

"One of our brothers has been shot," Neumann told us. "And the reason is all around us. The pigs! He died of pig poisoning!" Cries of "Oink oink! Oink oink!" came from the crowd.

"The official line for the media — and the story was probably written at one central office downtown because all the media say the same thing — is that he was stopped for supposed curfew violations and that he had a gun and shot at the cops at point-blank range. But we know we can't believe the media. We're suffering from pig poisoning and media poisoning!"

Shouts of "Media pigs! Media pigs!"

"However," Neumann went on, "there's a general body of rumor that has the smell of truth about it. According to the rumors, Dean Johnson was an American Indian and that's a bad thing to be in this country. And we know that he didn't have a gun. The question now is what are we going to *do*?"

"You're going to obey the law just like everybody else!" A short, burly man with a crew-cut and a short-sleeved white shirt was challenging Neumann from the back of the crowd. He looked like a marine sergeant in civilian clothes. Voices from the crowd answered him: "We didn't write the laws and we ain't obeying any laws."

The marine type fought back. "When we pay taxes, don't you call any man a pig!"

The crowd was angry now. The people standing around Neumann and his bullhorn looked ready to charge out and start swinging. Suddenly, blinding white lights flashed on us. A mobile television unit had quietly driven up beside the crowd.

People screamed, "Turn off those lights! Turn off those fucking lights!" After a few minutes' hesitation, the mobile unit did turn off its lights, and in the sudden darkness and confusion, the marine type drifted away.

Neumann introduced a girl from the Chicago Legal Defense Committee. "We're raising bail for the other guy," she told us. "But I just want you to know that the police got him to sign a full confession. God only knows how badly he was cut up." She sounded ready to burst into tears.

Neumann took the bullhorn again and said we would now hold a funeral service for Dean Johnson, but "I don't know what *we* do to hold a funeral service." Someone suggested we walk out of the park and down to the corner of North Avenue and La Salle, where Dean Johnson had been killed. A chorus of general consent came from the crowd. Neumann warned us that we didn't have a permit for this march and that this was not the time to force a confrontation with the pigs.

We straggled out of the park and down La Salle Street, past the plate-glass windows of a car showroom and the flaking dark green and brown stoops of old gingerbread houses that looked very nineteenth-century rural and out of place on a busy thoroughfare. At the corner of North Avenue, we cut across a gas station, and a man in a spiffy, old-fashioned glen check suit started snarling, "Dirty hippies." The crowd was indulgent. "Go home, old man. Your time is up," a long-haired boy in front of me said.

In a dirty vacant lot across from the gas station, a signboard advertised, "Carl Sandburg Village, one-, two-, and three-bedroom suites." We turned along North Avenue and paused across from the liquor store where the cops had stopped Dean Johnson. But there was no blood on the sidewalk and nothing to see. We moved on toward Wells Street. Behind me, two young Negroes were discussing the march.

"This kind of thing happens to us all the time," one of them was saying. "But look what happens when they do it to a white kid."

"You're right, man. You're right."

The corner of North Avenue and Wells Street was the heart of Old Town, Chicago's version of Greenwich Village. We stopped there for the funeral service, but it turned out that no one had made any plans to actually *do* anything. We just milled around and began to fill up the intersection. Two squad cars pulled up and the cops got out and told us to keep moving. They pushed us to the sidewalk with their night sticks but they were pretty gentle about it. I turned back to the park, passing people still marching dutifully to the corner.

We spent a lot of time in Old Town, and the action in Lincoln Park spilled down Wells Street. I never got over the feeling that all the attractions of Old Town had been cut out of cardboard and erected overnight, and then the Junior Chamber of Commerce had said, "Hoo boy! Look at us, now Chicago has its own real live bohemia!" The boutiques sold bad copies of Carnaby Street styles, posters and even plastic toilet-seat covers embossed with psychedelic flowers. The restaurants had cartoon names like The Pickle Barrel, The Paul Bunyan, and That Steak Joynt. The sophisticated Second City satire cabaret was there, but so were a "Believe It or Not" wax museum and a string of topless bars. Wells Street was cheap and cynical. Old Town was a hell of a place for some hippie kid to get killed in.

At ten o'clock there were still about 100 people in Lincoln Park. Some sat on the grass and some stood up and just talked. "We know that the man is all around us," one of them said. "We have to prepare ourselves inside and out. We have to be ready to defend our community."

In fact, plainclothesmen were circling the edge of the crowd. Their shiny handcuffs stuck out below their loose-fitting sport shirts. But the feeling in the park was still peaceful. A boy and girl who looked young enough to still be in high school sat on the steps of the washhouse playing a guitar and singing antiwar songs.

Lincoln Park runs for about two and a half miles along Lake Michigan, part of the city's waterfront green belt, but we were using only the southernmost corner of it. *Our* Lincoln Park was bound on the south by La Salle Drive, funneling cars in off Lakeshore Drive, and to the north, it sloped down to a small lake and a children's zoo. Coming in from Clark Street at the west were parking lots and a winding service road and then a shallow valley that was cut by two parallel asphalt paths. The little valley was broken up by random trees but the back half of the park was a huge playing field divided into baseball diamonds. The playing field was flat and hard and most of the grass had been ground into dust. The washhouse stood at just about the exact geographic center of the park and it became a natural gathering place. The Yippie communications center and hospital were to be set up on trestle tables around the washhouse. It was a solidly built brick rectangle. The washhouse looked like a small-town jail.

Keith, who had taken on the job of press relations for Yippie, had gone back to our room to make some telephone calls about the funeral service and march. When I met him later in the park, he was very excited. He told me that a media man in his late forties who held a very important job with one of the TV networks had been waiting for him in the hotel lobby. Keith had suggested they go into the park together, but the media man had said he'd better go back to his own hotel room first. He had some LSD caps on him and he wanted to get rid of them in case the cops stopped him. He had told Keith that he was a practicing acid head and Keith was delighted with him. The movement had allies all over the place.

By 11, the curfew hour, there were only a dozen or so people still hanging around the washhouse. The young folk singers had gone and the little bands "rapping" about self-protection had broken up.

At 11:15, the cops moved in and very politely told us that the park was closing and we would have to leave.

We left. But we walked slowly so that cops on little motor scooters had to warn us twice to keep moving. We stopped at the edge of the parking lots for a while and watched the cops stop a very straight-looking couple trying to take their enormous Russian wolfhound for a walk. The couple seemed amazed at what was going on. All those cops bouncing through the trees on motor scooters! It was obvious that these people were used to going into the park at all hours and that the cops were only enforcing the curfew because of the Yippies. We watched the couple retreat to the street, the wolfhound still tugging desperately at his leash, and then we strolled back to our hotel.

Dean Johnson never did make it as a martyr. The Legal Defense Committee lawyers got the other boy out on bail and he promptly left Chicago and disappeared for good. The lawyers could find no evidence to shake the police charge that Johnson had fired at them first. In the rush of events in Chicago, Dean Johnson was forgotten.

Life in Lawrence
ELSPETH CAMERON

Elspeth Cameron (born 1943) is the author of two important literary biographies, Hugh MacLennan: A Writer's Life *and the controversial* Irving Layton: A Portrait. *She is a member of the staff of the University of Toronto. Her impressions of a city in the American wheatbelt, below, derive from her work teaching Canadian studies at the University of Kansas.*

K ansas, of all places. Why would the University of Kansas want me to speak about Canadian literature? I pictured Dorothy and her wildly whirling farmhouse in *The Wizard of Oz.* Surely Kansas was not much more than an endless stretch of corn-fields populated by fresh-faced Norman Rockwell farmers in crisp checkered cotton shirts. Kansas. That mysterious dark heart of America, largely unknown and probably unfathomable to Canadians.

Wichita. Dodge City. Topeka. Abilene. The very names of Kansas towns spun me back in time to the television westerns that mesmerized me as a child in the 50's. Oxen-drawn wagons painfully inching their way along the panoramic Oregon Trail; or, awkwardly forming a hasty circle for defence against one of those nightmarish Indian blitzes that passed for plot. Screaming women. Sick children. Sometimes scalps. Then there were Wyatt Earp shoot-outs. Stage coaches held up by masked desperados whose horses sped away on jerky double-time film. Wild Bill Hickok. Buffalo Bill. Stampedes. Cattle-rustlers. In the 50's every Canadian home was at home on the range and "Home on the Range" is the state song of Kansas.

There were other songs too. All that idealizing of the railway: "The Atchison, Topeka and the Santa Fe." Or "Abilene, Abilene, prettiest town that I've ever seen." And, of course, Kansas City. It wasn't because everything's up to date that a later generation eulogized "Goin' To Kansas City." It was those crazy l'il women there.

Kansas is right in the middle of middle America. It harbours the geographical centre of the United States. Everything about the term middle America seems antipathetic to Canada: Bible-beating evangelism, rigid conformity, the slaughter of beef cattle and the Queen's English, a way of life galvanized by the alternating currents of vulgar commercialism and unsophisticated rusticity. A people who had taken to Ford panel trucks instead of horses and who were as bland and featureless as the land. Kansas, after all, was and is a Republican stronghold. It had not only produced President Eisenhower but also the vacuous slogan "I Like Ike."

Such were my thoughts as I took shelter on a Toronto plane from a March blizzard I wished I could call "unseasonal." I stepped out at Kansas City airport into a sunswept balmy landscape greening with buds Canada wouldn't see until May or even June. The burly graduate student who drove me west across the wide Missouri and on into Lawrence was not Kansan. He was, as his lilting speech at once betrayed, Irish. A graduate of Dublin, he had come to Kansas to do his Ph.D., thinking he'd quickly finish it off and go back. After two years in Lawrence, he explained with animated cheerfulness, he and his family wanted nothing more than to stay.

Suddenly, there it was on the horizon. Past the rounded hills moulded aeons ago when the southernmost tip of a glacier clawed at the Missouri and Kansas rivers with its icy fingers, rose Mount Oread. On its crest, arranged as if by some Renaissance artist, stood the buildings of the university. Nothing could have less resembled the Kansas I had expected to find. This scene conjured up the castles, fortresses and monasteries of northern Italy or southern France. There were tawny terra-cotta tile roofs on an array of handsomely proportioned buildings, many in the creamy yellows and subtle ochres of the native limestone. As we mounted the hill past intricately landscaped bushes, groves of dark pines and slim cottonwoods, fanning elms and tremulous poplars, the more impressive the architecture seemed. Classical arches turned windows into cloisters; plain square towers spoke of symmetry; doorways were embellished with intricate carvings and brick-work; winding walkways with wide flights of stairs laced in and out of each building making the campus a tracery on which chatting students walked or lingered in groups. But for their modern clothes — denims and bright T-shirts — I might have stumbled into

Zefferelli's film set for *Romeo and Juliet*. Everything seemed luminous and golden. The air was filled with the warm, intoxicating scents of spring. Looking north, I could see the Kansas River snaking its way through thick alders and cottonwoods. To the south, through clumps of pines I could glimpse the cobalt-blue Warakusa River; to the west, fields of corn and wheat. On this mountain about the size of Mount Royal, a campus of a thousand acres — more than twice the size of Toronto's vast York University — had existed for over a hundred years.

On the western edge of the hilltop, set apart from the main campus, lay a modest pioneer cemetery. In it had been buried some of the first abolitionist martyrs. For here, in and around Lawrence, the first skirmishes between pro-slavers and abolitionists had anticipated the Civil War and earned for the state the epithet Bleeding Kansas. It was in Lawrence, in front of the Free-State Hotel, that John Brown, the mythic American freedom-fighter, delivered fiery speeches calling for violence against pro-slavery men. That was in December 1855, and violence is what he got. Six months later, at what came to be called the Battle of Black Jack, a couple of dozen men under Brown attacked and killed a band of pro-slavery men in the first such battlefield confrontation.

The most spectacular clash for Lawrence was later, during the Civil War, in 1863: Quantrill's Raid. A band of Confederate irregulars from Missouri stormed the town one August night, killing many abolitionists and burning and looting most of the houses and shops. With characteristic pluck, the *Kansas Weekly Tribune*, whose office had been razed, issued a paper within a week, from Topeka. "Our town," the editor wrote, "will not be like a ruffian hole destroyed. It will rise from its ashes in a space of time that will astonish even Quantrill himself."

Such raiders were known as "border ruffians," coming as they did across the border from the slave state Missouri. Abolitionist bands who retaliated with raids into Missouri were known as "jayhawkers," an Irish term for a bird that delights in catching another bird and "bullyragging the life out of it like a cat with a mouse." This legend lives on in the Jayhawk, the University of Kansas mascot, a cocky little red-crested bird that might pass for Woody Woodpecker's younger brother. Today the Jayhawk is seen everywhere: on sweatshirts and posters, on key-rings and pennants, most boldly in a huge bronze statue outside the university's elegant Alumni Center. And jayhawker is the American nickname for a Kansan, akin to buckeye for an Ohioan or tarheel for a person from North Carolina.

Given its abolitionist history, it is not surprising that Lawrence later produced Langston Hughes, once known as "the Negro Poet Laureate," whose grandfather fought with John Brown; Hughes recalled that hearing Booker T. Washington speak at the University of Kansas was one of the most influential events of his childhood. Nor is it surprising that Lawrence opted in 1884 to house the first school for American Indians, now the thriving Haskell Indian Junior College.

Langston Hughes is not Lawrence's only legendary cultural figure. Frank Harris, the Irish pornographer, did his part to add to the yeasty history of the town. When Jim Harris (as he was then called) arrived in Lawrence in 1872 to live with his brother, he found the place surprisingly cultured: its citizens conversant with the works of George Eliot, Wilkie Collins or Victor Hugo, and appreciative of Chopin, Wagner and the ballads of Ireland and Scotland. Harris worked odd jobs — as a bouncer for a casino, waiting tables at the handsome Eldridge House (the hotel rebuilt after Quantrill's Raid and still going strong today), promoting acts for the old Liberty Hall, a splendid theatre restored in the 1980's, to which he brought minstrel shows, brass bands — even, in 1874, Martino, the Far-Famed California Illusionist, his Famous Talking Lion and Instantaneous Growth of Flowers in the Air. Harris finally settled on a butcher shop and began referring to himself as "the cowboy."

But as for Langston Hughes much later, a lecture at the University of Kansas transformed his life and set in motion a Lawrencian legend. Byron Smith, a brilliant and handsome young professor of Greek, inspired Harris to near-idolatry through his speech "Culture as Creed." Smith was already embroiled in a passionate (though never consummated) love affair with one of his students, Kate Stephens. The antics of this trio — Smith, torn apart by duty, friendship and love; Harris, who immediately sold his meat business and enrolled in Smith's classes; and Kate, who vied jealously with Harris for Smith's attentions — became increasingly bizarre. To impress Smith, Harris took his middle name Frank because that's what he now intended to become: a franker and better man.

Certainly he spoke and wrote more frankly than the citizens of Lawrence might have wished. As Kate Stephens tells it in her later exposé of Harris, *Lies and Libels*: "He would have us believe he could sweep horizontal at the merest touch a crowd of sighing matrons and virgins, penetrate them to the hilt and leave them sobbing for more... [But] probably most of the female bodies he saw or touched were veiled firmly in muslin, unyieldingly vertical." Harris, for his part, was almost inseparable from his mentor. He hung around his office, waited outside his classes, walked up and down Mount Oread with him to his lectures. For a brief time, he even managed to persuade Smith to share his lodgings with him. When Smith became ill, Harris quickly diagnosed his trouble as "nocturnal emissions" and somehow convinced Smith to try a series of cures, including tying himself up with whipcord and applying ice packs. Smith left Lawrence, his health broken, more perhaps from Harris' cures than from the consumption he finally succumbed to in Philadelphia in 1875. Furious and inconsolable, Kate Stephens spent much of her later life taking revenge on Harris in her books. All he was, she insisted, was "a little Irish immigrant in a senescent corduroy jacket and atrocious swagger."

As it once was for Harris, Lawrence continues to be a stimulating place for writers and artists. In its inimitable American way, the 1985 Rand McNally guide claims that Lawrence has "more culture per capita than New York City." It would no doubt please Harris to know that William Burroughs, author of *The Naked Lunch*, now lives here. For a town of 54,000 people, Lawrence flaunts an astonishing array of cultural happenings. Museums of anthropology, paleontology, natural history, local history; art shows in galleries, libraries, cafés — even in the hospital; concerts, string quartets, jazz combos, folk music, rock shows, opera; lectures on every conceivable subject; plays, musical comedies, vaudeville, foreign films. "It's a lot like Florence," quips a local wit. "Just put an F in front of Lawrence."

I begin to see why there could be an interest in Canadian literature here. It's true that one earnest professor asked me if "Bob" Davies had written any other novels — other than *What's Bred in the Bone*, that is. And it's true that the owner of a local bookstore swore he didn't have any Canadian books when volumes by Atwood, Munro, Davies and Leacock stood in plain view on his shelves. But Lawrence's longstanding sympathy for the underdog, its history of ethnic diversity and cultural ferment are clearly evident.

As I walked across campus past those towers that could be Florence silhouetted against a sky that shaded smoothly from apricot to a dusky grey-blue, the soft-spoken professor beside me commented almost sadly, "We love Lawrence, but we don't really want the rest of the world to find out what it's like here. It's an oasis that might get ruined."

Above Montana
and
Single World West
GEORGE BOWERING

*A fierce ambivalence about the United States is a significant element in
the works of George Bowering (born 1935), the prolific West Coast
poet. He is part of a distinct Canadian tradition that is nonetheless
derived from the literary theories of such American figures as William
Carlos Williams and Robert Creeley. At his most typical he shows a
greater sympathy for people, subjects and ideas from the American
West than with those from eastern Canada. Yet when he writes about
the actual United States (and one of his nearly 50 books is called* At
War with the U.S.*), he sees it in terms of dread, corruption and
almost unbearable sadness.*

above montana

The brown earth
back of the Rockies

patterned by men:
in stripes –

here I am
transient prairie man

in old shaky airplane
tipt sideways

to the sun
early morning
carving of the Rockies

the snow
apple pie sugar on them,

wrinkly little hill cluster
a puckered ass.

That crust down there,
men on it:

fleas
in the hair of my dog
asleep back home.

Here I am
sitting quiet twenty thousand feet
above the brown ground

for godsake,
& why not?

Looking out
I have visions of Russia
great tinder steppes

Australian cowboys
see great miles of cow country.

Sailors getting off plane
at Great Falls Montana

lo what ships
navigate this great calm sea?

Billings Montana,
these lonely towns

so far from
one another,

places to work,
lonely for America,
for Kanada, Russia.

Billings lumberman
neighbor to Australian cowboy.

Montana filled with
little airplanes,
traffic markers at airports.

No sense running
over this brown earth.

SINGLE WORLD WEST

(Bring it to you
or get right into it,

it is not a world parallel
to your own)

Have questions.

Would I have shot
John Wesley Hardin,
given the chance?

Two.

Would I have shot him
in the back
or dared him in sunlight,
thinking of the literature?

(When we stood on Custer's knoll
we stood, god damn it, where
men got their balls cut off,
where scared privates with children
lay with empty rifles
& arrows go in a foot deep)

Would I have hated Wild Bill Hickok
for being a drunk bully,
for killing his friend in panic,
for beating the shit out of women?

I could have been in Deadwood
among 20,000 criminals
a thousand miles from law,
where a dirty drunk American
might take it into his head
to point his gun at me
for being quiet & thoughtful.

（It is not a parallel fictitious world,
we haven't got away from it.

Did Kennedy ask himself those questions?

The radio is not a parallel universe,
and its messages are real as your brain)

What would you do
if your god told you
to kill his enemies for gain?

Right now
are you wishing I had more control
over my material?

(If you are not into it yet,
keep trying. Love & history
are like each other.

                              Be willing
to be carried closer. Lovers
are not parallel)

Three.

Would I want magic
in a poem about
killing John Wesley Hardin?

George Custer thought
his legend controlled his fate,
Crazy Horse rubbed his pony
with magic stones.

When they hit each other
it was not in literature,
it was in this single world,
my friend.

June 5/68

A Hobo's View of the Midwest
FREDERICK PHILIP GROVE

Frederick Philip Grove was the nom de plume — and alias – of Felix Paul Greve (1879–1948), a German-born writer who in 1909 faked his suicide and fled to the United States. About three years later he moved to Canada, where he became well known for such books as Over Prairie Trails, A Search for America, Our Daily Bread *and* The Master of the Mill. *Grove was seldom wholly truthful in his published reminiscences, but this excerpt from* In Search of Myself, *his 1947 autobiography, has the ring of authenticity. It also makes a fascinating comparison with Hugh Garner's short story beginning on page 67.*

What I am going to relate took place during one of the years shortly after the turn of the century.

As usual, I had started work in Kansas; and I had attached myself, as I mostly did, to a "pardner." Most hoboes did that; quite apart from the fact that a partner afforded company when one was travelling, he also facilitated many operations. Thus one man could get a camp ready while the other "rustled" food; or one of a pair could stand guard while the other scouted about for a chance of finding accommodation on a freight-train; if members of the train-crew happened to come along, a signal from the watcher told the scout to hide, for detection meant the loss of the opportunity of using the train. Finally, since most hoboes came to the farms in pairs, it was safer for everyone to have a helper.

During the very first week of the summer I am talking of I had joined forces with a Pole of ordinarily disreputable appearance. Like myself, who, perhaps, looked no less disreputable, he spoke half a dozen European languages and was, unsuspected by the Americans among whom we moved, capable of shaving and even of dressing like a dandy. Whenever he did so, which was, of course, on rare occasions, he assumed, with an inexpressibly comic effect, the irreproachable manners of a man of society. Unlike myself — at least if I could believe the stories he told — he made, on occasion, use of his accomplishments to "put one over" on gullible middle-class people by passing himself off as a *blasé* globe-trotter moment-arily embarrassed, alleging that he had outrun his base of supplies. Sometimes I suspected, again from the stories he told, that his harvest tramps were undertaken chiefly as a cloak for scouting purposes. What linked us together was that, as hoboes, we were both professionals, not, like so many others, mere amateurs who had been thrown on the road by adversity. If I judge by the amount of laughing we did, we must have been very good company, at least for each other.

Commonly we worked on large farms; which had the advantage that they offered a variety of buildings in which to find shelter for the night; while haylofts exposed one's clothing to the attack of crickets, they harboured neither fleas nor lice; an ounce of preven-tion is worth a pound of cure.

It was, of course, my, as well as his, invariable rule never to betray to the ordinary run of our fellow-workers that by birth, breeding, or education we were anything but common labourers. In speech and manner we made it a point to appear as nearly as we could their equals; for the average lower-class American hates the very suspicion of an education. Any other plan would have made our lives insupportable.

My newly-adopted friend, however, must have seen through my disguise at an early stage; and sometimes he allowed his own particular humour to run away with him. We were still in Kansas and engaged in haying when, standing on top of a load, in the blistering sunshine of a late-June or early-July noon, while I and another "pitcher" were tossing the hay up to him, he, in a sudden reckless mood, engaged me in a discussion of modern French poetry, with a ludicrous effect. It was done ostentatiously, with the pointed intention of making the other hoboes open their mouths. He even dropped his perfect American speech and changed to French; and in doing so, he adopted what, in these raw surround-ings, might have passed for aristocratic society manners, handling his pitch-fork with the fastidious nonchalance of a fop, parodying that nonchalance by its very exaggeration. Every now and then he stopped, looked at me, and laughed and laughed. I, laughing with him, though well aware of the probable consequences, entered into the fun.

At night, we found ourselves isolated. If there had not been two of us, both looking "tough," we should undoubtedly have been beaten up.

While we remained together, such things happened repeatedly, with the invariable consequence that we had to leave the place where we were working; and, towards the end of the season, when we were working on a "bonanza" farm, one last thing happened which I want to give in detail.

On the Saturday of our first week at the place it rained; and we had already discovered that we were not wanted at any of the diversions going on in the bunk-house: poker, horse-shoe quoits, and so on. I had a few books in my bundle but dared not take them out, even in the presence of my "pardner." Newspapers or even cheap magazines might have passed; but books! I proposed to walk to town, along the track, and to see the sights. My friend was willing. I do not remember the name of the town; nor does it matter; but it was pleasantly situated and extended over both banks of the Red River, its two halves being joined by a long, narrow, wooden bridge.

"Seeing the sights" meant to us very largely making fun of the false-front architecture and the ludicrous grandiloquence in the names of buildings — "Mandeville Opera House" — so commonly met with in the American small town. We laughed a good deal and generally, I am afraid, made ourselves conspicuous while present-ing a none-too-respectable exterior to the eyes of indignant burghers. We were in tattered overalls and carried a week's stubble on our chins; in a sort of defiance we had disdained shaving for the trip. While work was in full swing, Sunday was shaving-day, of course.

Having explored the west end of the town, with its pretentious residential quarter and its hectic business section, we came to the bridge and crossed to the east bank of the river.

By that time it had struck us that we were being followed by a tall, cavernous man in a buttoned-up blue serge suit and a quasi-official blue peaked cap. More than once, when casually turning back, we had seen him at some distance behind us. As we arrived at the far end of the bridge, I saw the tall, lank figure disconsolately halted at its west end. I called Stravinski's attention to it; and we both laughed.

I did not know it at the time, but the point was that the two halves of the town were separately administered; in fact, they were situated in different states, North Dakota and Minnesota. Never having been a consumer of alcohol in its undiluted state, I did not know either that North Dakota was "dry," while Minnesota was "wet"; had I known it, I should not have given the matter a further thought.

Suffice it to say that, when my friend and I returned from a half-hour's stroll on the far bank and recrossed the bridge, the tall man in blue was still standing at its west end. It turned out that he was waiting for us; as we approached, he bared a badge on the lapel of his vest, proclaimed himself, in a funereal voice, the Chief of Police, and informed us that we were under arrest. Leading the way, he enjoined us to follow him quietly, without making any attempt to escape.

In our exploration of the town we had seen the police station on Main Street, next to a little white frame building with an imposing false front which, in large, black letters, bore the legend "Town Hall and Municipal Office." I was surprised, therefore, when the chief, instead of continuing on Main Street, which was in line with the bridge, turned north along the bank of the river. However, scenting adventure, we followed obediently enough. Nothing could happen to us; we had done nothing to deserve arrest or punishment.

Meanwhile I tried to elicit some information as to the charge we were presumably facing. The chief received my overtures with a stony and reproving silence. I barely thought of the possibility that some major crime might have been committed in the vicinity and that we were suspected of being involved.

We went to the very end of the town, northward, before we turned west; from there on, the street was a mere trail skirting the endless fields of prairie wheat. After perhaps ten minutes we turned once more, this time south, and passed through a very poor street resembling the worst of the slums of a city. But when we reached the next side street, again running away from the river, the aspect changed into that of a cramped, middle-class respectability with diminutive but very smooth lawns in front of diminutive but up-to-date houses built of parti-coloured brick.

For a last time our guide turned, crossing one of the little lawns and pulling out a latch-key when he reached the front steps of the dwelling. He opened the door and motioned us to precede him into the narrow hall. Entering in our rear, he closed the outer door and threw open that into a small living-room which was neatly furnished in maroon mohair. My friend and I filed in, catching sight, as we did so, of a stout and forbidding woman in the kitchen at the back of the house. Our host or jailer closed and locked the door on us.

Left alone, we dropped into arm-chairs, laughed, and exchanged a few words, puzzled by the mystery.

Within five minutes, the chief returned; and, summoning me by an imperative gesture to stand up and to raise my hands over my head, he went through my pockets, laying everything he found on a little table the top of which was daintily carved in the form of an over-nourished clover-leaf. There were some papers, a few letters addressed to me, the manuscripts of half a dozen poems, some cigarettes, and, in a side pocket of my overalls, some money which he counted. Let us say that it amounted to $24.35.

Having finished, he motioned me to stand back and summoned my companion for examination. In his pockets, he found a pocket knife, some more papers, some more cigarettes, and some more money; all of which he arranged in a neat little pile on the clover-leaf table. Let us say that this money amounted to $13.32.

Then, to our surprise, our captor returned our possessions.

Having done so, he spoke for the first time since we had arrived. "You wait here till I get back."

With that he left us and again turned the key in the lock of the door.

We made ourselves comfortable, smoked, laughed, and wondered. Thus half an hour went by.

When our host returned, there was a marked change in his manner. He was curt, abrupt, almost grim. With a disapproving look at the stubs of our cigarettes in the diminutive fire-place, he told us not to try any "monkey-business" and to come quietly along. As we filed out, he held the door.

Again he took us a round-about way, but in a generally southward direction; and suddenly we emerged from a littered alley on Main Street, opposite the Town Hall. Having crossed the street and opened the door, he motioned us into an office so large that it seemed the whole building could hold nothing else.

His motions were quick and alert now; his manner, that of a

non-commissioned officer in front of the colonel. He ordered us about in a sharp voice. "Stand there; both of you; hats off!"

The room, a sort of board-room, was almost filled by a long table covered with black oil-cloth and surrounded by bare, clumsy wooden arm-chairs. We had been told to stand at the lower end of that table.

At its upper end sat a massive elderly man with a huge face framed by abundant iron-grey hair, tousled and not very clean. Over his eyes, the arched brows were so bushy and large that, his head being lowered over some papers, I at first mistook them for a moustache. When he looked up, I saw that his face consisted of several overhanging folds of heavy, greyish flesh. His eyes were extraordinarily mobile as he took us in and then focused his glance on the chief, without a word.

The chief, fingering his cap, stood at attention. "Your Honour," he began precipitously, "I've placed these men under arrest on a double charge, vagrancy and drunkenness. They have no regular domicile; I have had them under observation since Monday; at night they sleep somewhere along the river. This afternoon they crossed to the other side and came back dead-drunk. Whereupon I brought them here."

There was a pause of several seconds. Stravinski and I were dumbfounded and looked it. At last His Honour flashed us a look and grumbled, "What have you got to say for yourselves?"

I assumed the part of spokesman and, not disguising my indignation, replied that we had not been in town since Monday; that we were duly employed at the so-and-so farm, a fact easily verified; that we had tasted no liquor for weeks on end; that, if we had been dead-drunk an hour ago, we must surely still show signs of it which I defied anyone to detect. My companion stood with a contemptuous smile on his lips.

His Honour made an indeterminate noise. Then, as if on second thought, he hammered the button of a desk-bell with the palm of a pudgy hand.

Two burly men entered from the rear, looking more like thugs than like policemen, but jumping to attention at sight of His Honour.

The latter pointed a thick, inarticulate finger at them. "I want you to remain within call, do you hear? Dismissed."

They saluted after a fashion and withdrew.

His Honour turned back to us, saying curtly, "I fine you thirty dollars and costs. Total thirty-seven dollars and sixty-seven cents. Or a week in jail for each."

Thirty-seven dollars and sixty-seven cents — to a penny what we had between us!

My companion gave a contemptuous laugh. I smiled knowingly. Previous experience had taught me that any protest would be utterly useless. We threw our money on the table and filed out, free men once more.

But, though I accepted the thing, I did not mean to let it go without giving it a modicum of publicity. In the street I spoke to a grocer who was arranging a display of vegetables in front of his store and asked him for the name of a good lawyer in town.

He turned and, happening to glance along the street, said, "There he is now, talking to someone. Mr. McDonnell. The man standing with one foot on the curb."

I waited till the lawyer was disengaged and then approached him. While I was telling him the story, he nodded sympathetically more than once; but when I had finished, he seemed to change his mind and spoke with a sudden edge to his voice. "You'd better beat it," he said. "You can't tell such a cock-and-bull story about Judge O'Leary. Not in this town you can't." He veered on his heels and walked off, turning the nearest corner with accelerated step.

What he thought of us when our ringing laughter followed him, I cannot tell, of course.

When I say that such a thing was, by all of us hoboes, considered as being in the day's work, it will give a rough hint as to the foreground through which I was moving up to the fall of 1912; and, by readers of A Search for America, it will be observed that, in all essentials, the milieu was identical with the one through which I had been moving ten years earlier. There was fundamentally no change; in spite of the fact that I had already written such books as the one just mentioned, or Our Daily Bread, to speak only of such as have since been published, if in a considerably altered and abbreviated form. Manuscripts of these two books and of several others were circulating through the outer offices of many publishers.

Now the fall of 1912 was to prove a landmark in my life; and to explain how that came about, I must at some length speak of the agricultural distress prevailing over the whole west of the Ameri-

can continent — a distress due to meteorological conditions. For
the first time in my many years of life as an itinerant harvest-hand,
the result was, for me, that I experienced a serious difficulty in
earning the usual surplus for the ensuing winter. I had planned to
take a trip to Europe that year; even before I had become fully
aware of my predicament, however, I had realized that I could not
do so at the best, without drawing on my reserves; in striking
contrast to previous years I had begun that season without cash in
hand — a fact due to an extraordinary outlay made, in 1911, on
books. These books were, of course, never available in summer; at
least with the exception of perhaps two or three slender volumes
which I carried in my bundle; most of them were stored with some
friendly farmer in Manitoba. At the very start, therefore, having
found it impossible to secure work, I had had to draw fifty dollars to
go on with — a loan I considered it which had to be repaid to my
reserves.

I don't know whether that fact is in itself sufficient to explain the
mood in which the trip north was made and which, frankly, was
one of despondency. The sort of life I was leading suddenly seemed
repugnant.

Throughout the late summer and the early fall there were heavy
rains in the west, so heavy that there was no hay harvest worth
speaking of; one cannot cut grass when there is water standing on
the meadows. I might have waited in Kansas. I did wait for a short
time; but at last I began to move north. In some way I had heard
that Nebraska and South Dakota had had a dry summer and that,
there, the grain harvest would be early, though the crop was light.

From force of habit, I suppose, I travelled in my usual way,
"bumming rides" on freight cars, sleeping at night in stooks or
stacks or under culverts, buying bread and cheese for food. But for
the first time I failed to look at this sort of thing as an adventure.
Nor had I found a "pardner" for my companion.

When I reached the drought district, I found that the harvest was
finished. There was nothing to do but to go on.

Following roughly the state line between Minnesota and the
Dakotas, I came into more northerly latitudes; and it seemed for
the moment as if my reasoning had been correct; stooks of wheat,
oats, and barley dotted the fields in close formation; so far, the crop
was excellent. It seemed as if all I needed to do was to strike for

some really large farm — in those bonanza days we considered no farm as large which did not comprise between thirty and fifty square miles — in order to find, shortly, a steady run of work. Those farms I knew; and I was known to the people who operated them.

But I had hardly reached this favoured district when rain started here as well: the famous rains of the fall of 1912 which I later described, with their consequences, in *Fruits of the Earth*. It rained and it rained. Every town and village was crowded with its contingent of itinerant harvesters waiting for work, unable to find it. The fringes of every permanent settlement were occupied by the improvised, rain-bedraggled temporary settlements of the hoboes. Soon I found out — and this was a shock to me — that I could not continue my usual life when on the road. Painful twinges and sudden knife-thrusts in the muscles of my body warned me: I could not stand the wetness. In the past, I had often slept in the open in clothes that were soaked with rain; and in stooks or hay-stacks that were improperly cured. Even then I had, on occasion, suffered for it. I had caught colds which had disabled me for weeks at a time. With everything depending on it that, when work opened up, I should be fit, I felt I could not afford to do it again. I stopped long enough, at some town where I took up quarters at a boarding-house, to draw an additional fifty dollars from my reserves in Winnipeg which were thereby reduced to slightly over a hundred dollars; my dream of a winter in Paris or Rome received its death-blow. On the other hand, what were reserves for if they were not to be used in an emergency?

And then, having received the money, I again followed established habit and went on, sometimes even paying my fare for brief runs on local way-trains. Arriving in a new town, now in North Dakota, I promptly did what I had never done before; I shunned the hobo-camps and sought out some modest hostelry. Instead of laying steadily up treasure against the winter to come, I was rapidly consuming savings of happier times.

It worried me. No doubt there were, among the hoboes crowding the outskirts of the towns, many who were less fortunate even than I; men who, from one day to the next, never could thoroughly dry their clothes, even though they lit huge fires and erected make-shift shelters out of tin cans or box lumber; men who ulti-

mately had to subsist on garbage to keep alive. Slowly, but definitely, I succumbed to a sense of the utter insecurity of all life.

Yet I was still so much an animal obeying an initial impulse, that I
kept pushing on towards the Canadian border. I might have
stopped anywhere; what did it matter? As for my books, Canada
had shown itself no less indifferent than the United States. Yet,
somehow, I had come to look upon Canada as "my" country. There
was a subtle difference of atmosphere north and south of the
border; one felt it the moment one crossed the line. Canada had
never, so far, entirely severed the umbilical cord which bound it to
England. To the European I still was, it somehow seemed less alien.
Further, my own final interests had come to define themselves as
bound up with pioneering conditions which, in Canada, existed in a
purer culture, as it were, than in the country to its south.

PART
V
THE SOUTHWEST

Wonders in Arizona
DEAN HARRIS

The Very Rev W.R. Harris (1847 – 1923) — usually referred to as Dean Harris because he was dean of the Roman Catholic Archdiocese of Toronto — was a prolific amateur historian. He was also one of Canada's pioneer travel writers, with a special fascination for Mexico and other Spanish-speaking countries. But as this excerpt from his book Travel-Talks *shows, he was a shrewd observer of American locales as well. Although he seldom mentioned the fact, Dean Harris was the younger brother of Mother Jones, the famous or infamous American radical and labour organizer.*

I

After thirty days' traveling by train and burro, through Sonora and Arizona, I rode into Nogales last night, filled with amazement and admiration for the wonderful creations of God made manifest in the strange configuration of this land and in the marvels wrought by the hand of time. Dante Aligherie, when he breathed his last in the picturesque capital of the Exarchate, died 570 years too soon. If he were living to-day and travelled across this land of wonders, he would have seen upon the earth a region where Purgatory, Hell and Heaven had conspired to produce a bewildering viascope of all that is weird, terrible and awe-inspiring, side by side with the beautiful, the marvelous and romantic. With the possible exception of Sonora, in the Republic of Mexico, to which geographically and ethnographically Arizona belongs, there is not on the continent of America, perhaps not in the world, a land as full to repletion with all that is so fascinating in nature and startling to man.

Only a few months ago, a sailing ship from Honolulu reported that the lava from Mount Matatutu, then in active eruption on the Island of Savaii, had covered thirty square miles, while in places the flowing stream was two hundred feet high, and that in a part of the island a river of lava twelve miles wide was rushing to the ocean.

The tale was laughed down and ridiculed in San Francisco, where the captain of the ship made his report. Yet here, almost on the boundary line of California, there are indisputable, positive and visible proofs of a volcanic vomit compared to which the Matatutu discharge is but an intestinal disturbance.

The San Francisco mountain, 13,000 feet high on the northwestern edge of Arizona, is one of the most beautiful mountains in America. At some period, geologically recent, it was the focus of an igneous commotion of unequalled duration and violence. It poured out rivers and lakes of lava, which covered the land for two hundred square miles and raised it in places 500 feet. This statement may stagger belief, but any one who leaves the Santa Fe at Ash Fork and follows the trail to the Hupais village of Ave Supais, and begins the descent of Cataract Canyon, may verify for himself the enormous depth of this unprecedented flow.

Returning to Ash Fork, when the sun is declining and the sky flecked with clouds, the same man will see a sunset impossible of description, paralyzing the genius of a Paul Loraine and the brush of a Turner. Then the heavens are bathed in a lurid blood color, in purple and saffron, or gleam with vivid sheen of molten, burnished gold, when a falling cataract of fiery vermilion rests upon the purple peaks and ridges of the western mountains. I know not any land where the full majesty of the text of the inspired writer is more luminously present than here in the region of wonders. "The heavens declareth the glory of God and the firmament showeth His handiwork."

East of the Missouri river this is an unknown land, even to the well-informed Americans. Wealthy and presumedly educated citizens of the East spend millions annually sightseeing in Europe and Egypt, when here, within their borders, is a land where mysterious and pre-historic races dwell, where nature and nature's God have wrought incredible marvels unlike anything seen elsewhere upon the earth, and of which the people seem to have no appreciation. The hills and lakes of Switzerland, the Alps and Appenines, to which thousands, year after year, go from America ostensibly to admire the configurations and towering heights of these historically famous mountains, can offer nothing to the eye or to the imagination to be compared to the natural wonders of their own land and of which they appear to be unconscious.

Nowhere may there be found such extensive areas of arid deserts, crossed and recrossed in every direction by lofty mountains of strange formation, as in this comparatively unknown region. Here are fathomless canyons, dizzy crags and cloud-piercing peaks and a vast array of all the contradictions possible in topography. There are broad stretches of desert, where the winds raise storms of dust and whirl cyclones of sand, carrying death to man and beast. Here are to be found dismal ravines, horrent abysses and startling canyons, through whose gloomy depths flow streams of water pure and clear as ever rippled through the pages of Cervantes. Here are the cells of the cliff-dwellers, the burrows of the troglodytes, or pre-historic cave-men, the ruins of the ancient pueblo towns, and traces of pre-Columbian tribes who have gone down amid the fierce conflicts of tribal wars and have disappeared from off the earth.

Darwin, Huxley and Maupas are welcome to their theories accounting for the origin of Man and his expansion from the brute to a civilized being, but my life among and my experience with savages have convinced me that the territory separating the civilized from the savage man could never be crossed by the savage unassisted by a civilized guide, while all history proves that races at one time in possession of civilization have retrograded and descended into the gloomy depths of savagery, where many of them yet remain. In Arizona, at least, it was impossible for the Indian to lift himself out of his degradation, for when he began his rude cultivation of the lands, the ferocious mountain tribes swooped down upon him and drove him into the desert or to the inaccessible cliffs.

Following the instinct of self-preservation, he built his stone hut on lofty ledges or scooped from the friable mountain side, fifty, one hundred, two hundred feet in air, a cave which served for an observatory and a refuge for his wife and children. With a rope ladder, twisted from the viscera of the grey wolf, or the hide of the mountain lion, he climbed down from his lofty perch, returning with food and water for his miserable family. Thus began the now famous "cliff-dwellings," which seventy years ago many of our learned antiquaries thought were the dens of an extinct species, half animal and half man. Seeing and knowing nothing of the rope which was always lifted by the woman when the man was at home or on the hunt, the deduction was quite natural that no human being could scale the face of the almost perpendicular cliff.

The Moqui Indians still inhabit these strange rock lairs on the northern side of the Colorado Chiquito. There is no tribe of aborigines left upon the earth, there's no region of the world, more deserving of examination than the Moquis and the mysterious land they occupy. Here at the village of Huaipi, on a mesa or table land surrounded by sand dunes and amorphous boulders of old red sandstone, is held every second year the mystic rite of the "Feast of the Snake," when the tribal medicine men, or shamans, holding in their mouths and fondling venomous rattlesnakes, dance around and through the sacred fire, and rushing wildly through the assembled crowd of women and children, disappear behind the estufas and liberate the reptiles. These Moqui dwellings and the Zuni pueblos of New Mexico are the oldest continuously inhabited structures in America and probably remain more nearly in their original state than those of any other aboriginal people in North or South America.

For ethnological study it is hardly possible to overestimate the value of these strange people — the Moquis and the Zunis. In the accounts of their early explorations the Spanish missionary fathers found from eighty to a hundred cells of these pueblo and cliff dwellers inhabited in Sonora, Chihuahua and Arizona. Clearly the whole of New Mexico, Arizona and Northern Mexico was occupied by these semi-civilized people, who lived in caves, stone and adobe houses, cultivated the land with stone hoes, and irrigated it with water brought in channels from the nearest river. Centuries before the advent of the Spaniards, the decline of the race began, and eventually would have ended in total savagery if the European had not entered upon the scene. Internecine wars, drought, pestilence, and, above all, the coming into the land of the fierce Apaches, or Dinnés, and their many predatory and annihilating raids, wore down the ancient race and threatened its extinction. All the adobe and stone ruins, all the remains of ditches and canals from all over the lands of New Mexico and Arizona, are the relics of these strange people.

This is not the place to enter upon a disquisition into the origin or migration of the vanished race. I may, however, add that in the common use of adobe, for building material, in the plain walls, rising to a height of many stories, in the architecture of their terraced structures, absence of doors in the lower stories, the ascent by external ladders to the higher, their buildings were altogether unlike any found in Mexico, Yucatan or Central America. In the absence of arched ceilings, of overlapping blocks, of all architectural decorations, of idols, temples and buildings for religious rites, of burial mounds and mummies or human remains, rock inscriptions and miscellaneous relics, the monuments of the Zunis and Moquis present no analogies with those of the Mayas, Quichés or any known race of people now existing.

Returning from this digression, let me continue my explorations. Here in this land of wonders is the Petrified Forest, where are to be seen trunks of giant trees over ten feet in diameter and a hundred feet long, changed from wood into carnelian, precious jasper and banded agate. Here are hundreds of tons — a riotous outpouring — of Chalcedony, topaz, agate and onyx, protected from vandals by decree of congress. Here also is the Cohino Forest, through which one may ride for five days and find no water unless it be in the rainy season. There are places here where the ground is covered with pure baking soda, which at times rises in a cloud of irritating dust, and when driven by the wind excoriates the nostrils, throat, eyes and ears. There are depressions near the mouth of the Virgin River, where slabs of salt, two or three feet thick and clear as lake ice, may be cut; and mirages of deceiving bodies of water so realistic that even the old desert traveller parched with thirst, is sometimes lured to his death.

In this territory is the Mogollon Mountain, whose sides and summit are covered with a forest of giant pine trees. At some time in the remote past nature, when in an experimental mood, fashioned it, casting the huge freak to one side, and, laughing aloud, left it unfinished in the lonely desert. It is an unexampled upheaval, a marvelous oddity, from whose western rim one looks down 3,000 feet into the Tonto abyss, a weird depth, where ravines, arroyos, angular hills and volcanic settlings, conspire to produce one of the roughest and strangest spots on the earth's surface.

II

I cannot resist the temptation of enlarging and dwelling upon, what I may term, the natural miracles of this extraordinary region. North of Yuma, on the Colorado, there are hundreds of acres of mosaic pavement fashioned from minute cubes of jasper, carnelian and agate, a flooring of tiny pebbles so hard and polished that, when swept by the wind, is as visibly compact and regular as if each cube was set in place by an artisan and forced down by a roller. At times this floor of precious stones is entirely hidden by the sand, then a fierce desert wind enters and sweeps it clean. Nowhere, unless it be the Giant's Causeway, Ireland, have I seen stones laid with such mathematical accuracy.

In this land of contradictions is the Painted Desert, with its fantastic surface of ocherous earth and varieties of marls rivalling the tints and colors of a large palette. Here, in this weird and wonderful territory, was opened by the Spaniards the now exhausted and abandoned mines of the Silver King and the Plancha de la Plata, where lumps of virgin silver weighing two thousand pounds were discovered, and the Salero, where in Spanish times the Padre, who had charge of the little mission, wishing to entertain with proper respect his bishop, who was paying his first visit to the camp, discovered when the table was set that there were no salt cellars. Calling two of his Indian neophytes, he ordered them to dig ore from the mine and hammer it into a solid silver basin, which he placed on the table, garnished with roses and ferns, and presented to the bishop when he was leaving for Durango, his episcopal see.

In 1870 the last herd of wild horses was rounded up in Arizona, and here, too, corraled like the horses, and at about the same time, are the remnants of the Apaches, who, with no weapons, save bows and arrows, lance, knife and war club, defied for two hundred and fifty years the fighting men of Spain and the United States.

The Standard Iron Company is now tunneling earth near the Diabolo Canyon in search of the greatest meteor ever heard of by meteorologists. When this composite visitor struck the earth it cut a channel 600 feet deep and nearly a mile in length. The land for miles around was, and is yet, covered with fragments of this star rock. Some of these pieces weighed many tons, and when broken up and reduced, ran high in valuable minerals. The size of this meteor is said to be enormous, and judging from the value of the ore scattered around the great depression, the minerals embosomed in the meteor will amount to many millions of dollars. Distinguished mineralogists of Europe and America have expressed a wish to be present when the meteoric wonder is uncovered. Here, also, solidly perched on the breast of a small volcanic hill, is the only desert laboratory in the world. This hill projects from the base of a rugged mountain range, known as the Tucson, and was selected by the Spaniards as a site on which to build a blockhouse and observatory in the days when the Apaches terrified Southern Arizona. From the crest of this volcanic mount one may sweep a circular horizon within which repose in awful majesty fifteen ranges of mountains, stretching southward into Mexico, northward into Central Arizona, and extending toward the west far into California. Within this circle the Spaniards were making history when the states of the East were a wilderness, and New York had as yet no place on the map of America. The mountains and the deserts remain as they were when the Spanish priest, Marco, of Nizza, in 1539, crossed them on his way to the Moqui towns of Quivera. The vegetation even has undergone no change, for here, all around, and before you, are the giant Suaharos, or Candelabrum cacti, the ocotilla, the Spanish dagger plant, with bayonets all a-bristle, the palo verde, the mesquite, prickly pear, sagebrush, and all the wonderful varieties of desert flora for which the Arizona deserts are notorious.

The professor of botany in the University of Arizona tells me there are in Arizona 3,000 varieties of flower-carrying plants, and 300 different kinds of grasses. With the exception of the verbena and a few others, all the indigenous flowers are odorless, owing, it is said, to the absence of moisture in the air. All desert plants are protected against the greed or hunger, or, let us say, wanton destruction of man and animal, by spines or thorns. More than six hundred varieties of the cactus alone have been discovered, catalogued and classified. All deserts have a botany of their own and a flora of infinite possibilities of value, and in the deserts of Arizona are found plants of great medicinal value, many of them with unique and interesting characteristics. It is a very curious fact that the only varieties of the cactus without thorns known to exist in this region, are found growing in rock projections and ledges beyond the reach of animals. This was explained to me on the theory that, at some time in the past, this kind of cactus was common enough in the mountains, but the gophers, rabbits and other desert animals had long ago consumed all that could be reached. In "Wild West" books, and even in professedly historical novels, one reads occasionally of this and that family or clan of Indians perishing of hunger or thirst. It is impossible for a normally healthy savage to die of hunger or perish from thirst on the Arizona deserts. The white man? Yes, and often, the Indian never. It is a case of God tempering the wind to the shorn lamb, or fitting the back to the burden. Under the thorns of every variety of cactus there is refreshing, nourishing and indeed, palatable food. The desert and mountain tribes knew this from immemorial times, and until they were confined to the reservations, cactus food formed a large part of their ordinary diet. They had a way of their own of stripping the needles from the plant, reaching the pulp and eating it cooked or uncooked.

There are many fruit and berry bearing cacti, and these fruits and berries were gathered in season, eaten raw or boiled, and from which a delicious syrup or juice was extracted, and an intoxicating drink, called "chaca," distilled. The pitayha and suaharo cacti grow to the height of twenty and thirty feet, and yield, when properly tapped, from five to ten gallons of pure drinking water. All desert plants contain a large amount of moisture, and the professors of the Carnegie desert laboratory are now trying to find out how these desert plants, especially the cacti, extract water from a parched and sandy soil, and moisture from hot air. There is a cactus, christened by the early Spaniards the "barrel," which is forty per cent water, and, strange to say, thrives best in hopelessly barren lands in which no water is found within hundreds of miles, and on which rain seldom falls.

The desert laboratory for the study of the flora of barren lands, is the property of the Carnegie Institute at Washington, and was founded by Mr. F. V. Coville, of the United States Department of Agriculture, and Dr. D. Trembly MacDougal, who was for years assistant director of the New York Botanical Garden. Dr. MacDougal is now here in charge of the department of botanical research. In its specialty of purpose there is only one other institution in existence, even collaterally related to this desert laboratory, and that is the college of science established lately in Greenland by the government of Denmark, for researches in arctic regions and the study of the flora and fauna of the far north. This desert laboratory, under expert botanists, will include in its scope, the physiographic conditions of notable interest in the two great desert areas of

Western America, delaminated by the geologist, the botanist, and the geographer, and designated as the Sonora – Nevada desert and the Sinaloa – Chihuahua region of sand. These two regions embrace large sections of Idaho, Utah, Oregon, Colorado, Washington, Nevada, California, Arizona, Lower California, Sonora and Sinaloa. In this classification the beds of many ancient lakes are included, and among them the yet existing Great Salt Lake. Dr. MacDougal informs me that notable features in this vast body are the Snake river desert of Idaho, the Ralston sand lands of Nevada, the sage fields of Washington, the lava beds of Oregon, Death Valley, the Mojave Desert, the Colorado Desert, the Painted Desert in Arizona and New Mexico, the Salton bed and the great Sonora desert of Mexico. In the Californias — Southern and Lower — the desert vegetation and that of the coast lands meet, but, except in rare instances, never assimilate. I was surprised to hear from the distinguished professor, as without doubt you will be to read, that if the deserts of the earth could be brought into one area they would form a continent larger than all of North America. The wonderful and peculiar vegetation of the deserts has time and again invited and received the attention of learned botanists, but not until the founding of this Carnegie laboratory was any systematic and continuous study made of desert plant life. The assistant in charge of the botanical department corresponds with the famous botanists of the world, and is daily mailing to and receiving specimens of desert flowers and plants from all parts of Asia, Africa and Australia.

It may interest my readers to learn that, in the valley of the Salt River, in Arizona, the United States government reclamation service has well under way one of the most remarkable engineering enterprises for the irrigation of desert lands ever undertaken. Before a hole was drilled for the actual work in this almost inaccessible quarter of the Salt River Canyon, a wagon road twenty-five miles long had to be blasted from the side of the fearful gorge. Fifteen miles of this road presented almost insurmountable difficulties, for it had to be run through the wildest and most precipitous portions of the awesome canyons. Then began the herculean task of preparation for controlling the turbulent waters of the river, which in the late spring become a rushing torrent. In a narrow part of this canyon the men, under expert hydrographic and civil engineers, are now building a wall of solid masonry, which, when completed, will rise to a height of 270 feet. It will enclose a lake of storaged water twenty-five miles long and 200 feet deep. Sluices and canals will carry water from this artificial lake to the parched lands. This government contract will cost $6,000,000, and will reclaim 200,000 acres of arid land. At the southern level of the lake stands the town of Roosevelt, not very old, as you may judge by the name, but substantially built. Well, when the reservoir is finished and the waters are about to be let in, "Roosevelt must go."

III

Nowhere is the dividing line between the old and the new so sharply drawn as in Tucson. I do not mean the growth from a frontier or bush village into a city or that of a mining camp into a town, as in the mineral states. To this transition we are accustomed. Here, the modern city has grown away from the old Mexican pueblo which is yet a numerically strong part of it, growing out into the desert, leaving the quaint old Mexican village in possession of the fertile valley of Santa Cruz. It is not a divorce — *a mense et thoro* — from bed and board, nor yet a separation, but rather a spreading out, an elongation of the young giant towards and into the desert. The historic pueblo, so full of romance and story, is left in possession of its ground, its own religion, language, traditions and customs. Its people have a voice in the selection of the mayor and are eligible for any office in the gift of the citizens, are protected by the same laws and the same police as are those of whiter color.

Tucson had a name and was a rancheria of Pimas, Papagroes and Sobaipuri before the great missionary, Padre Kino, visited it in 1691. He was the first white man that ever crossed the Santa Cruz from the west and entered Tucson. In 1773 it was still a rancheria, but many of its swarthy denizens had already been received into the church; it was visited regularly by the priests of San Xavier del Bac and was now San Jose de Tucson. In 1771 the Spanish garrison or presidio at Tubac was shifted to Tucson, a resident priest appointed and the adobe church of St. Augustin built, the walls of which are yet standing on the east bank of the Santa Cruz, one of the disappearing rivers of the southwest. With the coming of the railroad in 1880, two meteoric bodies were found here weighing respectively 1,600 and 632 pounds. The rubbish that has been written about Tucson in the newspapers, books and magazines of the east, is only matched by the myths and fables published about Santa Fe. From before Father Kino's visit in 1691 Tucson was never heard of. Since then, down to the building of the Southern Pacific, its history is a record of blood and murders, of Apache raids, of Mexican feuds and American outlaws, gamblers and hold-up men who exterminated each other or were lynched by the law-abiding citizens. To-day Tucson is a city of law and order and will soon be the metropolis of Arizona. So much by way of a preface and now let us continue our impressions of the city.

The early Spaniards civilized and Christianized the Aztecs of Mexico and intermarried with them. From these unions were begotten the race known to-day as Mexican, though the average American very often confuses — and very annoyingly to the Mexican — the Indian tribes of the Mexican republic with the descendants of the Spanish colonists and military settlers and the daughters of the warriors of Montezuma. The Spaniards did something more. They imparted to their descendants courtesy, civility and high ideals. They taught them all those nameless refinements of speech and manner which impart a gracious flavor to association and a charm to companionship.

I cannot help thinking that the Americans of Tucson have profited very much from their intercourse with the Mexicans, for nowhere in the southwest have I met a more civil and companionable people.

The modern American is so full of the spirit of commercialism and the demon of material progress; so masterful in all that makes for political expansion and the achievement of great enterprises, that he is in danger of forgetting his duties to God and the courtesies of social life.

Today I took my second stroll through the Mexican section of Tucson and noted the slow but steady encroachment of Anglo-Celtic influence. I saw with regret that many of the old Spanish names of the streets had disappeared and that other and less euphonious ones had replaced them. The Calle Santa Rita had gone down in the struggle to hold its own with the "gringo" and Cherry street has usurped its traditional privileges, and our good-natured friend, McKenna, has his Celtic name blazoned where Santa Maria del Guadaloupe, by immemorial right, ought to be.

But, with the exception of these street names, the adoption of a more modern dress, and the absence of old time customs, fiestas and ceremonies, or their modification, the people are the same with whom I mingled two years ago in Zacatecas, Cuernavaca, and other towns in Mexico. Here are the narrow streets, with rows of one storied flat-roofed houses of sun baked brick, or adobes, with here and there a house whose floor is "rammed" earth. Remember that lumber here a few years ago cost $80 the thousand. In early times there were houses with not a solitary nail anywhere in or about them, for the window frames and doors were held in place by strips of rawhide. The women no longer wear the many-striped "Rebozo" or the "Tapole," which concealed all the face but the left eye. The Moors, who held possession of nearly one-half of Spain for almost 800 years, grafted on the Iberian race many of their own customs, manners and Oriental dress. The Spanish women inherited from them the "Rebozo," the "Tapole," and concealment of the face, and the Mexican senoritas adopted the dress of their Spanish sisters. I found the men leaning, as of old, against the door jambs and walls of the *mescal* shops, smoking their soothing cigarettes, made by rolling a pinch of tobacco in a piece of corn-husk, and apparently supremely happy. But I missed the picturesque "zarape" and the many colored blanket of cotton or wool, and the sweeping sombrero, wide as a phaeton wheel, and banded with snakes of silver bullion. Through the ancient street of the old pueblo — the main street of the town — there passed and repassed a motley aggregation of quaint people, Pima and Papago Indians, "greasers," half-castes, Mexicans and American ranchers, herders and cow-punchers. You must be careful here, for it is yet early in the forenoon, and the street is filled with horses, mules and burros loaded with wood or garden truck for the market and dealers, and with tawny-complexioned men and women carrying huge loads on their heads and followed by bare-footed children and half-starved and wild looking mongrels, first cousins to the sneaking coyotes of the Sierras.

The sure sign of racial absorption comes when a people begin to adopt the diet and cooking of the foreign element with whom they must live and with whom they must associate, at least commercially. To test how far this process of assimilation and incorporation had already advanced among the Mexicans, I dined to-day at one of their restaurants. Fortunately or alas! it was the same familiar and palatable meal I had so often sampled in the inland towns of the neighboring republic. Beginning with "soppaseca" or vegetable soup, I had my choice of one or all of the dishes of "enchiladas," "tamales," "tortillas," plates of "frijoles" and "chile con carne" seasoned with "chile Colorado" or any other kind of pepper. The dessert introduced "dulces," coffee or chocolate, cheese, cigarettes and Chihuahua biscuits. Evidently after fifty years of occupation the absorption of the Mexican by the Anglo-Celt is yet in its initial stage in Tucson.

The "enchilada" and the "tamale" are of Aztec origin. The enchilada is a cake of corn batter dipped in a stew of tomatoes, cheese and onions seasoned with pepper and served steaming hot. The tamale is made from chopped meat, beef, pork or chicken, or a mixture of all three combined with cornmeal, boiled or baked in husks of corn. These dishes, when properly prepared, are delicious and are gradually finding their way to American tables and restaurants. Cooked as the Mexicans cook them, they would be a valuable addition to the admirable menus of our eastern hotels.

After dinner I visited the half acre of ground which was at one time the "God's acre," the last resting place of the early "comers," many of whom died with their boots on. In those days — 1855 to 1876 — the Apaches swooped down from their mountain lairs, and attacking the suburbs of the town and the neighboring ranchos, killed the men and boys, drove off the cattle and carried back with them the women and children. As I may have to deal some other time with this extraordinary and crafty tribe and fierce race of men, I will say here, only in anticipation, that the Apaches of Arizona were the shrewdest and most revengeful fighters ever encountered by white men within the present limits of the United States. Fiercer than the mountain lion, wilder than the coyote he called his brother, inured to great fatigue, to extreme suffering of soul and body, to the extremes of heat and cold and to bearing for days and nights the pangs of hunger and thirst, the Apache Indian was the most terrible foe the wilderness produced. In those early days this neglected piece of ground, "where heaves the turf in many a mouldering heap," recorded the history of the pioneer days of the American Tucson. The headboards marking the graves informed the visiting stranger that this man was "killed by the Apaches," this one "died of wounds in a fight with the Apaches," this other "scalped, tortured and killed by the Apaches," and — this family in the little corner of the graveyard — "this whole family, wife, husband and six children, was wiped out by the Apaches." But these days are gone forever; the Apache is corraled on the reservation and we may safely say of him what Bourienne said over the grave of Bonaparte, "No sound can awake him to glory again."

To-day with a population of 17,000, and a property valuation of many millions, this city is the social and commercial oasis of Arizona. The city is well supplied with churches, schoolhouses and public institutions. The Carnegie free library, erected at a cost of $25,000, is surrounded by well kept grounds; it faces Washington Park, the military plaza of the old Mexican presidio, and the largest public park in the city. The Sisters of St. Joseph look after the parochial schools, have a very fine academy for young ladies and conduct one of the best hospitals of Arizona. There are twelve hotels in the city, and one of them, the Santa Rita, is architecturally one of the most novel buildings of the southwest. It is named from the Santa Rita range of mountains, and forms, with San Augustin's Cathedral, the most imposing structure in Tucson. The city council is experimenting in street oiling, not sprinkling the streets with oil, as in San Diego, Southern California, but soaking them, so that the fine triturated sand forms with the oil a fairly durable and smooth surface.

On these same streets one is always running up against some interesting and peculiar varieties of the Noachic stock. Here are Chinese in quest of the elusive dollar — stage ghosts in Oriental dress — quiet, unobtrusive, always looking down on the dust as if examining the minute particles entering into the composition of their material selves, and apparently doing a "heap" of thinking; here, also, is his cousin-germain — the gentle and innocent-looking Papago or Pima of the mysterious aboriginal race, sun-scorched and wind-tanned with long coal-black hair and keen snake-like eyes. He is in from the reservation of San Xavier del Bac, nine miles south of here, asking a dollar for a manufactured stone relic worth ten cents. The sons of Cush, the Ethiopian, monopolize the lucrative trade of shoe blacking, guffaws and loud laughter. Varieties of the Caucasian race — rare varieties many of them — half-breeds, mulattos and Mexican half-castes, all have right of way and use it on the beautiful streets of Tucson.

The Cowboy
GREGORY CLARK

Gregory Clark (1892 – 1980) was a journalist associated with the Toronto Star *from 1911 to 1947 and then, until his final years, with* Weekend Magazine; *during much of his career, his periodical writings were gathered together in frequent books. He was a type of writer now virtually extinct: the spinner of warm yarns and turner of light essays. When commenting on the United States (as in this piece from* Greg's Choice, *a 1961 collection) or on any other subject, he revealed the folk wisdom and trusting attitudes of what seems to us now a more innocent age.*

M otoring through Texas lately with some friends, we were struck by the absence of cowboys in this last stronghold of the breed.

We saw plenty of big hats with wide, upflaring brims; plenty of skin-tight blue jeans, and any number of fancy-stitched cowboy boots with high heels. But on inquiry, we discovered that, without exception, those wearing the authentic outfits were tourists from New York and the New England states. This dissuaded me, in San Antonio, from buying a very fine cowboy hat I could have got for only $8.

What we did find in Texas were oilmen. The Lone Star state is full of oilmen, and a more unromantic crew you would never want to see. They are toilers, wearing small safety hats not unlike undersize steel helmets. A far cry from the ten-gallon hat. It seems Texas isn't interested in ten gallons any more. Everything is by the barrel. A hundred, two hundred barrels a day; that's what they are interested in.

Far west of San Antonio, we pulled into a little highway snack bar, wide on the lone Texas range. Seated inside were a few dowdy gentlemen in khaki trousers and shirts, wearing ordinary old felt hats that looked as if they had been sat on instead of worn, most of the time.

They were not bow-legged from riding cayuses. They were

knock-kneed, from riding in jeeps. The cowhand of today rides herd in jeeps or sometimes in Cadillacs, depending on whether there is oil as well as cattle on his ranch.

They eyed us respectfully as we came in. They ceased their conversation and lowered their eyes modestly. There was a spinsterish look about them all.

"Know something?" I murmured to my companions, as we sat down at a table. "I bet you we are at last in the presence of cowboys!"

My friends, glancing pleasantly about the little snack bar, covertly inspected the half-dozen dusty, drab gentlemen of varied ages and sizes at the far end.

"Pah!" they said: "Cowboys?"

They had that sand-blasted rather than tanned look that outdoor Texans wear. But the impression of old-maidishness about them, a kind of withery, prim quality, was what I was going by, in my guess. For, having listened all these years to cowboy songs, those melancholy, wailing, lonely yodels and whines that are identified with this classic breed of men, I cannot help but know that real cowboys are moody and modest men bearing little resemblance to the cowboy of fiction and the movies.

"Want to bet?" I asked my friends.

A small bet, sufficient to pay me the price of a pair of skin-tight Levis, was agreed upon.

"Excuse me, gentlemen," I said, going over to the other table, "but we're strangers here. We're playing a little game called 'What's My Line?' I say you're cowhands. Is that right?"

They all smiled delightedly.

"That's right, suh," they chorused in their mild, Texas way. "We-all work on this ranch heah, on the both sides of the hahway."

"Horses?" I inquired. "You got horses outside?"

"Hosses?" checked the oldest of them, a wiry little tenor of about sixty-five. "Not heah, suh. We got some hosses back at headquarters, that's about thirty miles from heah. But mostly, we do our ranching by cah."

"Cah?"

"Jeeps," he explained, "pickups, cahs."

"I figure hosses," put in a very tall, lean youth, a baritone, "would scare our caows. Panic them, maybe."

"Cattle," submitted the bass-baritone, a middle-aged man who looked like ZaSu Pitts, "is used to cahs."

I thanked them, and went back and collected fifty cents all round my table.

At this moment, the door opened and in strode a terrific apparition. Six feet four, lean as an axe handle, his slender legs snug in skin-tight Levis, he was the picture of the cowboy, not of fiction but of dreams. He had a great silver-gray hat on, its crown rising like a quart sealer, its brim vast and upcurled on both sides. His boots were scarlet and tan, in arabesque design, stitched with white; and heels four inches high.

To my astonishment, he was greeted warmly and respectfully by all the cowhands. He was no tourist from Brooklyn or Toronto! As he strode past the cowhands, he patted a couple on the back, ruffled a head or two, and then went to the counter and took a stool in front of the bright-eyed waitress.

My friends closed in on me. They held out their hands for their fifty cents.

"Aha!" they whispered. "The boss! The head wrangler! Now you *are* seeing your first real cowboy."

I do not let go money that easy.

I sneaked over to my friends, the cowhands.

"Who's he?" I hissed.

"The local school teachah," they hissed back.

PART
VI
THE NORTHWEST

Looking from Oregon
EARLE BIRNEY

*The dean of Canadian poets, Earle Birney (born 1904), is best known
for his long narrative poem "David" and also has a large following for
the comic war novel* Turvey. *He is an indefatigable traveller to —
and poetic meditator on — many parts of the world, including the
United States, where he wrote this gentle but chilling commentary on
the Vietnam War. His* Collected Poems *appeared in 1975.*

LOOKING FROM OREGON

"And what it watches is not our wars" (Robinson Jeffers)

Far out as I can see
into the crazy dance of light
there are cormorants like little black eyebrows
wriggling and drooping

       but the eye is out of all proportion

Nearer   just beyond the roiling surf
salmon   the young or the sperm-heavy
are being overtaken by bird's neb
sealion's teeth   fisherman's talon

The spent waters
      flecks in this corner of the eyeball
falling past my friend and his two sons
      where they straddle the groin's head
collapse on the beach
      after the long race
from where?   perhaps from Tonkin's gulf
      on the bloodshot edge

There's no good my searching the horizon
    I'm one of those another poet saw
     sitting beside our other ocean
I can't look farther out or in

Yet up here in the wild parsnips and the wind
I know the earth is not holding
tumbles in body-lengths
towards thunderheads and unimaginable Asia

though below me on the frothy rocks
my friend and his two boys
do not look up from fishing

Florence, Oregon, August 7, 1964

They Don't Sell Much Quiche in Alaska

GARRY MARCHANT

Garry Marchant (born 1941) is a Vancouver travel writer who has visited 186 countries. He has been on the staff of the Brazil Herald *in Rio de Janeiro and both the* South China Morning Post *and the* Far Eastern Economic Review *in Hong Kong. His account of a cruise to Alaska subtly underscores the differences between that state and the Canadian North.*

A curious collection of passengers gathers on deck of the *MV Tropicale* as it departs Vancouver this mild spring afternoon: those few in jeans, plaids and hefty hiking boots are with the Westours combined cruise and adventure jaunt to Alaska; others, cruising the Inland Passage and back, wear black tie, frilly shirts or formal gowns. The well dressed look forward to a week of dining and dancing, the gaming tables and long hours of leisure. Those of us answering the call of the wild will disembark at Juneau for a week of hiking and white water rafting — and a lot more adventure than we had planned.

The ship itself, on its first Alaska cruise after a Caribbean winter, suffers an identity crisis. Busy waiters peddling trays of pina coladas hustle through the ship like marketplace hawkers. Dinner themes are Italian Night — waiters in red, or black and white striped shirts, serving pasta and Chianti — or Caribbean Night, with Jamaican bean soup, mutton curry and rum swizzles. The Baked Alaska, a shipboard tradition, is about as Alaskan as enchiladas, and we savor no sourdough pancakes, bannock, beans or baked salmon.

The view is northern enough — lonely, rugged, forest-covered mountains cleaved by foaming waterfalls, killer whales and a few isolated fishing communities, all of them smaller than this floating pleasure village of about 1,000.

Up on the sports deck, Mike, a New York ballet critic and travel writer, a marathon runner and fitness fanatic, leads a group of fellow journalists in a jogging and exercise class. In the Paradise Club casino, gamblers cluster round a croupier who explains the intricacies of blackjack, roulette and craps, and the jargon of split pairs, double down bets, hardway bets and passline; the background sound is muzak and the metallic clatter of one-armed bandits. Noisy children and tuxedoed adults hunch over Pac-Man and Space Invader toys, their backs to some of the world's most spectacular scenery.

A lazy few of us stretch out like great seals on the comfortable chairs of the sunny, glassed-in Port Promenade Deck. With a copy in my lap of Robert W. Service's *Songs of a Sourdough*, I doze off, dreaming of gold nuggets glinting in the rushing waters of a Klondike creek.

Early the second morning we dock at Ketchikan, Gateway to Alaska, which looks like a soggy set from the movie *Popeye*. Frame houses on wood pilings climb the mountainside, joined by steps zigzagging from platform to platform. They look from the ship like model houses on matchsticks. Thickly forested Deer Mountain looms 5,000 feet behind the town, wisps of mist caught in the branches of tall conifers. While boxy, orange school buses take passengers to the Totem Heritage Center (Ketchikan claims the most totem poles in the world), the Salmon Hatchery and the Tongass Historical Society Museum and Heritage Cultural Center, a group of journalists visit the local bawdy house.

Donning our Ketchikan Sneakers (high rubber boots), necessary in this wet coastal town (12 feet of rain a year), we hike down Front Street. This is frontier U.S. of A; a town of low buildings with white picket fences on the second-floor canopy and the Stars and Stripes hanging everywhere. A political sign declares, "Protect your rights and freedom of choice. Vote against early bar closures."

Ketchikan started at Creek Street, this row of houses on pilings; the most infamous house on the boardwalk was Number 24. From 1919 until 1953, a more liberal age than ours, Thelma Dolly Copeland kept this little two-story, green with red trim, clapboard house. The sumptuous strumpet of stamina, last cited for prostitution when she was 63, died in 1975 at 87. Now her cozy home is a museum where giggling high school girls show off Dolly's receipt book, a coin box in the hallway for bootleg drinks and a kitchen with one of Ketchikan's first electric stoves. Dolly's handstitched pillows in the upstairs bedroom are scattered over the pink satin bedspread, and the walls are decorated with interbellum wallpaper, paintings and a seminude photograph of the proprietress. In the 1920s and 1930s, the "ladies of utlimate accessibility" entertained loggers, miners and fishermen at $3 per service in some 20 Creek Street houses. In 1953, when the shrill voices of righteous indignation closed the brothels, the girls held closing-out sales: "Three glorious weeks of exotic bargains on Creek Street; a variety of sizes and all popular colors; no exchanges, no refunds, no charges." The street has since degenerated to a row of arts and crafts shops, an art gallery, civic club and apartments.

As we pause on the Stedman Street Bridge to watch the dark forms of giant salmon in the clear water below, a passing native says wistfully of the good old days, "This used to be the only place in Alaska where both fishermen and fish went upstream to spawn."

We disembark next day at Juneau, the state capital, where the men are like great hairy bears dressed in wool. At the Triangle Bar, where it is a Juneau tradition to drink beer and eat hotdogs every day at both noon and 5 p.m. (they don't sell much quiche in Alaska), the bartender boasts he has never left Juneau. Recognizing *cheechakos*, newcomers, he booms, "Know what happiness is to an Alaskan? A Texan flying south with an Okie under each arm." Roustabouts from the Valdez pipeline must have passed this way. We retreat across the street to the Red Dog Saloon, a sawdust-on-the-floor, beer-by-the-pitcher place, where the angelic folksinger from California sings the requested *Why Don't We Get Drunk and Screw?*

Juneau is one of the few Alaskan towns not leveled by fire, earthquake or flood, the waitress says, as she demands $5 for a plastic pitcher of cold brew. That explains the number of turn-of-the-century, Victorian buildings decorated in Carpenter's Gothic. The "jewel of the city," St. Nicholas Church, with its gilded onion dome topped by the double-barred Russian Orthodox cross, recalls the early history of the Alaskan coast — and the Russians just across the Bering Strait. The rest of the town, though, including the marble-pillared state capital, with replica of the Liberty Bell and the white Governor's Mansion, is as American as the bald eagles soaring high above the four-lane freeway out of town.

Skagway, a four-hour cruise up the Lynn Canal on the *MV Fairweather*, has the dirt roads and board sidewalks of a Gary Cooper western. After a simple meal of Alaska king crab in the Klondike Hotel, we meet our guides. They are strong, silent mountain men, all whiskers and Copenhagen snuff. Briefly taking over the lobby of the hotel, we spread out clothes, boots, tents, camp gear and food to pack into rucksacks for tomorrow. Then we clump out onto the raised wooden sidewalks to tour the town. That takes 10 minutes.

During the gold rush of 1898, Skagway was a boom town of 15,000 people, the largest in Alaska. The numerous sourdoughs climbing the backbreaking Chilkoot and White Pass trails looked like solid lines of human ants, and their lawless, frontier headquarters was described as "little better than a hell on earth." But tonight its 800 citizens, supported by the Whitepass and Yukon Railway and by visiting cruise ships, pass the time more serenely: they listen to Willie Nelson on the jukebox in Moe's Frontier Bar, shoot pool in the Golden North Hotel or cram in for live music at the Red Onion Saloon. In the eerie half-light of the midnight sun, a group of teenagers sits drinking on the boardwalk at 1 a.m. The largest gets down on all fours to bay at the moon, startling the passing cruise ship passengers. The northern lights have, indeed, seen strange sights.

Next day our motley crew of city-bred journalists and photographers gets off the White Pass and Yukon Railway in the middle of nowhere. The pile of gear thrown out of the baggage car evokes Robert Service:

This is the law of the Yukon, and ever she makes it plain:
"Send not your foolish and feeble; send me your strong and your sane . . .
The pallid pimp of the deadline, the enervate of the pen,
One by one I weeded them out, for all I sought was — Men."

Hoisting heavy packs, a dozen pallid pimps of the deadline march single file through the open hill country of moss-covered rocks, sparse trees, gentle streams and trails cushioned by pine needles. This warm, bright day in the little panhandle of B.C. between the

Yukon and Alaska, with impertinent jays hopping through the trees and the sun warming our backs, belies the agonies suffered by the sourdoughs in grim northern winters.

At placid Bare Loon Lake, while the guides set up tents and cook dinner, a few of the brave plunge into the glacial water. Mike, the New York ballet critic, swims happily for half an hour wearing only a fluorescent red wool cap. No "enervate of the pen" that man. After bannock, beans, barbecue beef and Sara Lee cake, we sit late into the night sipping Yukon Jack while the guides read excerpts from *Songs of a Sourdough* — tales of lonely, desperate men, barroom shootouts and the love and hate of the north. By 3 a.m. it is still faintly light; suffering a sort of jet lag, we have trouble sleeping.

The morning's cold drives us out of sleeping bags to huddle around the giant black coffee pot. After a two-hour hike up part of the Chilkoot Trail, we overlook jade-green Lake Lindeman, which in 1898 was one of the largest tent cities in the world. From our height we see only a few log cabins and tents — and boot hill, a reminder of grimmer times. Thousands wintered here that year, building boats and rafts to take them down a series of lakes to the Yukon River and the Klondike. In the spring thaw of May, 1898, some 7,124 boats left loaded with men and supplies. Many didn't make it. We recreate part of the run, paddling rubber rafts through brief, exhilarating rapids between Lindeman and Bennet Lakes, whooping happily through the deadly waters that shattered so many boats and dreams.

From the six-man float plane flying 1,000 feet above, the waters of the Alaska panhandle's Whiting River look innocent enough. But when the planes drop us off on Bates Lake, 60 lonely miles upstream, then take off in formation playfully waggling their wings, we feel alone and vulnerable. There is no human habitation in this valley, and without a radio we are more than three days from contact with the outside world.

In a subdued mood, we struggle into wool shirts, wet suits, rain gear and life jackets and stumble around the chilly beach like awkward, multi-colored penguins. With four passengers and one oarsman to a boat, we push off from the rocky shore. Almost immediately, we are bouncing down a liquid slide of churning, boiling water.

We shoot the wildest rapids the first day, including the melo-dramatically named Holy Gardens. Our boatmen, who have run whitewater rapids all over Canada and the U.S., treat these with a solemn respect. Pulling over to shore, they walk ahead to study the foaming water and jagged rocks. It is all incomprehensible technical talk of eddies, holes, walls, waves and haystacks.

From the last raft, we silently watch the first two crash through the Gardens, disappearing from view under a wall of seething water and then popping in the air again like rubber ducks under a pouring faucet. Our boatman studies every move intently. Then we are sucked from the quiet water into the roar and foam and confusion. Water hammers at the bottom, spews over us, blinds us; suddenly we pop out the other end of the rapids. Hey, that wasn't so bad, let's do it again. It is a Catch-22 of river running, the boatman explains, that it must be done exactly right or it can be deadly. And when it is done right, it looks easy.

The danger has past, we think, by our last afternoon. The valley has widened so it no longer feels forbidding, the sun has broken through the clouds. With time to spare before the float planes pick us up down river, we fish at a side stream for Dolly Varden, listen to the woodpeckers and watch a family of ducks glide by. In our rubber raft, with our yellow rain gear and red life jackets reflected off the still water, we look like a *Field and Stream* cover.

Half an hour before pickup time, my nap in the front of the drifting raft is shattered by a shriek: "Look out!"

A giant cottonwood, roots eroded by the river, has crashed into the raft a few hundred feet behind us, driving five people into the rushing water. Somehow, they manage to stay with the raft.

The boatman shoves off the branches, changes his broken oar and rows for shore while we watch helplessly. Mike clings to the raft, his leg twisted at a crazy angle. I think of the drowning victim in *Deliverance.* Our lazy joy ride is suddenly serious, the river no longer warm and friendly but cold and cruel. The sun disappears behind a black cloud. Even the current seems to run faster.

Our boatmen quickly row to shore to set the leg, then float Mike down to the rendezvous point with the float planes. (Later we find the injury, more serious than a broken leg, would have been fatal if left unattended even a few hours.) Exactly on time, three planes sweep low over the water, banking to take a closer look when they see the orange smoke from our distress flare.

Less than an hour after the accident, Mike is loaded on to the Cessna on his way to a Juneau hospital. The rest of us — cold, wet, and somber — climb into the other two planes. They turn downstream and bank steeply to get out of the valley. When we break past the clouds into sunlight, I feel suddenly grateful for living in the machine age.

PART
VII
THE FAR WEST

Berkeley and the Higher Learning in America
JOHN KENNETH GALBRAITH

John Kenneth Galbraith was born in 1908 in Iona Station, Ontario, and is probably North America's best-known economist, certainly the best-known liberal one. He was United States Ambassador to India during the Kennedy administration, taught for many years at Harvard University and is the author of 24 books including The Affluent Society, The New Industrial State *and* The Age of Uncertainty. *Below is an excerpt from his 1981 autobiography,* A Life in Our Times. *It recounts his arrival, during the Depression, at the University of Southern California at Berkeley, following his undergraduate years in a rather different environment — at the Ontario Agricultural College at Guelph.*

My life has been spent in greater or less communion with five centers of higher learning, as that term, often loosely, is used. Two of these, Guelph and Princeton — respectively the least and the most aristocratic in tendency — did not engage my affection. Two, the University of California at Berkeley and the University of Cambridge, I greatly loved. Harvard, where I've spent most of my life, does not lend itself easily to classification. In all five universities, as they all now are, I suffered from a problem in personal relations that I never quite overcame. This was not so much from being more versatile, more diligent or perhaps more able than my colleagues. Such can be tolerated. The damage arose from my fear, which I earlier indicated and which I never quite suppressed, that my superiority would not be recognized.

Princeton was an especially serious case. There I was employed for three years immediately before and following the outbreak of World War II, two years of which I spent on leaves of absence. Much of Princeton I remember with distaste; even someone with a greater instinct for social grace and adjustment might so remember it from those years. The economics faculty of the time was firmly committed to teaching what a decade of depression had shown to be irrelevant. There were exceptions; one was Frank D. Graham, a professor of money and banking and the historian of the great German inflation of the early twenties. I also became very fond of Frank A. Fetter, by then retired, an old-fashioned liberal of exceptionally strong fiber. He once told me that he had never allowed the promotion to tenure of any economist in his department who testified on behalf of a corporation in an antitrust case, for such behavior meant the man's views could be had for money. He was, I think, right.

The low quality of the economics faculty was, however, less depressing than the scholarly and social tendencies of the Princeton undergraduates. They were even more deeply anti-intellectual, though in a more refined way, than those at Guelph. In Canada there was a certain sense of aspiration; at Princeton students, with rare exceptions, felt that they had already arrived. From time to time, as a conscientious young instructor, I sought to correct some of the more egregious archaisms which my Princeton colleagues had written into a set of small green-jacketed textbooks. These — "the little green terrors" — they had then assigned to their classes to exploit a financially insignificant conflict of interest. I was repeatedly and indignantly asked by students if it wouldn't be the textbook version, not my corrections, that would be required on the examinations. If so, why confuse them with the truth?

Those then responsible for admission to Princeton favored what was called "the Princeton type." So far as ever defined — ambiguity in these matters greatly enhances freedom of choice — a Princeton type was like a Princeton graduate. He was affluent, white, Anglo-Saxon and usually a Protestant; from a reasonably acceptable preparatory school, a substantial family or suburb, often on the Philadelphia Main Line; and with a commitment to sound personal hygiene. Scholarly aptitude was neither a requisite nor a handicap. Many of the faculty, reflecting the instincts, ambition or conditioning for academic achievement of the offspring of schoolteachers, ministers of the gospel, Jewish immigrants and the more eccentric of the American middle class, were much less distinguished in their social origins than those they taught. So at Princeton before World War II, quite a few faculty members looked with admiration on the superior social assurance and behavior of their students.

For a week or so each spring all academic work at Princeton, however frivolous, came to a complete halt while the precise social rank of each member of the freshman class was appraised and established. In an appalling procedure called "the bicker," social precedence was recognized by selecting students for the several dining clubs, buildings of sub-Georgian architecture which lined the two sides of Prospect Avenue near the campus. Each club had its exact position in the general order, beginning at the top with one called the Ivy. I was never quite sure which came last. Jews and other outcasts were firmly excluded from all clubs. At first I was rather indifferent to these awful proceedings. Then two or three students sought me out to confide their terrible fear that they would not be selected. For all of their bright college years they would be formally designated as undesirables. There was nothing one could do. I learned that Woodrow Wilson, when president of the university, had also been appalled but was equally helpless to change the system.

After World War II, women, racial tolerance and suspicion of prescriptive social position as adumbrated by John O'Hara — who, with his unerring sense of scene, came to live in Princeton — intruded on undergraduate life as civilizing forces. And two talented young economists, Richard A. Lester and Lester V. Chandler, became influential in the economics department and brought it abreast of the century. To the undoubted distress of many whom in a manner of speaking it had educated, the university moved on. My memory, alas, is of the earlier frame.

The two academic institutions that engaged my affection, Berkeley and the University of Cambridge, could have done so partly because of their beauty. Cambridge, England — Trinity Great Court, the Wren Library, King's Chapel, the other more initimate quadrangles, the Backs — has no equal in Europe, and certainly not in the spring when first the crocuses and then the daffodils cover great stretches of field and lawn. One learns also at Cambridge how architecture has declined geometrically in taste and excellence — by roughly half in each century since the first Elizabeth. There much is good because so little is new.

Berkeley depends for its enchantment less on architecture,

though this is not universally offensive, than on location. The campus is so arranged that from a hundred places one can look out on the Bay, the Golden Gate and the Marin mountains, all in the hazy distance. The live oaks and lesser flora are a rich admixture of light and dark greens, and over all is an especially rich and lingering aroma of eucalyptus. Above is the gently Gothic Campanile mocking the white-to-cream Moorish façades with their tiles and arches that were once the compulsory California fashion. Those buildings vastly improve on their aggressively sensible successors.

I arrived in Berkeley one late summer evening in 1931, having left Ontario by ship ten days earlier, the ship being one that plied from Port Stanley, twenty miles from our farm, to Cleveland. At the casino in Port Stanley during my youth the dance orchestra was thought by all to be very good, a shrewd judgment. It was from the nearby city of London and was led by the then uncelebrated Guy Lombardo.

The journey from Ohio to California was with another graduate student in an ancient and enfeebled Oakland automobile with an uncontrollable appetite for gasoline and oil. However, the depression was heavy on the land, and even the oil companies were succumbing to the relentless pressures of deflation so by watching attentively for the battle zones of the gasoline wars that had broken out across the country, we were able to fill up the tank and a spare can for just upward of ten cents a gallon. From Lincoln, Nebraska, west in 1931, the main crosscountry roads were unpaved to the California line.

My travel to Berkeley was to acquire a Ph.D. and to take up a research assistantship in the Giannini Foundation of Agricultural Economics. There my ultimate benefactor was Amadeo Peter Giannini, a California banker and entrepreneur, who, a year or two earlier (following a temporary loss of control of his enterprises), had launched a major effort to improve his ethnic and political image. The ethnic transformation involved the renaming of his Bank of Italy the Bank of America. The political improvement was principally accomplished by having the Bancitaly Corporation, the parent enterprise, give the University of California a million and a half dollars in what may not have been an arm's-length transaction to establish the A.P. Giannini Foundation of Agricultural Economics in honor of its president. From early in his career Giannini had been a major source of financial support to California farmers. He had also learned not to doubt their political power.

Years later, as an editor of *Fortune*, I returned the Giannini favor with a major story on his life and enterprises. The research was done by a tall, slender, highly intelligent woman named Janet McEnany to whom Giannini, by then well along in his seventies, was much attracted. Janet returned to New York to tell of going to lunch with him one rainy day in San Francisco. There was doubt as to whether the great banker's car had arrived so his secretary asked a distinguished-looking gray-haired man who was in the outer office to accompany her employer down to the street and get him a taxi should this be necessary. One was needed, and when the man came back with the vehicle, Giannini gave him a twenty-five-cent piece. The recipient was visibly embarrassed and explained to Giannini that he was an officer of the company, the head of the Los Angeles Bank of America, and as such, one of the larger bankers of the nation. Giannini apologized, took back the quarter and gave his man a dollar.

I spent three utterly contented years at Berkeley.[1] During the third I commuted into the Sacramento Valley to the university's agricultural branch at Davis, an institution now, like Guelph, promoted to separate university rank and with the added distinction recently of having sought to exclude the litigious Allan Bakke from its medical school. At Davis I was in charge of teaching in economics, agricultural economics, farm management and accounting and, apart from assistance from an elderly dean, provided all the instruction in these subjects. During that year I also wrote a Ph.D. thesis, which was without distinction, on the expenditures of California counties. The purpose was to get the degree.

The College of Agriculture of the University of California was then divided between Davis and Berkeley, with a further branch at Riverside. The Berkeley part consisted of three buildings in subdued Moorish revival making three sides of a rectangle, one of which was the gleaming new building of the Giannini Foundation. An older one proclaimed its agricultural purpose: "To rescue for human society the native values of rural life." There was frequent speculation as to why human as opposed to other society was specified, what the native values of rural life were and why these already needed rescue in a state where there was no land that had been farmed for more than three or four generations. Some nit-picking is inevitable.

The University of California in those days existed in a unique political equilibrium in which my fellow agriculturalists played an important part. The instincts of the arts and sciences faculty members were generally liberal; the professors expressed sympathy for the migrant field-workers, including the Okies and Arkies who were now swarming into the state from the drought and depression of the southern Great Plains. Paul Taylor, a phenomenally durable reformer in the department of economics, valiantly urged the enforcement of a law prohibiting the distribution to farms of more than 160 acres, of irrigation water that was provided by the federal government at public expense. However, since much of the water had for long gone to much larger landowners, suggestions that the law be enforced were held to be subversive. This was still the response as late as 1977, when the Secretary of the Interior held that so long as the law was on the books, it should be obeyed.

Other professors spoke sympathetically of trade unions, which in the circulation area of the *Los Angeles Times* were then regarded as instruments of extreme sedition. And of the public ownership of utilities and the writings of Lincoln Steffens. With faculty members venturing onto such dubious ground, it was inevitable that the graduate students in economics would go further. In consequence, the most distinguished of my classmates were Communists. We looked up especially to Gregory Silvermaster, who was rather older than the rest of us and who had a regular teaching job at nearby St. Mary's College, a Catholic academy of high religious and athletic reputation. Silvermaster later moved on to Washington and was much celebrated by Whittaker Chambers as a leader of the Communist underground in that city. Robert Merriman, another contemporary, had come down to Berkeley from the University of Nevada where, handsome and popular, he had been a big man on campus and a pillar of the local ROTC. At Berkeley he became the head teaching fellow in economics under Professor Ira B. Cross, a stalwart conservative who prided himself, rightly, on his tolerance of the aberrant political views of the young. In due course, Merriman was awarded one of the rare traveling fellow-ships in the gift of the university — foreign travel was not for everyone in those days. He turned both this and his ROTC training to unexpected use by going on to Spain where he commanded the Abraham Lincoln Battalion in the Spanish Civil War and was eventually chief of staff of the XV International Brigade. He was killed in Aragon in the retreat from Belchite in 1938, but he lives on as the Robert Jordan of Hemingway's *For Whom the Bell Tolls*. I think of him with admiration.

The mood of the university, ranging from liberal to revolution-ary in those years, could have been expected to arouse the antago-nism of conservative California citizens and taxpayers. The reaction was far less than might have been imagined. A tradition of academic freedom helped but not much; California conservatives were not then greatly deterred by such abstractions. More of the protection lay in the fact that much of the liberal and all of the revolutionary tendency was without serious operative effect. It expended itself verbally and within a closed circle; what filtered out was not understood. This is not exceptional in the American aca-demic experience. Until relatively recent times, the most radical of the major economics departments in the United States was that of the University of Texas. Here in mid-century years even active Marxists were tolerated. A few hundred yards distant from the campus was the Texas legislature. The economists at the university survived because the legislators, though politically adverse, were also intellectually obtuse, and a great and useful barrier of ignor-ance thus separated the enemies of academic freedom from their prey.[2]

At Berkeley, however, academic freedom had a yet more effec-tive defense. My fellow agriculturalists were highly regarded prac-titioners of what Thorstein Veblen called exoteric learning. (Veblen made a distinction between esoteric knowledge, which enjoys the greatest academic prestige but is without economic or industrial effect, and exoteric learning, which, in contrast, has negligible academic prestige but is very useful.) My colleagues at Berkeley and Davis had gone on from the simple-minded empiri-cism of the early colleges of agriculture to a scientific and effective response to the numerous afflictions and opportunities of Califor-nia agriculture. Animal disease, plant disease, declining water tables, soil disorders, bankrupt irrigation districts, even low prices, brought prompt remedial effort from the College of Agriculture. Often, if not invariably, it helped. To this part of the university the politically conservative and very influential California Farm Bureau Federation and the unabashedly reactionary and even more influential Associated Farmers of California were deeply indebted. The revolutionaries and the liberals and their rhetoric were the price the farmers had to pay for the exoteric help. Thus the balance between liberty and utility.

No one should think this a theoretical construct. In the early thirties the finances of the State of California were in very poor condition. Payrolls were being covered with tax anticipation certificates which the recipient sold at a discount. State expenditures were reduced, and this included the university budget. The university promptly announced that its savings would be achieved in the College of Agriculture — the Agricultural Extension (Farm Adviser) Service was held to be expendable. At once the legislative mood became more generous, and the budget cuts were restored. As Veblen had indicated, the agriculturalists at the University of California were, indeed, second-class citizens. But we protected the first-class citizens and never ceased to wish that we were better appreciated.

Within the Giannini Foundation there was also a certain balance between the esoteric and exoteric worlds. The Foundation was headed by Howard R. Tolley, recently arrived from the United States Department of Agriculture where he had headed the work on farm management. A lovable, well-loved and extremely homely man, he had the appearance and something of the posture of an elongated frog. He was soon recalled to Washington to serve in the Agricultural Adjustment Administration, of which, yet later, he became the head. When the war restored farm prices and made that activity irrelevant, he came contentedly to work for me controlling food prices.

Quite a few of the Foundation professors were new arrivals, brought in by the Giannini largesse. One recalls with wonder how much could then be done with the income from a million and a half dollars. Full professors were paid three or four thousand dollars a year, worked in narrow offices without secretaries and, when called on the telephone, dashed down the hall to the main office in response to a buzzer. Although all were judged by their usefulness, not all were useful. Peach, prune, grape, avocado, artichoke and citrus growers were told what they might expect as to prices, how in principle they might limit shipments to get higher prices, how they might better manage their cooperatives or their orchards, groves or farms. This service failed of complete success, for economics, then as now, was less than a predictive science. Our price forecasts were based almost entirely on market influences that had yet to reveal themselves. Efforts to limit shipments in order to raise prices broke down when each farmer suspected his neighbor of selling more than his quota and then proceeded to sell more himself. What a farmer could usefully be told about how to manage his farm was somewhat unclear. Still, the effort was made and appreciated.

To earn my $60 a month, I was first assigned to work with Edwin C. Voorhies, a charming bachelor wholly free from economic knowledge but with a certain distinction as the only native-born Californian on the agricultural economics faculty. Our task was to ascertain ways of improving the economic position of the California bee industry. I thought it would be useful to visit retail establishments in various parts of Los Angeles, San Francisco and their environs to see what the owners knew of their customers' tastes and preferences. To these the apiarists could then respond. Eventually we published two substantial monographs, but by neither, I judge, was the well-being of the apiarists much improved.

I did learn that for a young economist, publication, even on so exoteric a subject as the preferences of consumers for orange blossom honey over sage, is a prime measure of academic worth. Those passing judgment on a scholar avow their interest in the quality of his published work, but, in the end, most settle for counting the number of printed pages. In the depression years, the principal, indeed the nearly total, preoccupation of graduate students, outranking sex, alcohol or even revolution, was the question of an eventual job. Few expected ever to achieve one; at Berkeley many kept postponing their final examinations, for then one descended from the modestly honorific stature of a student to the wholly derogatory status of the unemployed. In addition to my more monumental work on bees, I set about writing articles for the *Journal of Farm Economics* and eventually, also, getting my thesis published. I became known as a prolific scholar, and in the spring of 1934, this reputation, unsullied by any consideration as to the quality of the contributions, brought me an offer of an instructorship at Harvard for that autumn. I could have remained happily at Berkeley, which I loved, and Davis, which I endured. But Harvard offered me a great deal more money — $2400 a year instead of the $1800 that I was now being paid for my numerous courses at Davis.

Agricultural economics left me with the strong feeling that social science should be tested by its usefulness.[3] This, as Veblen urged, is a considerable professional handicap. The economists who are most highly regarded in their own time have almost always been those who confined themselves to abstract speculation unmarred by social purpose. Joseph Schumpeter, in later years one of the most admired of my senior Harvard colleagues, once accused John Maynard Keynes of being, like David Ricardo, subject to the curse (his word) of usefulness. Again the prestige of the esoteric as opposed to the exoteric.

However, usefulness causes problems for the teacher. At Berkeley the instruction in agricultural economics — farm management, land economics, marketing, agricultural cooperation, prices — was intensely practical. And much of it encountered the same difficulty that had emerged at Guelph — there was nothing much to teach. All the information useful to students that was possessed by R.L. Adams, the tall and confident professor of farm management, could have been conveyed in an hour or two. So with marketing, agricultural cooperation and other practical subjects. What remained was often tedious description, which one could more easily have read. Or classroom time was spent in discussion. Discussion, in all higher education, is the vacuum which is used to fill a vacuum.

Some instruction I do remember with gratitude. Howard Tolley lectured on statistical methods and left his students with the one indispensable attribute of an economist, which is a sense of magnitudes. This allows one to respect the income tax for the money it raises and forget customs duties since they are insignificant. In personal affairs it causes one to concentrate on important items of revenue and ignore unimportant items of outgo. From Tolley I also learned to add a column of figures by inspection and know for nearly all purposes that the resulting 10 percent error could be ignored. George M. Peterson, an exceptionally roughhewn product of the Minnesota farm country, drilled us in the nature of the production function — roughly the behavior of costs with different mixes of labor, capital and land. And even some of the practical information served an eventual purpose. When lecturing or making political speeches in California in later years, I could always astonish my audiences by showing that a Harvard professor could be richly knowledgeable on the details of rice cultivation in the Sacramento Valley or lemon marketing in Ventura County.

Agricultural economics forty-five years ago was an unformed subject. Provision of money to finance its teaching and research had run far ahead of the available subject matter and talent. The Berkeley agricultural economists did have one advantage over my professors at Guelph: they sensed that they were beginners with a good deal to learn.

The teaching of economics proper in those years was in South Hall, a tall, ungainly red-brick building at the base of the Campanile. Two lines of instruction had for me a permanent effect. The first was in the economics of Alfred Marshall, which was taught with great diligence and precision by E.T. Grether, who became a lifelong friend. Marshall, who lived from 1842 to 1924, nearly all that time at the University of Cambridge, was the preeminent figure in what has come to be called the neoclassical school. This is the economics of numerous, competitive firms, each intelligently committed to maximizing its profits and meeting in the market the even more numerous consumers, all rationally distributing their income between products so as to maximize enjoyment. This process is facilitated by an equally rational state, which recognizes the primary role of the market and confines itself to rendering those services, from education to the enforcement of laws to providing for the common defense, that are beyond the scope of the market. In this system prices settle out at cost plus a minimum necessary profit.

Workers can find employment by slightly lowering their wage demands, thus making it worth the while of some employer to hire them. There are occasional flawing monopolies, but these are the exception. The Marshallian world is a tidy thing without unemployment, inflation or depression or anyhow not much. Not surprisingly, many who studied Marshall found it pleasant to live in his world forever.

By the time of my exposure, Marshall's *Principles of Economics* had reached its eighth edition and totaled 871 learned pages. We were required, more or less, to know it all. The feeling that I was meant to be an economist emerged when I discovered that I had grasped the essentials of Marshall and had escaped the despair that afflicted many of my contemporaries.

In 1937, when I was at the University of Cambridge as a postdoctoral student, Alfred Marshall had been dead for thirteen years, but Mary Marshall, his widow, survived and maintained the prophet's house on Madingley Road as a shrine. In the garden was the study where Marshall worked, one side of it open to the air, the whole structure mounted on a pivot like a Dutch windmill so that it could be turned to catch the light or the sun. Mary still rode her bicycle with perilous abandon through the Cambridge traffic until one day John Maynard Keynes, himself a protégé of Marshall, took it away from her.

Marshall's world of competitive entrepreneurs, maximizing consumers and a suitably reticent state continues to serve the ends of comfortable orthodoxy today. It does not describe the world as it is. The great modern corporation — of which a thousand do around half the American business — the unions, the farm organizations and the welfare and garrison state have captured the reality, as one day they will capture the economic mind. But to have mastered Marshall was a good thing. To know what is right, one must have a firm grasp on what is wrong.

In the Berkeley years I was also introduced to Adam Smith, David Ricardo, Karl Marx, the early John Maynard Keynes and the great German economists who sought truth in history and of whom only Werner Sombart seriously entered my consciousness. This instruction was led by Leo Rogin, a teacher who established himself firmly in the affections of all of my generation. However, after Marshall, the major influence on me from those years was Thorstein Veblen.

Veblen is the most interesting social scientist the United States has produced. With Henry George, he is also one of the few with roots in the last century who still have a substantial and appreciative audience. In 1931, Veblen was two years dead, his last years having been spent near the Stanford campus from which he had been ejected for conspicuous philandering, as then judged, two decades before.

Veblen was perhaps dangerously attractive to someone of my background. The Scotch in Ontario owned and farmed the land, dominated the political life and, in the case of the more prestigious clans, sought educational advancement with some enthusiasm. As I have told, we felt ourselves superior to the merchants and tradesmen of the towns. But the townspeople, more often of English origin and prideful supporters of the Church of England, took their superior social position for granted. Town folk, not hicks. We disputed that eminence without being clear as to what our recourse, if any, should be. The Veblens were a highly intelligent and cultivated family, relatively affluent, at a time when Norwegian farmers in Minnesota were considered awkward, uncouth, unmannered and even slightly stupid. Veblen's scholarship was an eruption against all who, in consequence of wealth, occupation, ethnic origin or elegance of manner, made invidious claim (a Veblen phrase) to superior worldly position. I knew the mood.

Veblen's treatment of the manners and social observances of the American rich dealt with their dwellings, entertainments and dress on the same level as an anthropologist would examine the orgiastic observances and ceremonials of a primitive New Guinea tribe. In consequence, he made the rich the object not of envy, which concedes superiority, but of ridicule, which does not. The Veblenian ridicule persists in the language, most notably in the still-current reference to eye-catching social extravagance as "conspicuous consumption." In the United States, in contrast with France or Italy, a too overt display of wealth has come to be thought a trifle gauche. This — a raised eyebrow at conspicuous consumption — was the achievement of Veblen.

He was not a constructive figure; no alternative economic system and no penetrating reforms are associated with his name. There was danger here. Veblen was a skeptic and an enemy of pretense. Those who drank too deeply could be in doubt about everything and everybody; they could believe that all effort at reform was humbug. I've thought to resist this tendency, but in other respects Veblen's influence on me has lasted long. One of my greatest pleasures in writing has come from the thought that perhaps my work might annoy someone of comfortably pretentious position. Then comes the saddening realization that such people rarely read. There is a theorem to this effect. At Harvard in 1934, I took over the course previously given in agricultural economics by Thomas Nixon Carver, a notable conservative of his time. Were he to be remembered for anything, it would be for Carver's Law: "The trouble with radicals is that they only read radical literature, and the trouble with conservatives is that they don't read anything."

In the war years one of the recruits to the staff of the Office of Price Administration was a leading Berkeley Veblenian, Robert Brady. Brady came up with the sensible thought that lubricating oil could be conserved by not having it changed every 1000 miles as the oil companies then demanded. I did not approve the idea; such was the pressure on my office that I never got around to his paper. As would any good follower of Veblen, Bob accused me not of negligence but of shielding the oil companies.

And there has been yet more. In 1970, the nominating committee of the American Economic Association entertained a proposal that I be the next president. Nomination within the AEA is equivalent to election; democratic centralism is not confined to the Soviet Union. My selection was opposed by Professor Milton Friedman, and he offered as his clinching argument that Veblen had never been president. I learned after the election that this got me by. Later I wrote the introduction for a new edition of *The Theory of the Leisure Class* for Houghton Mifflin and Penguin Classics and led a drive to rescue from the ravages of time and casual tenants the fine house built by Thorstein Veblen's father with his own hands on the family homestead south of Northfield, Minnesota.

Over the Christmas holidays in 1933, I used some of my new wealth from my teaching at Davis to make the first trip home to Canada in two and a half years. (In accordance with the thrifty family compact by which the older educated the younger, I was already using some of it to send my younger sister Catherine to college.) I went on to Philadelphia to attend the meetings of the American Economic Association. There, except among the agricultural economists, the reputable opinion was powerfully against the New Deal. The budget was unbalanced. The value of the dollar on the international exchanges was being depreciated deliberately by the gold-buying program. The National Recovery Administration was allowing businessmen to get together to stabilize prices and wages in an especially egregious conflict with Marshallian market principles. The Agricultural Adjustment Administration was cutting back on agricultural production. Every one of these actions violated the accepted canons of economic wisdom. All were sternly denounced. Yet there was also a strong undercurrent of excitement at the meetings over what was going on in Washington. I decided to go down to see for myself, my first visit. Everything was entirely up to my expectations.

Early the following summer, now with a Ph.D., I left Berkeley to go back east and, eventually, take up my job at Harvard. With a fellow graduate student who, like nearly all of my contemporaries, now had a job with the federal government, I again journeyed across the country by car, this time through Yellowstone National Park, over the northern Great Plains and stopping, as was obligatory that year, to see Sally Rand at the Century of Progress in Chicago, her performance being the major current breakthrough in soft-core pornography. This was one of the years of the great drought, and in South Dakota the soil was in drifts in the manner of snowbanks behind the fence rows. Cars were being driven with last year's license plates. A stone thrown up from one of the dry gravel roads took out our windshield. One was surprised on reaching Illinois to see green fields again. Since I wasn't expected in Cambridge until the autumn, I decided to accompany my friend to Washington before going north.

NOTES

1 Of which I have told in *Economics, Peace and Laughter* (Boston: Houghton Mifflin, 1971), pp. 344-360.
2 Not entirely, of course. There were recurrent outbursts in the legislature and one or two efforts to persuade the university to sack Robert H. Montgomery and Clarence E. Ayres, the most distinguished and inimical of the economics professors. Once, when under investigation by the legislature, Montgomery

was asked if he favored private property. "I do," he said, "and so strongly that I want everyone in Texas to have some." The department was also not without its distinguished defenders. When he was Vice President, I commented to Lyndon Johnson that I thought the department of economics at the University of Texas was the most interesting in the country. He replied, "How long did it take you to find that out?"

3 Some forty years later, in a notable presidential address to the American Economic Association, the Nobel laureate and my friend Wassily Leontief surveyed the research achievements of the various branches of economics and concluded that agricultural economics had earned a special distinction in consequence of this test.

Born Again in Babylon
RON GRAHAM

Ron Graham (born 1948) is an associate editor of Saturday Night *and the author of* One-Eyed Kings, *a study of recent Canadian political leaders, published in 1986. His June 1983 article on the expatriate Canadian community in Los Angeles grapples with the countries' differing mythologies.*

T he huge gates of the Playboy Mansion West in Los Angeles are guarded by a rock with the authority of St. Peter. The rock asks for one's name, one's purpose, and the colour of one's car; the gates are swung open by invisible forces. At the end of a steep and winding road through green and sunny gardens, paradise turns out to be a vast Tudor home with a Rolls-Royce in front. Flamingos and bunnies cavort around the pool, the pond of rare koy fish, the cages of parrots and monkeys, and the forty-person Jacuzzi. This is heaven to all red-blooded playboys, whose prophet Hugh Hefner is upstairs starting his work-day at four in the afternoon, but no one could be more surprised and delighted to be there than the tall, lean, blonde Canadian being served toast and hot chocolate in the panelled dining-room.

"It's a Cinderella story," says Shannon Tweed, sitting at the head of the table in pink sweater and jeans.

Raised on a mink ranch in Newfoundland, Tweed — "Mortimer" to her family — passed her adolescence in Saskatoon before love wafted her off to the bright lights of Ottawa. Love proved fickle, and she found herself slaving over her own bar on Bank Street. There must be an easier way to make money she thought, and she remembered her childhood ambition to be in the Eaton's catalogue. She became a model. She had some success in Montreal and Toronto, but she was too smart and articulate to be content with smiling silently forever. She wanted to talk, she wanted to get to Hollywood, and she figured the best way was to be a *Playboy* centrefold. Alas, they told her she was too thin to appear nude, and she humiliated herself three times before she got the message.

Enter fate. The TV programme *Thrill of a Lifetime* was looking for someone whose thwarted thrill was to be a playmate. Shannon's agent said, "Have I got a gal for you," and Shannon Tweed had her thrill. But fate was not finished with her. She was invited to the midsummer-night pajama party at the mansion in Los Angeles, the city of angels. It was the first time she'd flown first class to a waiting limousine, and there was the rock, the house on the hill, and Hef in the front hall.

"My agent and I had spent days in Toronto looking for what I should wear," she recalls, dragging on a cigarette and tickling her white Maltese, Vanilla. "I didn't want to look like a prude from Canada. We settled on a $40 outfit, panties and a lacy bra under a see-through, floor-length gown, sort of showing everything while showing nothing. I had a long talk with Hef — we still have it on videotape — and things started to snowball, and I fell in love, and I didn't go back home." She giggles at the wonder of it all.

And that's not all, as they say on the Hollywood game shows before yanking another curtain. She was chosen playmate of the year, which netted her $100,000 and a new Porsche; she landed a bit part on *Falcon Crest*, the TV series; and she became the mistress of the mansion. Now she's doing movies, and there's talk of a bigger role in the series. She's taking singing lessons to record an album of love songs, and she's a hostess on the Playboy channel, the pay-TV package that drove at least one of her Canadian sisters to destroy her Eaton's credit card.

Tweed is unperturbed by the controversy, which she dismisses as "ridiculous." After all, she survived the jealousy of the Toronto girls who shunned her for taking off her clothes and who now, in her frank opinion, can eat their hearts out. She's more bothered by those who believe that Hef bought her success and that all play-mates are airheads. "I would like to validate my acting ability. I don't mind being seen as sensual and a sex object as long as that is not all I am. I would like to be a film star who also works in TV and cable, versatile enough not to be typecast. That may not be possible, but if I set my goals higher I work harder and have more to look forward to. It must be unfortunate for the men who walked on the moon. I mean, my God, where do you go?"

Certainly there seems little chance of getting Tweed back to the mink ranch after she's seen L.A. This is where fantasies come true.

The best ending is a happy one, and Shannon Tweed's life to date is worthy of the supreme L.A. accolade, "What a great movie idea!" "I'll go with the flow," she says, "wherever the offers are. I'm not here because of luck. I'm here because of goddamn perseverance!"

Southern California has made the Cinderella story its own myth, partly by capturing the world's most influential film and television industry and partly by being itself the ideal rags-to-riches tale. The pioneers, the gold-seekers, the drifers, the Okies — no one came here unless he or she was leaving something worse and hoping for something better.

Desert was transformed into tropical gardens, orange groves were turned into industrial parks, and the dippy sister of the American union emerged as the fairy princess of the twentieth century with Los Angeles as her glittering crown. If California were an independent nation, it would be the eighth industrial power in the world. The sixty-mile circle of greater L.A. is now the second-largest city in the United States, the second-largest banking and financial centre, and the third-largest port. It has a gross regional product exceeded by that of only thirteen nations. It has given the nation Richard Nixon and Ronald Reagan, it has received the lion's share of multi-billion-dollar defence and aerospace contracts that have spun off giants in electronics, high-technology, construction, and aircraft manufacture. And it has gained control of mass culture through films, television, and records, with all that implies for ethics, trends, and politics.

Jim Nutt, Canada's consul-general in L.A., guesses that there is a ten-year gap in Canadian appreciation of how important southern California has become. But the message must be seeping through, for greater Los Angeles is now the fourth-largest Canadian city in the world. The dreams of fame, money, and perpetual sun have proven more durable than the quickly repressed nightmares of Vietnam, Charles Manson, and the San Andreas fault, and Canadians, even with the dignity and infrastructure of a separate nationhood, have shown themselves no less susceptible to the allure than any similarly ambitious Kansans or Virginians. Mary Pickford and Walter Huston, Joni Mitchell and Robert Goulet, Margot Kidder and Monty Hall, Norma Shearer and Donald Sutherland — their names are invoked over and over like a litany of saints.

There are at least 850,000 people of Canadian origin in greater Los Angeles, and the number could well go as high as ten per cent of the 12-million people in the sixty-mile circle; most people settle on an even million. There is a Canada-California Chamber of Commerce, a Québec-Californie Association, a Royal Canadian Legion, and a Canadian Students' Union at USC. The actors and actresses are the best known, but there are Canadians to be found in every occupation from professor to prostitute, from senator to surf punk. The chairman of Union Oil, Fred Hartley, was born in Vancouver, the notable architect Frank Gehry was born in Toronto, and there's a Canadian waitress who'll keep working — illegally — in a coffee shop on Van Nuys Boulevard until she gets discovered by a producer or an immigration officer.

Moreover, Canada is California's second-largest trading partner after Japan, with trade totalling more than $6-billion in 1981. That has brought a large commercial section into Nutt's office; delegations from Alberta, British Columbia, Ontario, and Quebec; offices of the major Canadian banks; and a host of firms trying to get a piece of the lucrative defence, aerospace, and high-technology contracts under the Canada-U.S. Defence Development and Production Sharing Agreements. Telidon is competing in the videotex market, the Toronto-based Cable America is winning a major cable contract in the San Fernando Valley, and Cadillac Fairview is developing a five-block area of downtown into California Plaza. The ten-year, billion-dollar project designed by Vancouver's Arthur Erickson will have three office towers, stores, condominiums, and possibly such Canadian features as a Four Seasons Hotel and a Cineplex.

"We've always felt welcomed here," says Martin Seaton, president of Cadillac Fairview U.S. Western Region. "Much of downtown Los Angeles is owned by foreigners. There are Japanese and British companies with major investments here, and the Americans have bragged about being so attractive. They're far less xenophobic than Canadians. And there's a pro-business attitude here on the part of the mayor, the council and the civil service. If you're profitable here, you almost become a hero, whereas in many parts of Canada, particularly in the Toronto area, the prejudice is against earning money."

Prejudices aside, the possibility of making money seems greater. Bolstered by record defence spending and the entertainment industry, the L.A. economy has not been grievously affected by the recession and is in the best position to boom after it. Access to the Pacific Rim, a firm agricultural base, and the post-industrial nature of its business suggest that southern California will continue to outpace the antiquated and sluggish northeastern U.S. Christopher Gadsby, a young banker who came to Los Angeles with the Toronto-Dominion in 1980, jumped at the chance to stay on as president of First Pacific Bank, a medium-sized operation headquartered in Beverly Hills with $100-million in assets, four branches, and a staff of 114. Not only can he enjoy the excitement of navigating a business through a challenging period, he's poised to enjoy the financial rewards to come.

"The individual opportunities to progress in a career or financially are significantly greater here than they would be in Canada at the moment," he says. "The Canadian economy has some very serious structural problems that will take years to be resolved. And in a business sense, people are more open. It seems as if most have arrived within the last ten or fifteen years, so there aren't the traditional old-school-tie social barriers."

"I wasn't getting anywhere in Toronto," says Gary Turnbull, a successful criminal lawyer in the valley. He's wearing jeans and a sweater in his corner office overlooking Santa Monica Hills. The son of a *Toronto Star* linotype operator, he worked as a cop, a fireman, a bouncer, and a salesman before heading to California in 1973 with $200 and a nine-year-old son. "It was hard for a guy like me in Canada. The law schools were closed if you weren't the elite or didn't have the money to buy your way in. But here, if you want it and if you're willing to give a little bit, you can make it, I don't care who you are. It's unbelievable."

At first he slept on the beach, then got a job in the district attorney's office while studying law at night. Eventually he discovered that his true talent was handling twelve people in a box. He's never lost a drunken driving or prostitution case before a jury. He once scored a $4.2-million personal injury decision against Volkswagen from a jury, and his reputation has brought him the business of hockey players and "organized crime people." It has also brought him a large house in Van Nuys with a pool, a hot tub, and a gamesroom, a boat on the ocean, and season's tickets to the Los Angeles Kings hockey games at the Forum. The house has been dubbed the "Canadian Embassy" for all the Canadians who have passed through or settled at Turnbull's urging, and there's always Canadian beer at the parties he loves to throw. But he has no sentimental attachment to his native city.

"I hate it. Too many bad memories," he says. "Whatever I want to do I can do here, and it's a very easy place to make friends. But you have to be very careful. There are a lot of people who just want to rip you off so badly, and there are a lot of flaky people, and the drugs are out of sight. It's pathetic. My son got arrested for cocaine. But I did the case myself and ended up getting it dismissed. There are a lot of serious people here too, however."

What about crime in Los Angeles?

"None of my clients are guilty," he deadpans.

Despite a crime rate that has produced a society of paranoids, despite the rapid deterioration of the state's once-proud education system, despite smog and mud-slides and the price of houses, the gung-ho optimism of the place seems pervasive and infectious. Whether it's the sun and the palm trees, the Hollywood myth, the 1950s feeling to the town, or the realization that this is the last chance to make good, Los Angeles exudes a kind of Rotary Club boosterism that is touching and naive. The prevailing ethos is that of a white, Anglo, fundamentalist, middle-American pioneer, engineer, or technician whose common desire was to settle in a neat suburb by the sea. There is a real downtown now, but it's still denied as something of an eastern pretension; there is a real Broadway, but it's left to the blacks and the Chicanos; and there is, of course, the extravagance of the entertainment crowd, but it's resented by the sober majority.

"This whole town is about new ideas, freshness, and experimenting," observes Sheena Paterson, who was recently lured from *The Toronto Star* to become associate editor of the *Los Angeles Herald-Examiner*, one of four people responsible for recasting the Hearst newspaper in its battle against the titan *Los Angeles Times*. She was successful and happy in Toronto, but she's effervescent about her new job and her home under the "H" of the Hollywood sign. "They never put ideas down initially, and there's so little of the carping and destructive knifing that seem to exist in Toronto. I mean, the first week I was here, I got a phone call from the publisher of the *Times* saying, 'Good to have you here. It's important for newspapers in this city that we attract fresh talent. Come and have lunch with me.' Can you imagine the publisher of *The Globe and Mail* doing that?

"And people work very hard here. Laid-backness is a veneer. Even on the phone by the pool or playing tennis or having meetings in a sauna at lunchtime, they never let up. People don't socialize here. The parties and the dinners are working, networking, making contacts, talking deals. Everyone is on the make every minute of the day."

Like Toronto, Los Angeles feels inferior to New York. Because of the time difference, for example, many executives have to be on the freeways by dawn and always feel at least three hours behind. But with L.A.'s economic advancement, its cultural insecurity is turning into a rather snide self-satisfaction. As the city wrests more and more political, social, and financial clout from its snobbish and sophisticated big sister, it revels in the illusion that it has done so effortlessly, on its own terms. Hard work and hustle have been hidden behind another Hollywood effect. In Los Angeles they know that a great tan means a tourist, a retiree, or an unemployed actor.

"The other odd thing," Paterson continues, "is that, for the sex capital of the world, there is almost no sexism here. The editor of my newspaper is a woman, I've met young women who are presidents of companies, and there are women who have been holding important jobs in the movie industry for years. Women have been pioneers here in so many things that nobody blinks an eye when they get into positions of power. It's almost expected."

In fact, the two most celebrated Canadians in local history were women, and both Mary Pickford and Aimee Semple McPherson demonstrated a business acumen that probably surpassed their respective talents in acting and evangelism. Today Janet Blair Fleming, who left a job on Parliament Hill in Ottawa despite the direst warnings of the cabinet minister for whom she worked, is the senior vice-president of the Producers Sales Organization, a highly successful film-distribution agency she helped found in 1977. Monty Hall's wife, Marilyn, has started a mid-life career with her own film production company after her auspicious debut as associate producer of the award-winning TV movie *Golda*.

Aimee Semple McPherson once said that California is "God's great blueprint for man's abode on earth," but most Californians believe that man deserves the real credit. The predominant cult in the land of cults is free enterprise; the opportunities, the optimism, the hard work, and the openness all flow from it. This is the cult of the John Wayne movie, the automobile, Howard Jarvis, Arthur Laffer, Howard Hughes, the MX missile, Walt Disney, and twenty-four-hour supermarkets. Californians can get mystical talking about free enterprise, and its appeal for many immigrants was no less exciting than pamphlets showing pretty girls posturing beside lemon trees. Nor has the appeal waned in light of the artificial economy of government defence spending, the invasion of foreign competition, the near-bankruptcy of the state government, or the seething discontent of the black and Chicano underclass.

Michael Gilbert, a young Montreal investment banker specializing in real estate, heard this particular call of the West. "Around 1976 a host of things began to trouble me: Canada's strident unionism, the indulgent attitude toward strikes, a too-extensive social welfare system, the punitive taxes, the excessive government involvement in business affairs. There I was selling free enterprise in a country where I was increasingly discouraged by the social democratic leanings of government. It's hard to think of a sophisticated, democratic, Western country that's been more ill-served by its politicans both nationally and provincially. Add to that the fact that I was in Quebec, and, though I have near-fluency in French, I was feeling increasingly isolated in a ghettoized community."

In 1977, after scouting the U.S. for acquisitions for Canadian real-estate companies that were looking south, Gilbert settled in L.A. "The United States will be the last country to relinquish free enterprise, and within it the southwest will be the last bastion. The difference is palpable. A couple of years ago Reagan *fired* 11,000 air-traffic controllers, and the postal workers settled in about an hour shortly thereafter. The Canadian postal workers went out for *six weeks.* You tell that to people down here and they think you're crazy, that you can't be talking about any place civilized. Canada is in for a terrible time.

"A friend of mine who moved here at my urging wants to throw a testimonial dinner just to thank me for his lifestyle. He's done well, he's the boyfriend of a popular local TV star, and he's deliriously happy. Most people who come here are."

Certainly the 150 men and women who gathered for drinks in an art gallery one recent Saturday afternoon seemed to confirm Gilbert's statement. They looked healthy and prosperous, their laughter was louder than their summer clothes, and their Mercedes and BMWs sat within sight of a long soup-line outside the Mission Hall. The unusual thing was that everyone was speaking French. This was a meeting of the 500-member Québec-Californie Association to elect a new executive and to see a film on the Quebec Winter Carnival. The film was brought along by Quebec's delegate to Los Angeles, Pierre Jolin, whose office provides some assistance to the association and sponsors a one-hour radio programme of Quebec news and music. Most people were too busy drinking to pay much attention. It's a minor duty in Jolin's job, which is primarily to assist small- and medium-sized Quebec companies doing business in L.A.; it was more a good-will gesture to those who retain links to their language and homeland through a Christmas ball, a Saint Jean-Baptiste celebration, a corn-husking beach party in August, an oyster party in November, and a maple-syrup feast in February.

There are more than 50,000 French Canadians in California. Prudent Beaudry was a great mayor of Los Angeles in the 1870s, Geneviève Bujold has been followed by such talented young actresses as Lisa Langlois and Marie Laurin, and Marcel Dionne is the most popular player on the Kings. When Montreal or Quebec play at the Forum, half the crowd is likely to be French Canadians, who are in Los Angeles for the same reasons, and with the same tendency to assimilate, as other Canadians.

"Your opportunity here is limited only by your capacity to work," says Luke Bouchard, sounding the common refrain. "If you have enthusiasm, you'll beat the next guy."

Bouchard, fifty-eight, came from Coaticook in Quebec's Eastern Townships in 1949. He had met a pretty girl named Dorothy on an overnight bus trip, proposed to her in the morning, married her, and returned with her to her parents' home in California. His education was limited, his English incomplete; it took him a while to find a job as a helper to two men starting up a steel-construction business. Fifteen years later he owned twenty per cent of it and now he and a partner own the whole thing. They have annual sales of more than $10-million, defence-industry sub-contracts, and a work force that's usually over 100 men. He's president of the Steel Fabricators Association of Southern California, and his "feel for steel" has awed engineers with PhDs at Rockwell International. His son, Donald, is the plant superintendent, and Bouchard is making room for any of his other children who show an interest.

"We're on a growth curve and could double in four years," he says in his office in Santa Fe Springs, which describes itself as an "All-American City." "I'm building my dream, setting the stage, doing my homework so that it's ready for my children if they want it." None of the children speaks French, though they sometimes visit their grandmother in Coaticook. "I don't regret that they're Americans, though I try to compensate — maybe overcompensate — by stressing I'm a French Canadian. I want them to be Americans, but I also want them to remember that the French had a glorious history on this continent. And I think my career can be an inspiration that French Canadians are just as good as anyone else."

Bouchard has become an American citizen, changed his name from Luc to Luke, and abandoned the Liberal tradition of his family to become a Republican. He still misses Quebec, returns at least once a year, and dreams of owning a resort on Lake Memphremagog. "But I gather it's tough for Americans to buy land there," he says rather wistfully.

In Coaticook he went to school with Normand Houle. Houle used to read his sister's fan magazines, worked at the Rivoli theatre, and watched his father do sets for the little plays of the Zouaves and the Knights of Columbus. From an early age his dream was Hollywood. In the RCAF during the war he transformed the officers' mess into a nightclub, did shows with YMCA theatre groups, took classes at an art school near the base in England, and emerged with his dream intact. He continued his studies in Montreal and New York, where he hobnobbed with Tony Curtis and Simone de Beauvoir, and in 1948 Coaticook held a dance to raise $200 to send him to Los Angeles. He enrolled in the prestigious Chouinard Art Institute, supplemented a grant from the RCAF benevolent fund by working as a breakfast chef in a hotel, compressed four years of study into eighteen months, added an accent to the end of his name, and became an art director for

films and television. As a TV pioneer in the 1950s, he designed for
Lawrence Welk and met "all those people who became people, like
Betty White and Liberace." He worked with Danny Thomas at the
Hollywood Bowl, did sets for Dalton Trumbo's *Johnny Got His Gun*,
and won awards for his commercials.

"I like to call it Houlé-wood," he says. "Recently I was asked to be
the art director for an evening honouring Bette Davis at the Coco-
nut Grove. This is the crown of making it, when they call you five
years after you've retired and it's not to make a ketchup
commercial."

In 1968 he founded Design Arts, an independent set-design and
-construction firm which grew into a complex of four sound studios in Hollywood, with more than 40,000 square feet of space to be
rented for films, television, and commercials. Ronald Reagan taped
his campaign commercials in one of Houlé's studios, and the walls
of Houlé's cluttered office display a snapshot of the president, an
invitation to the inaugural ball, awards, civic citations, and photographs of Mary Pickford, Dick Cavett, and Leonard Nimoy. There
are pictures of his splendid house in the Hollywood Hills and his
chalet in the mountains, souvenirs from travels around the world,
and boxes of memorabilia being sorted for the national archives
in Ottawa, the Cinémathèque in Montreal, and a Hollywood
museum he's planning for Coaticook. A recent sale of one of his
studios to CBS has made him a millionare. At least part of the
money has gone into the restoration of an old hotel near Hollywood and Vine, once associated with the golden era that lured
Houlé in the first place, now an ugly corner in one of L.A.'s sleaziest
districts.

"Hollywood is just one of the city's sixty-two communities, with
about 120,000 residents," Houlé explains. "When I first came here,
there were still orange groves and a good class of people. But the
civil-rights movement destroyed the whole shebang. We lost control of our destiny, and when the illegals started invading that did
it. It's no more what we used to call Hollywood. Universal, Burbank, Disney, NBC, they're all out in the valley. The nucleus of the
film industry, the technical side like Glen Glen Sound and Techni-
color, is still here, Goldwyn and Columbia and Paramount are
nearby, but the people who used to work here used to live here.
Not anymore."

Houlé's hotel seems like a gesture toward recovering his adolescent dream, a set behind which he can hide the grim reality of the present. He is a strongly built man who has had to fight hard and ruthlessly at times, but his exuberance and innocence are charmingly Los Angeles when he mentions that he might be getting a star in the pavement on Hollywood Boulevard. "I remember crying when they sold the MGM studios," he admits. "I saw them giving away props that I'd used in movies years ago, and when they destroyed the back lot to build condominiums, that hurt. We were much in love with all these things. Today kids want to know about the pay and the hours. In those days we just wanted to be in the business. We just wanted to make movies."

To most of the world Hollywood and Los Angeles remain interchangeable descriptions of the same fantasy, also known as Tinsel Town, Lotus Land, and the Big Orange, a kind of magic kingdom of movie stars, white mansions, Rodeo Drive, the Brown Derby, Schwab's Drugstore, Disneyland, palm trees, the Pacific Ocean, and the sun. The entertainment industry, like a colossal public-relations campaign, has sold southern California with the same hyperbole, positivism, and outright fabrication with which it sells its products and its celebrities. And the city is spread over so wide an area that it's not difficult to hide its missile plants and black ghettos by distracting tourists with maps to the homes of the stars.

Thus Beverly Hills is more famous for Pickfair than for the world headquarters of the high-tech giant Litton Industries, Burbank is more famous for Johnny Carson than for Lockheed Aircraft, and Pasadena is more famous for the Rose Bowl than for the Jet Propulsion Laboratory. Show business is far from the biggest business in town, but its glitter and success and high-stake gambles have come to define the city in its own eyes. *The Hollywood Reporter* is available on most street corners, Cher is invited to lecture at UCLA, and a banker brags of having Ricky Nelson and Richard Dreyfuss as his neighbours.

All this, plus the fact that the studios were established before airplanes and electronics were taken seriously, explain why Los Angeles can feel like a one-industry town. Everybody seems to have a movie deal on the side. Everybody mentions seeing Dustin Hoffman in the bar of the Westwood Marquis, and everybody is interested in William Shatner's hairpiece. Michael Gilbert, for example, is applying his real-estate expertise as a consultant on a $70-million office project aimed to attract producers and related show business. Set at the edge of the MGM-United Artists studio, the complex is envisaged as a kind of motion-picture stock exchange, designed by Maxwell Starkman, a Canadian, and financed by the Filmcorp Group whose president is Bruce Mallen, another ex-Montrealer, marketing consultant, and economist.

"Much of the real estate that's developed in Los Angeles is oriented toward the entertainment industry," says Gilbert, "at least in west L.A. and the valley, just as much of the real estate in Calgary is oriented toward the energy industry. After all, this is the home town of the film industry, the music industry, and most TV production."

Gilbert and Mallen have become film producers themselves. In Canada, Gilbert was involved with *Two Solitudes* and Mallen was an expert in Canadian film financing. Their real-estate ventures may be merely the means of indulging their fascination with movies. They are developing story ideas, putting up seed money to hire writers to write screenplays, and assembling packages of scripts, stars, and directors to sell to the major studios and networks. The risk is great, the competition fierce, and even a success might not bring in any return for two or three years, but they've got the bug.

"This is the entrepreneurial frontier," Gilbert enthuses, wearing slacks and a white sweater in an office decorated with movie posters. "You don't even start with a product, you start with an intangible idea, and not only is it the toughest thing I've ever done, it's the toughest thing I've ever heard about in the field of business. You're cut loose in a glamour business where some people are motivated for reasons other than money, where drugs are fairly pervasive, and where there are a lot of sick people and a lot of very ambitious people.

"If you're at the end of the industry where the odds are the toughest, like an aspiring actor, director, writer, or producer who doesn't have financial resources to fall back on, this can be a rough, rough town indeed. But given that I have a modicum of resources, I have the opportunity to be a midwife to the principal artistic medium of the latter half of the twentieth century, the movies. And that's about as creative as a businessman is going to get."

Like the sun, the entertainment industry exerts a particular fascination for Canadians. Unlike real estate or banking or even high technology, it is an industry that doesn't really exist in Canada. Often it's not a question of greater opportunity in Los Angeles, it's a question of no opportunity at home. Since the days of Mack Sennett and Marie Dressler, Canadian talent has found expression in Hollywood. When a government official estimated that sixteen per cent of the film industry was made up of Canadians, Ronald Reagan arbitrarily upped the figure to twenty per cent because, in his own experience, there were Canadians everywhere. In front of the cameras and behind the scenes, in movies and television, Canadians would constitute a visible minority if they were a different colour or dressed like Bob and Doug McKenzie; as it is, the most distinguishing features are the sounds of "about," "Z," and "bean" instead of "bin."

"The other way of recognizing Canadians here," observes Monica Parker, an actress and comedy writer who moved from Toronto three years ago with her French-Canadian husband, Gilles Sevard, "is that we're constantly saying, 'Please, excuse me, and thank you.' We're a very polite, well-bred, better-dressed, tidy, and dependable people, and we know how to fit in. 'Oh, you're Canadian!' the Americans say. 'But you're so much like us!' But we also have a bond with each other, so that sometimes the Americans say, 'You Canadians! You just stick together, don't you? You just have to help each other out!' All but two or three of my closest friends in Toronto have moved, and we're always on the phone or driving around and we still can't believe we're all here."

There have been three major migrations from Canada to Hollywood. The first was the Pickford wave, which survives in the revered form of Raymond Massey or Sidney Guilaroff, the hairdresser to the stars since the golden age of MGM. The second was the Lorne Greene gang, which got its start on television at the CBC and craved the bonanza; it's still represented by William Shatner, who became a cult figure by applying his Stratford voice and posture to the role of a space commander in green pajamas. But the largest wave is the most recent, when the collapse of the tax-supported Canadian film boom left a horde of talented young people with experience, ambition, no jobs, and plenty of offers in the United States. Film Centre Canada in Beverly Hills lists fifty pages of Canadian actors, actresses, directors, writers, producers, technicians, and musicians in Los Angeles, and the list is only a partial one. Both the King of Kensington and the McKenzie brothers are working there, and the Directors Guild of Canada has twice as many members in Los Angeles as in Canada.

Two generations of Canadian comedians share a small office on Ventura Boulevard. The elder ("I'll admit to fifty-five") is Jackie Kahane, who came out of Montreal and the vaudeville tradition and reached his peak as Elvis Presley's opening act for eight years. With the easy manner of George Burns and a smile that's a flash of big, bright teeth, Kahane could retire on his memories and the enormous pinkie ring — "J.K." in diamonds — that Elvis gave him. But he's partners with his protege, Stuart Gillard, an affable and skilled comedy writer who's developing and producing movies, TV pilots, and pay-TV variety shows. In Canada Gillard had won a Canadian Film Award as the star of *Why Rock the Boat?* and had written and acted in the TV sitcom *Excuse My French.* He was lured to Los Angeles in 1975 to write for Sonny and Cher.

"I remember when I won a Montreal film award for best actor," he recalls, laughing, "an old man came up and said that he had won it in 1943. I was so depressed thinking that this would happen to me if I stayed in Canada. Then there was no work, so I came here and I loved it. I did *Sonny and Cher, Donny and Marie, The Captain and Tenille, Mork and Mindy,* and I've written and produced feature films. When I arrived, most of the variety shows were written or produced by Canadians, and the number of Canadian comedy writers is amazing for a country with no sense of humour. I think it's the Canadian education system. I felt I had a better education than most of the people down here, a better feel for language, and our British tradition of dry, zany humour seemed to work better for television than the American vaudeville background."

"Also," Gillard continues, "Canadians have done just about everything to survive up there — TV, radio, commercials, industrials, school plays — and that's why our actors are so good. It's magical when you come here, though reality can set in pretty quickly. The first time Cher throws your script on the floor, you come down to earth pretty quickly."

Education and experience are the keys to Canadian success in Los Angeles. Both are virtually unavailable to many young Americans, especially now that the Hollywood unions have limited the opportunities for apprenticeship. The standards of Canadian schools and the subsidized cultural institutions such as the CBC, Stratford, the NFB, and regional theatres give Canadian talent skill and confidence. And if this is true in entertainment, it's equally true in most other fields. Cadillac Fairview was able to win the California Plaza project because the Canadian tax and banking systems had taught the company about mega-projects while its American counterparts were encouraged to stay small and local. Christopher Gadsby was able to win the presidency of the First Pacific Bank because the range and sophistication of his Toronto-Dominion apprenticeship made him uniquely qualified for the job. Sheena Paterson was offered her position at the *Herald-Examiner* because of her record at *The Toronto Star*, a newspaper more admired in the American industry than in Toronto. And, of course, there are no Americans on the L.A. Kings. Canada is not completely owned by the United States, and Canadians still have a freedom of choice, but there's a case to be made that Canada serves as a farm team for more American businesses than hockey and comedy. When the weak are weeded out and the strong emerge, there's often an American at the dressing-room door waving a dazzling contract.

"After my first year," says Monica Parker, "I thought it was my divine right to have a Rolls-Royce, a tennis court, a Jacuzzi, a pool, and a Bel-Air mansion full of servants. It's easy to lose perspective here."

After happy and successful work in Toronto in films, theatre, and television, Parker was invited to write for the *Helen Reddy Show* by two Los Angeles producers who saw her doing a stand-up comedy routine at Yuk Yuk's. She's acted in a film with Alan Arkin and received encouragement from studios and networks to develop her script ideas, but she's not yet become established enough or blase enough to lose perspective about her new home. The remoteness of Los Angeles, its sunny climate, its apparent prosperity in the midst of world recession, and the absorbing fascination of its make-believe industry give the town an air of unreality and, when friends like British Columbia actress Kim Cattrall drop by Parker's house full of news about an audition with director Steven Spielberg, it's easy to understand how trade talk and gossip become the be-all and end-all of human existence.

Parker deliberately defends herself against this addiction by choosing a wide range of friends and getting out of town as often as possible. But the resolution is as difficult to maintain as her diet, and she has to retreat into the sanity of her wit and her unpretentious house, which she accurately describes as a Lake Simcoe cottage set in a canyon just past the posh residences of Bel-Air. Henry Miller used to live in it. The rooms are bright and informal and look out on a tropical bush garden, and there are coyotes in the hills beyond. After the extravagances of the Playboy Mansion down the street, it feels therapeutic to sink into an overstuffed sofa in a cosy room with a decent cup of coffee and Seeya the chow basking in a sunspot and listen to Parker's observations of life in L.A.

"I was very happy in Toronto. But if you were a plant in Canada, you'd die of dehydration. Here you're overwatered. It's a cliché, but there *is* that negative feeling in Canada. We're afraid, so we're always covering our bets, while Americans will take the chance to fail publicly in a big way. It's enthusiasm and it's competition. You come from being the best in your class to find that everyone was the best in his class, so it's much more competitive. Everyone's here to rape and pillage. You don't come to Los Angeles to be an artist. You come to make money and to be successful and to do good work if you're lucky.

"And I wanted more opportunity. I didn't know that I was that ambitious, but ambition gives you choice. And though I was afraid, moving from Toronto to L.A. is not a big deal. It's the same language, the same food, and both places are pretentious cities with lots of delusions and trendy restaurants.

"I feel blessed about being here. Hollywood and Vine is not the Hollywood and Vine of anyone's imagination, but there's something magical in seeing those street signs, and my heart still flutters when I go through the gates of Paramount and I think of all the people who have been there before me. I think, 'Ah, this is show business, this is what I love to do so much.' People in showbiz don't grow up. I mean, we're an embarrassment. We're all walking around in jogging suits with little peak caps, for God's sake! We're in our mid-thirties and we're like complete fools. And we're loving it, by the way.

"Some wit once said that you dive into a pool in Los Angeles when you're twenty-five and you come out at the other end when you're sixty. The days slip away here. There's no sense of a week or a month. Time disappears, and if that's what they mean by 'laid-back,' then it scares me. It robs you of real living, and that's why you have to get away. I worry about losing my sense of reality, and 'mellow' may mean the wearing down of your resistance because it is so easy to live here. This is like a pleasure cruise. That's why I can't take the Pacific Ocean seriously. People surf on it — it's not real. The Atlantic is a worker ocean with Pilgrims and all those strange moral ideals.

"I have no time for those easterners who come here and spend their energy hating it. But I don't like the paranoia that's developed here, I don't like the obsession with vanity, and I miss our politeness. I also miss cheddar cheese, small grocery stores (though I love being able to go to a supermarket at three in the morning), lakes, the really green landscape that doesn't look like it's been done by a set designer, and that intrinsic Canadian substance known as *stuff*.

"I appreciate being a Canadian more than I did when I lived there, and I don't want to lose my ties to Canada. Nor do I want to be selling my wares here forever, because the hustle is just too great. In fact, I think I'd rather get old in Canada. Somehow it's closer to God. Besides, I want my medicare!"

Hollywood has always loved courtroom dramas as much as car chases and gunfights. The set for this particular drama could have been the scene of a hundred *Perry Mason* episodes (starring Raymond Burr, another Canadian). During the lunch break the cameraman was practising long pans from the witness stand to the defence table, where the star was sitting, eyes closed, lips moving, obviously rehearsing her lines. Twice her nervousness overcame her, and she rushed past the extras milling around the door to check her make-up and compose her jitters. Though an actress in Stratford and New York, she had never had a leading part until now, and she seemed to realize that this performance would make or break her.

Eventually everyone was brought to order. The jury indeed

looked like a random selection of ordinary people, and a gutsy immigrant defence counsel was pitted against a stern establishment lawyer. Only the judge, a blonde woman named Jacqueline, seemed miscast. The Shakespearian actress, with short red hair and a stunned expression, took her place on the witness stand as the camera zoomed in on her pursed lips, which occasionally cracked into an odd smile. Her glasses and make-up accentuated her dazed vulnerability.

"State your name," the clerk intoned.

"Marilyn Fleming," she whispered, her voice in danger of breaking. "But Erin is my nickname."

"Speak up, please!" someone barked.

Erin Fleming looked up as if expecting a director to yell, "Cut!" But no one did: this was real. She was being sued by the Bank of America, which was seeking to recover $400,000 it claimed she had weaseled from the late Groucho Marx. The suit had driven her to the point of destitution and mental breakdown, and she had already thrown tantrums in the courtroom. Now she sat in a kind of mesmerized panic waiting for the next assault from the bank's hostile lawyer, trying to control herself, perhaps wondering how she came to this crowded scene in Santa Monica, California, from the northern Ontario town of New Liskeard.

The dream, of course, had brought her. First the dream of Broadway and then the dream of Hollywood, where chance introduced her to the great comedian, fifty years her senior. She became his personal manager, his companion, and a partner in Groucho Marx Productions. He gave her houses and gifts out of love and gratitude or through her deceit, intimidation, and extortion, depending on which lawyer one believed. She presided at his star-studded parties, appeared in Woody Allen's *Everything You Always Wanted to Know About Sex But Were Afraid to Ask* as a girl eating lasagne and talking about Proust, and heard Groucho praise her at the Academy Awards as the one "who makes my life worth living."

Life did have its little problems, however. According to Marx's former chef, Fleming once threatened to kill Groucho if he didn't adopt her, once shoved a plate of food into the old man's face, and once stuffed a napkin into his mouth. Others testified that she was a loyal and devoted helper who gave zest to Marx's final years. Her seven years of good fortune turned into seven years of bad when

Marx died in 1977. The bank launched its suit despite Erin's having inherited only $150,000, compared to the $2.6-million left to Marx's three children.

Fleming appeared in court on a mixture of tranquilizers and stimulants. Her outbursts had the bank's attorney fearing for his life, and a court-appointed psychiatrist stated that Fleming was suffering from an incipient psychosis and severe grandiose paranoia. Among other things, she believed that the television series *Dynasty* was based on her family (which must have been a surprise for the rest of the country doctor's children in New Liskeard), that the cast members of the television series *Dallas* were her cousins, and that she would be murdered before all this was over.

"Erin!" a brash TV reporter had yelled in the corridor. "The psychiatrist's said you're psychotic! What's your reaction to that?"

"What does that mean?"

"It means you're *crazy*, Erin!"

"Oh," she mumbled, bewildered. "Permanently?"

The presence of the news cameras, including one in the courtroom, contributed to the make-believe quality of the trial. The lawyers behaved like actors, the witnesses included Archie Bunker and George Burns, the jury and the spectators laughed at the good lines, and the ghost of Groucho Marx hovered over the proceedings. When Erin got into a brawl, cursing and pummelling the bailiff who was trying to search her, one almost expected Hackenbush to fly through the door in his famous half-crouch, eyebrows and cigar aflutter, pursued by Harpo, Chico, and Zeppo, who would tweak the lawyers and chase the judge.

Instead there was only glum reality. "Plaintiff has been living in dire poverty," her lawyer reported. "Plaintiff has been unable to buy the most elementary necessities nor pay her taxes." In April the jury would conclude that she had breached the fiduciary trust that had been given her, and Erin Fleming would be ordered to pay more than $500,000 to the bank. There would be appeals she could not afford, a counter-suit against the bank for $1-billion in general damages, and Erin Fleming would wish that she had died with Groucho Marx.

During the lunch break Fleming sniffed and fondled the bouquet of flowers a friend had sent. She seemed more like Ophelia than Lady Macbeth, half-crazed by the vagaries of fate. The dream was not supposed to turn out like this. The coach had turned into a pumpkin and Cinderella was returned to the ashes. Where was the happy ending she had been promised? Erin Fleming murmured to someone nearby, "Remember the parties when Groucho used to sing? Remember all the beautiful flowers we had on the dining-room table? Remember?"

Los Angeles is not a good place to fail or grow old in. There are no slow lanes on the L.A. freeways. The dark side, Hollywood Babylon, whether a murdered Canadian Playmate or a Canadian woman caught up in the death of John Belushi, gets hidden behind the klieg lights. An aged and infirm Norma Shearer becomes inaccessible in the Motion Picture and Television Country House and Hospital lest the truth of time destroy the golden image. Many Canadians have come and failed to find their star on Hollywood Boulevard. Their stories rarely get told, partly because the only grace of failure is that it guarantees anonymity, partly because the siren call of southern California is louder than the real police sirens howling in a disenchanted city of crime, drugs, and smog. The town is full of statuesque, forty-year-old blonde cashiers, most of whom no doubt came with bigger ambitions. The L.A. ethos of youthful optimism demands success and happiness as much as it demands thin bodies and face lifts, fronts as bold as movie sets and as cheery as "Have a nice day."

Ken Finkleman, late of Winnipeg and Toronto, is as unlikely in this cultural atmosphere as his bushy hair and green plaid woodsman's shirt are in his large corner office at Universal Studios. The writer and director of *Airplane II*, with a contract to work on new scripts at an exorbitant salary, he's a success; but he's damned if he's going to be happy too. A tall, lean bundle of nerves fuelled by contradictions, Finkleman is burdened by a Woody Allen *angst*, complete with references to his shrink and his lost girlfriend, and made worse by his lack of Allen's detachment and his reputation for making *schlock*. He espouses a radical political line that never comes to terms with his job, except that he's trying to write an anti-capitalist comedy.

"This is a disgusting place," he says, drinking a beer from the bottle at his desk. "It takes so much time and money to produce a movie that you can't make anything provocative or interesting. It's a corporate world, so profits are important, so success is important, so everyone's racing for the number-one spot. It can drive you crazy. I don't do *schlock* well, but I was picked for it because I'm so cynical about money making the rules that I was always agreeable to doing whatever was wanted. I'm here to make money, not to express myself, but living in an atmosphere that you're rejecting all the time can make you feel dead. I just want to go home. That's why I live in the Chateau Marmont. I'm afraid of putting down roots.

"It's ridiculous. You come to this terrible place where the only pleasure is the accumulation of material goods, where you don't want to be, and it's a trap. If you're in Winnipeg, you can go to Toronto, from Toronto to New York, from New York to L.A., but from Los Angeles there's nowhere else to go except up into aerospace, into psychic space — or back, with your tail between your legs. It's silly, but if the idea of success plays on your mind, then you either have to stay in the trap or return home as some kind of failure. It's a roach motel: you walk in and, bang, you're dead."

Hollywood does produce excellent work, of course, but it's also the *schlock* factory of the Western world. Decisions are in the hands of accountants and TV programmers, and the hustle for financing leaves producers with less and less energy and room for expression. The irony is that, if any Canadians were prepared to forsake the fame and money of the American mass entertainment industry for the chance to do quality work back home, they probably would be judged as fools or failures even in Canada. Canadians seethe with resentment when their talented people abandon Canada for the United States, but the national inferiority complex inevitably defines Canada as the small pond. Those who stay might become big fish and gain a rather heroic stature; those who go gain an authenticity that's irrelevant to the quality of their work. And those who return from time to time trail clouds of glory that obscure the possibly finer achievements of those who stayed. Stuart Gillard remarked that if he wanted to succeed as an actor in Canada the first thing he'd do is take a room near the Los Angeles airport. And George Mendeluk, a talented young director now living in L.A., agreed that bonus points are given just for the courage and prestige of moving into the Big Pond.

This psychological factor is gaining a practical importance with the growth of Canadian pay-TV and the possible rebirth of a Canadian film industry. The producers and bankers who put together "packages" are obsessed with a product that can draw on American funds by appealing to the vast American market while satisfying Canada's content regulations. There are a limited number of Canadians who are "bankable" in the United States as stars, directors, or writers, and the overwhelming majority of them are "bankable" because they have a Los Angeles reputation. A bit role on *Starsky and Hutch* is worth more than a season on *The Beachcombers*, and anyone interested in mingling Canadian and American financing for cable or films will draw heavily on the Canadians in Los Angeles. Lisa Langlois and Shannon Tweed are brought back to do movies in Montreal, Stuart Gillard and Jackie Kahane are doing pay-TV shows in Toronto and Alberta, Norman Jewison and George Mendeluk are developing bi-national film projects, and Donald Sutherland and Margot Kidder are every Canadian producer's fantasy. Recently there has arisen a Canadian equivalent to the "bi-coastals" who commute between L.A. and New York — a subspecies of "snowbird" in constant migration between L.A. and Toronto.

Al Waxman now commutes between his family in Toronto and his job on *Cagney and Lacey*, a television sitcom in which he plays a New York cop. "I'm very much a nationalist, but I'm also a realist," he says. "I put out a lot for Canada and got a lot back, but I like what's happening here. Here they welcome you to make yourself a star, while in Canada you have to compete not only with all the American networks but with the apparent apathy of the audience and the cynicism of the fucking communications industry.

"We've never really set out to win our own audiences, but it can be done. If we told an honest story, if we didn't deny who we are, if we were universal without losing our identity, then we'd win over our audience. The international audience would follow, and there would be less need to leave home. All those Canadians who get subsidies ought to be charged with the responsibility of winning over their own fucking audiences but, goddammit, when the fuck are they going to learn?

"I'm happy here. The only thing I'm not happy about is that when I go home at night, I can't hug my wife and kids. But I think of my poor dad who came to Canada from Poland in 1927 and had to work three years before he could afford to bring his wife over. So when I have to wait three or four days before I see my wife and kids, I just think of my dear old dad. All I really want to do is pay off my mortgage. Many don't believe me, but I've had enough of a taste just to want to go back and put on a tweed jacket and teach drama or philosophy or something."

The memory of home touches the entire Canadian community in Los Angeles. Most never give up their citizenship, even after decades in Los Angeles. They hate the word "expatriate" because it sounds too much like "ex-patriot." Burt Metcalfe, the executive producer of M*A*S*H, left Montreal when he was fourteen, but he still has his "green card" as a resident alien and he always attends Norman Jewison's annual Canadian party at Malibu. There are potential tax advantages for remaining Canadian and, in the entertainment business, there are potential career opportunities, but the essential factor is the emotional magnet of their home and native land, part childhood, part family and friends, part the elusive but undeniable sense of a separate and proud culture. Oddly enough, the cultural links between Canada and the United States ensure that Canadians don't lose sight of those who've gone to L.A. and made it.

In February, for example, Neil Young gave a concert in Toronto, and the hometown crowd in Maple Leaf Gardens was as enthusiastic as the one a couple of weeks earlier at Universal City, California. Young had left Canada for the Promised Land in 1966, heading off in a hearse bearing Ontario licence plates and dreaming of being a star. Today he is one of the most revered figures in the American rock pantheon, and he wasn't sure how the Canadian kids would react to his paean to his new home, California. They seemed to gain a kind of self-respect from his success and, when he sang his touching song about the Ontario of his youth, he lifted their experience to the world dimension that they craved.

By leaving, Young had gained a power among his own people that Bruce Cockburn or Gordon Lightfoot will never achieve by staying — but only at the cost of depleting the cultural strength of his own country. His songs such as "Ohio" and "Heart of Gold" became part of Canada's legacy, but the legacy is a diminished one: its own national images will never be transmitted to the world by a talent that might have made them great. Neil Young has written a classic about Kent State that he will never write about the October Crisis, for example. That's this country's loss when Canadians go to work for the American dream factory.

Meanwhile, in Los Angeles, the Canadians flock to the hockey games, watch Canadian football on the sports network, and band together like a garrison on the edge of the American frontier. They're proud to distinguish themselves as Canadians, they work hard, and they manage, as a rule, to stay married and sane. However they might blend into the scene, they often retain an innate suspicion about the falseness and shallowness around them. Like the Hollywood movies whose production values are far superior to their content, Los Angeles is preoccupied with technique. The freeways, the space shuttles, the fast foods, the electronic computers, the nuclear missiles, and the television shows are all geared to smooth function rather than any moral or artistic end. Like the children of stern parents, the Canadians in southern California seem to keep a grudging respect for the disciplines and codes that shaped them. They respond well to their release from winter, strikes, government regulation, occupational hardships, or oppressive negativity, but they worry that the easy living of climate and do-your-own-thing is another deception behind which lurk torpor, violence, and evil.

They have settled in the land of the lotus eaters, and, despite their new optimism, they can feel themselves drifting into an eternal spring, in which quick victories, lower standards, glib hypocrisies, and selfish individualism become irresistible. As they grow older, a remarkable number of them think of home. But often it's too late. They've become warm-blooded and accustomed to chewing the leaves.

PART
VIII
POSTSCRIPTS

The Salesman's Son Grows Older
CLARK BLAISE

The award-winning novelist and short story writer Clark Blaise (born 1940) is a rare hybrid. Born in North Dakota to a French-Canadian father and an English-Canadian mother, he has lived, studied and taught at various locations in both countries. The resulting duality is a key element in his often quite openly autobiographical fiction, such as this story from his book A North American Education.

Camphor berries popped underfoot on a night as hot and close as a faucet of sweat. My mother and I were walking from the movies. It was late for me but since my father was on the road selling furniture, she had taken me out. She watched the sidewalk for roaches darting to the gutters. They popped like berries underfoot. I was sleepy and my mother restless, like women whose men are often gone. She hadn't eaten supper, hadn't read the paper, couldn't stand the radio, and finally she'd suggested the movies. Inside, she'd paced behind the glass while I watched a Margaret O'Brien movie. The theater was air-cooled, which meant the hot air was kept circulating; even so the outdoors had been formidable under a moon that burned hotly. The apartment would be crushing. She'd been a week without a letter.

I think now of the privileges of the salesman's son, as much as the moving from town to town, the post cards and long-distance calls; staying up late, keeping my mother company, being confidant, behaving even at eight a good ten years older. And always wondering with her where my father was. Somewhere in his territory, anywhere from Raleigh to Shreveport. Another privilege of the salesman's son was knowing the cities and the routes between them, knowing the miles and predicting how long any drive would take. As a child, I'd wanted to be a Greyhound driver.

The smell of a summer night in Florida is so strong that twenty years later on a snowy night in Canada I can still feel it. Lustrous tropical nights, full of roaches and rats and lizards, with lightning bugs and whip-poor-wills pricking the dark and silence. I wanted to walk past our apartment house to the crater of peat bogs just beyond, so that the sweat on my arms could at least evaporate.

"Maybe daddy'll be home tonight," I said, playing the game of the salesman's son. There was a cream-colored sedan in our driveway, with a white top that made it look like my father's convertible. Then the light went on inside and the door opened and a drowsy young patrolman with his tie loosened and his Stetson and clipboard shuffled our way.

"Ma'am, are you the party in the upper apartment? I mean are you Mrs. Thee...is this here your name, ma'am?"

"Thibidault," she said. "*T.B. Doe* if you wish."

"I wonder then can we go inside a spell?"

"What is it?"

"Let's just go inside so's we can set a spell."

A long climb up the back staircase, my mother breathing deeply, long *ah-h-h's* and I took the key from her to let us in. I threw open the windows and turned on the lights. The patrolman tried to have my mother sit. She knew what was coming, like a miner's wife at a sudden whistle. She went to the kitchen and opened a Coke for me and poured iced tea for the young patrolman, then came back and sat where he told her to.

"You're here to tell me my husband is dead. I've felt it all night." Her head was nodding, a way of commanding agreement. "I'll be all right."

She wouldn't be, I knew. She'd need me.

"I didn't say that, ma'am," and for the first time his eyes brightened. "No, ma'am, he isn't dead. There was a pretty bad smash-up in Georgia about three days ago and he was unconscious till this morning. The report we got is he was on the critical list but they done took him off. He's in serious condition."

"How serious is serious?" I asked.

"What?"

She was still nodding. "You needn't worry. You can go if you wish — you've been very considerate."

"Can I fetch you something? Is there anybody you want me to call? Lots of times the effect of distressing news don't sink in till later and it's kindly useful having somebody around."

"Where did you say he was?"

He rustled the papers on his clipboard, happy to oblige. "Georgia, ma'am, Valdosta — that's about two hundred mile north. This here isn't the official report but it says the accident happened about midnight last Wednesday smack in the middle of Valdosta. Mr. Thee . . . Mr. *Doe*, was alone in the car and they reckon he must have fell asleep. The car . . . well, there ain't much left of the car."

"Did he hurt anyone else?"

"No, ma'am. Least it don't say so here." He grinned. "Looks like it was just him."

She was angry.

"Why wasn't I notified earlier?" she asked.

"That's kindly irregular ma'am. I don't know why."

She nodded. She hadn't stopped nodding.

"We can call up to Valdosta and get you a place to stay. And we'll keep an eye on this place while you're gone. *Anything you want*, Mrs. Doe, that's what I'm aimin' to say."

She was silent for a long time as though she were going to say, *Would you repeat it please, I don't think I heard it right:* and there was even a smile on her face, not a happy one, a smile that says *life is long and many things happen that we can't control and can't change and can't bring back.* "You've been very helpful. Please go."

If my father were dead it meant we would move. Back to Canada perhaps. Or west to the mountains, north to cities. And if my father lived, that too would change our lives, somehow. My mother stayed in the living room after the officer left and I watched her from the crack of my door, drinking hot coffee and smoking more than she ever had before. A few minutes later came a knock on the front door and she hurried to open up. Two neighbor women whose children I knew but rarely played with stepped inside and poured themselves iced tea, then waited to learn what had brought the police to the Yankee lady's door.

My mother said there'd been an accident.

"I knowed it was that," said Mrs. Wade, "and him such a fine-looking gentleman, too. I seen the po-lice settin' in your drive all evenin'-long and I said to my Grady that poor woman and her li'l boy is in for bad news when they get back from the pitchershow — or wherever you was at — so I called Miz Davis here and told her what I seen and wouldn't you know she said we best fix up a li'l basket of fruit — that's kindly like a custom with us here, since I knowed you was from outastate. What I brung ain't much just some navels and tangerines but I reckon it's somethin' to suck on when the times is bad."

"I reckon," said Mrs. Davis, "your mister was hurt pretty bad."

"Yes."

"They told you where he's at, I reckon."

"Yes, they did."

"Miz Davis and me, we thought if you was going to see him you'd need somebody to look after your li'l boy. I don't want you to go on worryin' your head over that at all. Her and her Billy got all the room he's fixin' to need."

"That's very kind."

I was out of bed now and back at the crack of my opened door. I'd never seen my mother talk to any neighbor women. I'd never been more aware of how different she looked and sounded. And of all the exciting possibilities opened up by my father's accident and possible death, staying back in an unpainted shanty full of loud kids was the least attractive. I began wishing my father wasn't hurt. And then I realized that the neighbor women with their sympathy and fruit had broken my mother's resistance. She would cry as soon as they left and I would have to pretend to be asleep, or else go out and comfort her, bring her tea and listen to her; be a salesman's son.

Audrey Davis was plump and straight-haired; Billy was gaunt, red-cheeked, and almost handsome. The children came in a phalanx of older girls who'd already run off, then a second wave ranging from the nearly pubescent down to infancy. At eight, I fell in the middle of the second pack whose leader was a ten-year-old named Carrie, with ear-rings and painted nails.

They ate their meals fried or boiled. Twenty years later I can still taste their warm, sweet tea, the fat chunks of pork, the chick peas, and okra. I can still smell the outhouse and hear the hiss of a million maggots flashing silver down the hole. The Davis crap was the fairest yellow. The food? Disease?

But what I really remember, and remember with such vividness that even now I wince, is this: sleeping one night on the living room rug — it was red and worn down to its backing — I developed a cough. After some rustling in the back Miz Davis appeared in the door, clad in a robe tied once at the waist. One white tubular breast had worked free. The nipple was poised like an ornament at its tip. It was the first time I'd ever seen a breast.

Even as I was watching it, she set to work with a mixture for the cough. By the time I noticed the liquid and the spoon, she was adding sugar. I opened wide, anxious to impress, and she thrust in the spoon, far enough to make me gag, and pulled my head back by the hair. She kept the spoon inside until I felt I was drowning in the gritty mixture of sugar and kerosene. I knew if I was dying there was one thing I wanted to do; I brought my open hand against the palm-numbing softness of her breast, then for an instant ran my fingertips over the hard, dry nipple and shafts of prickly hair. She acted as though nothing had happened and I looked innocent as though nothing had been intended. Then she took out the spoon.

After Audrey Davis's breast and kerosene my excreta turned a runny yellow. The night after the breast I was hiding in the sawgrass, bitten by mosquitoes and betrayed by fireflies, playing kick-the-can. The bladder-burning tension was excruciating for a slow, chubby boy in a running game, scurrying under the Davis jeep, under the pilings of the house, into the edges of the peat. My breath, cupped in the palm of my sweating hand, echoed like a deep-sea diver's as Carrie Davis beat the brush looking for me. Chigger bites, mosquito welts, burned and itched. I wanted to scream, to lift the house on my shoulders, to send the can in a spiraling arch sixty yards downfield, splitting imaginary goal posts and freeing Carrie's prisoners but I knew — knew — that even if I snuck away undetected, even with a ten-foot lead on Carrie or anyone else, I'd lose the dash to the can. Even if I got there first I'd kick too early and catch it with my glancing heel and the can would lean and roll and be replaced before I could hide again. I knew finally that it would be my fate, if caught, to be searching for kids in a twenty-foot circle for the rest of the night, or until the Davis kids got tired of running and kicking the can from under me. Better, then, to huddle deep in the pilings, deeper even than the hounds would venture till I could smell the muck, the seepage from the outhouse, the undried spillage from the kitchen slops. No one would find me. I wouldn't be caught nor would I ever kick the goddam can. Time after time, game after game, after the kids were caught they'd have to call, "Frankie, Frankie, come in free," and it would be exasperation, not admiration, that tinted Carrie's voice.

My mother came back four days later and set about selling all the clothes and furniture that anyone wanted. There were brief discussions with the neighbor women who shook their heads as she spoke. Finally I drew the conclusion that my father was dead, though I didn't ask. I tried out this new profound distinction on Carrie Davis and was treated for a day or two with a deference, a near sympathy ("Don't you do that, Billy Joe, can't you see his daddy's dead?") that I'd been seeking all along and probably ever since.

But how was it, in the week or so that it took her to pack and sell off everything that I never asked her what exactly had happened in Valdosta? Her mood had been grim and businesslike, the mood a salesman's son learns not to tamper with. I adjusted instead to the news that we were leaving Florida and would be returning to her family in Saskatchewan.

Saskatchewan! No neighbor had ever heard of it. "Where in the world's that at?" my teacher asked when I requested the transfer slip. When I said Canada, she asked what state. The Davis kids had never heard of Canada.

One book that had always traveled with us was my mother's Atlas. She had used it in school before the Great War — a phrase she still used — a comprehensive British edition that smeared the world in Imperial reds and pinks so that my vision of the earth had been distorted by Edwardian lenses. Safe pink swatchs cut the rift of Africa, the belly of Asia, and lighted like a rash over Oceania and the Caribbean. And of course red dominated and overwhelmed poor North America. The raw, pink, bulging brow of the continent was Canada, the largest and reddest blob of Britishness in the flat projection of the world. Saskatchewan alone could hold half a dozen Texases and the undivided yellow of the desert southwest called the "Indian Territories."

It was the smell of the book that had attracted me and led me, even before I could read, to a tracing of the Ottoman Empire, Austro-Hungary, and a dozen princely states. That had been my mother's childhood world and it became mine too — cool, confi-

dent, and British — and now it seems to me, that all the disruptions
in my life and in Mildred Blankenship's have merely been a settling
of the old borders, an insurrection of the cool gazetteer with its
sultanates, Boer lands, Pondichérys, and Port Arthurs. All in the
frontispiece, with its two-toned map of the world in red and gray
emblazoned, *WE HOLD A GREATER EMPIRE THAN HAS BEEN.*

We rode for a week without a break. Too excited for sleep, I
crouched against the railings behind the driver's seat with a road
map in my hand, crossing off towns and county lines, then the
borders of states. We'd left in April; we were closing in on winter
again. The drivers urged me to talk, so they wouldn't fall asleep.
"Watch for a burnt-out gas station over the next rise," they'd say,
"three men got killed there ... Down there a new Stucky's is going
up ... Right at that guardrail is where eight people got killed in a
head-on crash. . . ." And on an on, identifying every town before it
came, pacing themselves like milers, "Must be 3:15," they'd say,
passing an all-night diner and tooting a horn, knowing every night
clerk in every small-town hotel where the bundles of morning
papers were thrown off. It had seemed miraculous, then, to master
a five-state route as though it were an elevator ride in a three-story
department store. Chattanooga to Indianapolis, four times a week.
And on we went: Chicago, Rock Island, Ottumwa, Des Moines,
Omaha, Sioux Falls, Pierre, and Butte, where my uncle John Blankenship was on hand to take us into Canada.

I watched my uncle for signs of foreignness. His clothes were
shaggy, the car was English, and there were British flags in the
corners of the windshield. But he looked like a fleshed-out Billy
Davis from Oshacola County, Florida, with the same scraped
cheeks, high coloring and sky-blue eyes, the reddened hands with
flaking knuckles, stubby fingers with stiff black hair. John's accent
was as strange as the Davises'. The voice was deep, the patterns
rapid, and each word emerged as hard and clear as cubes from a
freezer.

The border town had broad dirt streets. A few of the cars parked
along the elevated sidewalks were high, boxy, prewar models I
couldn't identify. The cigarette signs, the first thing a boy notices,
were foreign.

"How does it feel, Franklin? The air any different?"

"It might be, sir."

"You don't have to say 'sir' to me. Uncle John will do. You're in your own country now — just look at the land, will you? Look at the grain elevators — that's where our money is, in the land. Don't look for it in that chrome-plated junk. You can *see* the soil, can't you?"

The land was flat, about like Florida, the road straight and narrow and the next town's grain elevator already visible. It was late April and the snow had receded from the road-bed. Bald spots, black and glistening, were appearing in the fields under a cold bright sun. Three weeks ago, when my father was alive, the thermometer had hit ninety-five degrees.

"Of course you can. Grade A Saskatchewan hard, the finest in the world."

The finest what? I wondered.

"Far as the eye can see. That's prosperity, Mildred. And we haven't touched anything yet — we're going to be a rich province, Mildred. We have the largest potash reserves in the world. You'll have no trouble getting work, believe me."

"And how's Valerie?" my mother asked. "And the children?"

Around such questions I slowly unwound. My uncle was no bus driver and Saskatchewan offered nothing for a map-primed child. I was a British subject with a Deep South accent, riding in a cold car with a strong new uncle. So many new things to be ashamed of — my accent, my tan, my chubbiness. I spoke half as fast as my uncle and couldn't speed up.

"Ever been to a bonspiel, Franklin?"

"No, sir, I don't think so."

"You'll come out tonight, then. Your Aunt Valerie is skip."

I decided not to say another word. Not until I understood what the Canadians were talking about.

Uncle John Blankenship, that tedious man, and his wife and three children made room for us in Saskatoon. A cold spring gave way, in May, to a dry, burning heat, the kind that blazed across my forehead and shrunk the skin under my eyes and over my nose. But I didn't sweat. It wasn't like Florida heat that reached up groggily from the ground as well as from above, steaming the trouser cuffs while threatening sun stroke. The Blankenships had a farm out of town and Jack, my oldest cousin, ran a trap line and kept a 22 rifle in the loft of the barn. During the summer I spent hot afternoons firing at gophers as they popped from their holes. Fat boy with a gun, squinting over the wheat through July and August, the combine harvesting the beaten rows, months after believing my father dead, and happy. As happy as I've ever been.

I looked for help from my cousins, for cousins are the unborn brothers and sisters of the only child. But they were slightly older, more capable, and spoke strangely. They were never alone, never drank Cokes which were bad for the teeth and stomach (demonstrated for me by leaving a piece of metal in a cup of Coke), never seemed to tire of work and fellowship. They were up at five, worked hard till seven, ate hot meaty-mushy breakfasts, then raced back to work and came to lunch red in the brow, basted in sweat, yet not smelling bad at all. They drank pasteurized milk with flecks of cream and even when they rested in the early afternoon they'd sit outside with a motor in their lap and a kerosene-soaked rag to clean it. I would join them, but with an ancient issue of *Collier's* or *National Geographic* taken from the pillars of bundled magazines in the attic, and all afternoon I'd sit in the shade with my busy cousins, reading about "New Hope for Ancient Anatolia" or "Brave Finland Carries On." I was given an article from an old *Maclean's* about my grandfather, Morley Blankenship, a wheat pool president who had petitioned thirty thankless years for left-hand driving in Canada.

What about those cousins who'd never ceased working, who'd held night jobs through college, then married and gone to law school or whatever? *My* cousins, *my* unborn brothers with full Blankenship and McLeod blood and their medical or legal practices in Vancouver and Regina and their spiky, balding blond heads and their political organizing. Is that all their work and muscles and fresh air could bring them? Is that what I would have been if we'd stayed in Saskatoon, a bloody Blankenship with crinkles and crow's-feet at twenty-five?

And what if we'd stayed anywhere? If we'd never left Montreal, I'd have been educated in both my languages instead of Florida English. Or if we'd never left the South I'd have emerged a man of breeding, liberal in the traditions of Duke University with tastes for Augustan authors and breeding falcons, for quoting de Tocqueville and Henry James, a wearer of three-piece suits, a user of straight razors. What calamity made me a reader of back issues, defunct Atlases, and foreign grammars? The loss, the loss! To leave Montreal for places like Georgia and Florida; to leave Florida for Saskatchewan; to leave the prairies for places like Cincinnati and Pittsburgh and, finally, to stumble back to Montreal a middleclass American from a broken home, after years of pointless suffering had promised so much.

My son sleeps so soundly. Over his bed, five license plates are hung, the last four from Quebec, the first from Wisconsin. Five years ago, when he was six months old, we left to take a bad job in Montreal, where I was born but had never visited. My parents had brought me to the U.S. when I was six months old. Canada was at war, America was neutral. America meant opportunity, freedom; Montreal meant ghettos, and insults. And so, loving our children, we murder them. Following the sun, the dollars, the peace-of-mind, we blind ourselves. Better to be a professor's son than a salesman's son — better a thousand times, I think — better to ski than to feed the mordant hounds, better to swim at a summer cottage than debase yourself in the septic mud. But what do these license plates mean? Endurance? Exile, cunning? Where will we all wind up, and how?

Because I couldn't master the five-cent nib that all the Saskatoon kids had to use in school, and because the teacher wouldn't accept my very neat Florida pencil writing, a compromise was reached that allowed me to write in ball-point. I was now a third-grader.

The fanciest ball-point pen on sale in Saskatoon featured the head and enormous black hat of Hopalong Cassidy. The face was baby-pink with blue spots for eyes and white ones for teeth and sideburns. It was, naturally, an unbalanced thing that hemorrhaged purpley on the page. The ink was viscous and slow-drying and tended to accumulate in the cross-roads of every loop. Nevertheless, it was a handsome pen and the envy of my classmates, all of whom scratched their way Scottishly across the page.

One day in early October I had been sucking lightly on Hoppy's hat as I thought of the sum I was trying to add. I didn't know, but my mouth was purpling with a stream of ink and the blue saliva was trickling on my shirt. My fingers had carried it to my cheeks and eyes, over my forehead and up my nostrils. I noticed nothing. But suddenly the teacher gasped and started running toward me, and two students leaped from their desk to grab me.

I was thrown to the floor and when I opened my mouth to shout, the surrounding girls screamed. Then the teacher was upon me, cramming her fingers down my throat, two fingers when the first didn't help, and she pumped my head from the back with her other hand. "Stand back, give him air — can't you see he's choking? Somebody get the nurse!"

"Is he dying?"

"What's all that stuff?"

What was her name — that second woman who had crammed something down my throat? I could see her perfectly. For fifty years she had been pale and prim and ever so respectable but I remember her as a hairy-nostriled and badly dentured banshee with fingers poisoned by furtive tobacco. I remember reaching out to paw her face to make her stop this impulsive assault on an innocent American, when suddenly I saw it: the blue rubble on my shirt, the bright sticky gobs of blue on the backs of my hands, the blue tint my eyes picked up off my cheeks. *I've been shot*, I thought. Blood is blue when you're really hurt. Then one of the boys let go of my arm and I was dropped to one elbow. "That's *ink*, Miss Carstairs. That's not blood or anything — that's *ink*. He was sucking his pen."

She finally looked closely at me, her eyes narrowing with reproach and disappointment. Her fingers fluttered in my throat. *Canadians!* I'd wanted to scream, *what do you want?* You throw me on the floor because of my accent and you pump your fingers in my throat fit to choke me then worst of all you start laughing when you find I'm not dying. *But I am.* Stop it. You stupid Yank with your stupid pen and the stupid cowboy hat on top and you sucking it like a baby. I rolled to my knees and coughed and retched out the clots of ink, then bulled my way through the rows of curious girls in their flannel jumpers who were making "ugh" sounds, and, head down because I didn't want anyone else to catch me and administer first aid, I dashed the two blocks to the Blankenship house in what, coatless, seemed like zero cold.

I let myself in the kitchen, quietly, to wash before I was seen. In the living room a voice was straining, almost shouting. It wasn't my mother and I thought for an instant it might be Miss Carstairs who somehow had beaten me home. I moved closer.

"John says you're a bloody fool and I couldn't agree more!"

Aunt Valerie held a letter and she was snapping the envelope in my mother's face. "A bloody litle fool, and that's not all —"

"I see I shouldn't have shown it to you."

"He's not worth it — here," she threw the letter in my mother's lap, "don't tell me that was the first time. *She was there* — doesn't that mean anything to you? *That woman* was there the whole time. How much do you think he cares for your feelings? Does he know how you felt when you got there —"

"No one will ever know."

"Well someone better make *you* know. I don't think you're competent. I think he's got a spell on you if you want my opinion. It's like a poison —"

"I'm not minimizing it," my mother broke in, and though she was sitting and didn't seem angry, her voice had risen and without straining it was blotting out my aunt's. "I'm not minimizing it. I know she wasn't the first and she might not be the last —"

"That's even more —"

"Will you let me finish? I didn't marry a Blankenship. You can tell my brother that I remember very well all the advice he gave me and my answer to all of you is that it's my life and I'm responsible and you can all..."

"Go...to...hell — is that it?"

"In so many words. Exactly. You can all go to hell."

Go *to hell:* I remember the way she said it, for she never said it again, not in my presence. More permission than a command: *yes, you may go to hell.* But it lifted Aunt Valerie out of her shoes.

"Now I *know!*" she cried. "I *see* it."

"See what?"

"What he's turned you into. One letter from him saying he wants you and you're running back — like a... like an I-don't know what! Only some things a woman can guess even when she doesn't want to. I don't deny he's a handsome devil. They all are. But to *degrade* yourself, really —"

Then my mother stood and looked at the door, straight at me, whom she must have seen. Her face was a jumble of frowns and smiles. I moved back toward the kitchen. "This will be our address," I heard her say. "Mrs. Mildred Thibidault."

She didn't come to the kitchen. She went upstairs, and Aunt Valerie stayed in the living room. I pictured her crying or cursing, throwing the porcelain off the mantel. I felt sorry for her; I understood her better than my mother. But minutes later she turned on the vacuum cleaner. And I returned quietly to the kitchen then slammed the outside door loudly and shouted, "I'm home, Aunt Valerie!" And then, knowing the role if not the words, I went upstairs to find out when we were leaving and where we would be going.

This long afternoon and evening, I closed my eyes and heard sounds of my childhood: the skipping rope slaps a dusty street in a warm southern twilight. The bats are out, the lightning bugs, the whip-poor-wills. I am the boy on yellow grass patting a hound, feeling him tremble under my touch. *Slap, Slap,* a girl strains forward with her nose and shoulders, lets the rope *slap, slap, slap,* as she catches the rhythm before jumping in. The girls speed it up — hot pepper it's called — they begin a song, something insulting about Negroes. The anonymous hound lays his head on my knee. Gnats encrust his eyes. *Poor dog,* I say. His breath is bad, his ears are frayed from fights, his eyes are moist and pink and tropical . . .

All day the slap, slap. The rope in a dusty yard, a little pit between the girls who turn it. As I walked today in another climate, now a man, I heard boots skipping on a wet city pavement, a girl running with her lover, a girl in a maxi-coat on a Montreal street. *Tschiptschip:* I'd been listening for it, boots on sand over a layer of ice. A taxi waited at the corner, its wipers thrashing as the engine throbbed. And tonight, over the shallow breathing of my son, an aluminum shovel strikes the concrete, under new snow.

What can I make of this, I ask myself, staring now at the license plates on the wall. Five years ago in Wisconsin on a snowy evening like this, with our boy just a bundle in the middle of his crib, I looked out our bedroom window. Snow had been falling all that day, all evening too, and had just begun letting up. We were renting a corner house that year; my first teaching job. I was twenty-four and feeling important. I was political that year of the teach-in. I'd spoken out the day before and been abused by name on a local TV channel. A known agitator. Six inches of new snow had fallen. An hour later a policeman came to our door and issued a summons and twenty-dollar fine for keeping an uncleared walk.

America, I'd thought then. A friend called; he'd gotten a ticket too. Harassment — did I want to fight it? I said I'd think about it, but I knew suddenly that I didn't care.

Watching the police car stop at the corner and one policeman get out, kick his feet on our steps then hold his finger on the bell for a full thirty seconds, I'd thought of other places we could be, of taking the option my parents had accidently left me. Nothing principled, nothing heroic, nothing even defiant. And so my son is skiing and learning French and someday he'll ask me why I made him do it, and he'll exercise the option we've accidentally left him . . . *slap-slap,* the dusty rope. Patrolmen on our steps, the shovel scraping a snowy walk.

I'm still a young man, but many things have gone for good.

Their America, and Mine
ROBERT FULFORD

The following piece by Robert Fulford (born 1932) was written in 1968, the year he became editor of Saturday Night. *He contradicted its bald pro-Americanism two years later in a famous confession of nationalism, which was itself invalidated by a further essay of 1986. What the sequence shows is not prevarication but the mixed feelings so common — so essential, one might say — to the Canadian psyche. Fulford's books include* Crisis at the Victory Burlesk *and* Marshall Delaney at the Movies.

Once I spent a golden week in America. It seemed to me that within six magic days I went almost everywhere in the United States I could want to go. I was in Washington, New York, Cleveland, Pittsburgh. I was in Kentucky, Maryland, Delaware, Iowa. I was even in Oshkosh, Wisconsin. And everywhere it was beautiful: the sun was bright and the air bracing, the crops were good, the people were happy and prosperous. It was like a holiday, and I woke every morning full of joyful expectancy.

Just one thing was wrong: the purpose of my visit was Senator Barry Goldwater, whose presidential campaign I was following as a newspaperman. He struck me, in this one-week exposure, as a thoroughly nasty personality. I'd read a dozen times that he was, behind all his unfortunate political ideas, a good man; but as I watched him I came to the opposite conclusion. By the end of the week, the ideas seemed to me preferable to the man.

At that point, fortunately, Goldwater no longer mattered. The ninety or so reporters who flew in his jets and then trailed after him in press buses had come to regard him with a certain contempt. He was now a sure loser, and so (I, for one, tried to believe) was his kind of America — the rotten, half-dead, conservative, paranoid America. Liberal America, *my* America, was winning, easily. I would never have chosen as representative of liberal America the man who was then in the process of beating Goldwater, but I was confident that Lyndon Johnson was the servant of those American ideals and impulses I trusted most. Goldwater was thus a figure of no real consequence, and I could relax and enjoy my week in his company. Most of the other newspapermen on the plane — liberals, like myself, with one or two exceptions — shared this attitude.

All that was long ago, of course, much longer than the years which chronologically intervene. Everything has changed. It has for a long time been evident that, in some ominous way, Goldwater *won* that election, and we admirers of liberal America lost it.

For anyone who loves the United States, the years since 1964 have been torture. I am, to state a fairly vital point, pro-American. Some good friends of mine are basically suspicious of the American idea, and many Canadians who are otherwise sensible are given to the view that Americans as a class are "immature" or "irresponsible" or just plain obnoxious. Not me. I like America and Americans. I admire them. I've always been profoundly grateful that Canada shares this continent with the American people: God bless America, as I think both Frank Underhill and Marshall McLuhan have said, for saving us from the fate of Australia.

This affection, like most affection, proceeds not from a conscious decision but from my personal history and from the nature of what might be called my interior design. For the fact is that some large part of the furniture of my mind and imagination has always been clearly stamped "Made in U.S.A.". My first heroes were American musicians: Ellington, Armstrong, Peewee Russell, later Charlie Parker and Miles Davis. The novelists I first took seriously — Mark Twain, Hemingway, Fitzgerald, Salinger, eventually Bellow — were all American. The painters of my lifetime who have meant most to me have been those same painters who made New York the centre of their world: Pollock, de Kooning, Kline. And in my own trade, literary journalism, my heroes (with two major exceptions, Shaw and Orwell) have all been American: Lionel Trilling and Clement Greenberg, Leslie Fiedler and Edmund Wilson, Dwight Macdonald and Murray Kempton. Why, even my favourite English poet, W. H. Auden, has been an American citizen for a long time.

These people, more than any Englishmen or Frenchmen or Canadians, have taught me what art is, what is going on in the world out there, and who I am. I would not, looking at it objectively, recommend them to anyone else, nor would I suggest them as the basis of a course in civilization. They are merely the basis of *my* sense of civilization, such as it is. Heroes and models, I discovered only a few years ago, *happen* to you; as with parents, you don't choose them. You wake up one morning and discover they are there. You can hardly defend them or explain them, any more than you can defend or explain your parents. Most of mine are American, and that's all there is to it.

Still, I confess to an even deeper pro-Americanism than all this suggests. In the early 1950s, when I was in my twenties, I came to realize — "believe", perhaps, would be a more objective and defensible way to say it, but even now I'll stick with "realize"— that the world was involved in a basic conflict of values and that this conflict involved me. Some people in Moscow, whom I had every reason to despise, were trying to take over the world — *they* said this was so, and I for one believed them. And some people in Washington, whom I had no reason to despise, were opposing them. The issues were complicated, as all issues are, but that was the basic point. Ottawa had little to do with it. London was involved rather more, but was not important. Moscow versus Washington: this was what counted. I knew what side I was on, and through the 1950s, indeed up to (and past) President Kennedy's death in 1963, I had few doubts.

Now, of course, doubts swarm around me. I find myself susceptible to even the most tenuous arguments of the Cold War revisionist historians, not because their view of the past is so persuasive but because the present in which I read them is so poisoned. Vietnam is a terrible disaster for everyone involved; the Vietnamese suffer horribly, but what may finally be even worse is that the American spirit, on which so much of the future of mankind depends, is buckling under the strain. American intellectual life, for instance, has gone rotten. The typical American intellectual today is a man who hates the United States and everything for which it stands, who in his heart joins those demonstrators who so enthusiastically pissed on the walls of the Pentagon. Susan Sontag has said America is doomed; her only hope is that it won't pull down the rest of the world when it goes under. The black ideologues are desperate, their white opponents grow more vicious every day. For once all the people feel that a terrible cloud hangs over them; they differ only in describing its nature — is it Communism, is it Johnsonian imperial-ism, is it Black Power, is it anarchy? Whatever it is, it is breaking the heart of America, and someone in my position can only look on in impotent sorrow. My love for my kind of America is permanent. But can my kind of America endure? For the first time, I now take seriously the possibility that it cannot.